Worlds of Written Discourse

Advances in Applied Linguistics
General Editors: Christopher N. Candlin and Srikant Sarangi

Editorial Board: Charles Goodwin (UCLA), Jim Martin (University of Sydney), Yoshihiko Ikegami (University of Tokyo), Kari Sajavaara (University of Jyväskylä), Gabriele Kasper (University of Hawaii), Ron Scollon (Georgetown University), Günther Kress (Institute of Education, London), Merrill Swain (OISE, University of Toronto)

This series offers a number of innovative points of focus. It seeks to represent diversity in applied linguistics but within that diversity to identify ways in which distinct research fields can be coherently related. Such coherence can be achieved by shared subject matter among fields, parallel and shared methodologies of research, mutualities of purposes and goals of research, and collaborative and cooperative work among researchers from different disciplines.

Although interdisciplinarity among established disciplines is now common, this series has in mind to open up new and distinctive research areas which lie at the boundaries of such disciplines. Such areas will be distinguished in part by their novel data sets and in part by the innovative combination of research methodologies. The series hopes thereby both to consolidate already well-tried methodologies, data and contexts of research, and to extend the range of applied linguistics research and scholarship to new and under-represented cultural, institutional and social contexts.

The philosophy underpinning the series mirrors that of applied linguistics more generally: a problem-based, historically and socially grounded discipline concerned with the reflexive interrogation of research by practice, and practice by research, oriented towards issues of social relevance and concern, and multi-disciplinary in nature.

The structure of the series encompasses books of several distinct types: research monographs which address specific areas of concern; reports from well-evidenced research projects; coherent collections of papers from precisely defined colloquia; volumes which provide a thorough historical and conceptual engagement with key applied linguistics research and scholarship from specific areas of the world.

Other titles in the series:
Multimodal Teaching and Learning: The Rhetorics of the Science Classroom
Günther Kress, Carey Jewitt, Jon Ogborn and Charalampos Tsatsarelis
Metaphor in Educational Discourse
Lynne Cameron
Language Acquisition and Language Socialization: Ecological Perspectives
Edited by Claire Kramsch
Second Language Conversations
Edited by Rod Gardner and Johannes Wagner
Applied Linguistics as Social Science
Alison Sealey and Bob Carter

Worlds of
Written Discourse

Vijay K. Bhatia

continuum

Continuum
The Tower building, 11 York Road, London, SE1 7NX
15 East 26th Street, New York, NY 10010

First published in 2004 by Continuum

Reprinted 2005

British Library Cataloguing-in-Publication Data
A catalogue record for this book is available from the British Library.

 3BN: 08264 5445 3 (hardback) 08264 5446 1 (paperback) ✓

Library of Congress Cataloguing-in-Publication Data
A catalogue record for this book is available from the Library of Congress.

Typeset by Tradespools, Frome, Somerset
Printed and bound in Great Britain by MPG Books Ltd, Bodmin, Cornwall

Contents

Acknowledgements

A book of theory like this one essentially represents the work of a lifetime: a reflection of one's thinking and interaction with colleagues, fellow researchers, students and a number of other professionals one comes in contact with, either face-to-face in conferences, or indirectly through their published work. Considering the immense contribution that all such people have made to my thinking and work, I find it impossible to express my gratitude to these members of the precious discourse community that I have interacted with in the last several years. All of them in a number of ways have made a contribution to this book. It is impossible to name each one of them individually, but I would like to mention some of them.

I owe my greatest debt of gratitude to Chris Candlin, who has contributed to my thinking in a number of ways, as a colleague, friend, co-researcher, co-teacher and as one of the editors of the series. I distinctly remember numerous occasions before, during and after the MAESP classes discussing with him intricacies of genre analysis. During the period that we worked together at City University of Hong Kong, we collaborated in research, teaching and other professional activities, and it is difficult for me to specify explicitly his influence on my thinking and work. It certainly has been more than I can specify, and will be visible in several ways throughout this work. Equally important is the influence of John Swales on my thinking and work in a more general sense. I have benefited most from my interactions with them. My special thanks are also due to Srikant Sarangi, as the other editor of the series, whose detailed comments on the draft version were extremely helpful.

I also owe gratitude to Jan Engberg with whom I have had numerous discussions on my concept of 'genre colonies' during my several visits to Arhus. He was always a willing and enthusiastic participant in discussions and contributor to my thinking in most aspects of genre analysis. In addition to these I would like to thank Anna Trosborg for offering me the Valeux visiting professorship, which made it possible for me to visit Arhus several times and have interactions with colleagues, researchers and friends at Arhus Business School. I am also thankful to my colleagues John Flowerdew and Bertha Do-Babcock for reading through the draft version and for giving comments on it.

I would also like to offer special thanks to my students on 'Discourse Variation in Professional Communities', who were the first guinea pigs for many of the ideas in the book when these were still in the process of development. Their portfolios of 'dirty analyses' of hundreds of texts were often interesting confirmations of a number of my ideas and beliefs. In particular, I would like to mention Jane Lung who never got tired of participating in my classes, giving reactions to my analyses, and reading through my drafts.

I am especially grateful to Aditi, the most recently initiated member of the professional discourse community, who not only read all the earlier drafts, but also proofread the subsequent version of the book with great enthusiasm and patience.

And last but not least, I am very grateful to Archana and Astha for being very supportive of my work and putting up with my tedious and annoying schedule for so many years. I would not have survived without their support.

Vijay K. Bhatia
Department of English and Communication
City University of Hong Kong

General Editors' Preface

This editorial which accompanies Vijay Bhatia's *Worlds of Written Discourse: A Genre-Based View* marks the closure of the *Advances in Applied Linguistics Series*. In our original blurb for the Series we had signalled that there would be opportunities for key scholars to write individually authored books which would focus cumulatively on their scholarly contribution to a field of study. In a sense, advances in disciplinary knowledge, or genre, cannot be assessed in separation from advances made by individual scholars in a committed way over a considerable period of time. This present volume by Bhatia is an example of just such a commitment in the field of genre studies, with regard to both its analytic expansion and application potential.

Genre studies have to an extent reached a certain plateau in applied linguistics. Scholars and practitioners have acknowledged the distinctive perspectives that the study of genre offers: as typified rhetorical and social action (Miller 1984); as a staged, goal-oriented social process (Martin 1985); as a conventionalized communicative event closely associated with communities of practice (Swales 1990). They have acknowledged a range of analytical perspectives on an increasingly broad range of genres, including close textual and linguistic description focusing on specific choices of lexico-grammar and discursive structures; ethnographic accounts of critical moments in key sites from institutional, professional and organizational perspectives displaying how particular genres are characteristic of such cultures, their aims, objectives and constraints; socio-cognitive perspectives exploring tensions in the construction of genres between personal and professional intention. In his earlier influential book, Bhatia (1993) made a plea for an integration of different perspectives in the overall descriptions of genre in particular sites and contexts. This present book both consolidates such a position and anticipates future challenges to genre studies.

The main challenge facing genre studies comes with the changing times. In the face of extensive and pervasive hybridity in terms of textual realization and modes of representation, a stable notion of generic integrity belies the evidence. As Bhatia indicates, the real world of discourse does not neatly fit into the established theories and practices of genre analysis. The suggestion that genres are clearly demarcated and closely and identifiably attached to particular communities of practice can hardly be maintained. This is in large measure a consequence of the extraordinary contemporary flux in certain communities of practice as their own boundaries become less secure in response to social pressures and to changes in their own institutional, professional and organizational structures, or simply because of the sheer accretion of knowledge. As a prime example, a glance at the textbooks of fifty years ago in even one field, say, in nursing, or in business studies, or in law, would suggest that there has been a considerable shift in the discourse practices of such professionals, in terms of what they regard as useful knowledge, the view they take of the novice and expert practitioner, the purposes assumed for the profession, the stance they take towards their audiences, and the like. By a similar token, especially in fields like advertising, we note the deliberate and engaged construction of hybrid genres, mixing in different configurations discourse features of promotion and information. By extension, other fields of practice, not themselves within such a domain as advertising, have willingly borrowed some of its key generic characteristics for their own purposes, academic institutional writing being only one such example (Fairclough 1993).

Genres are not only complex internally, with uncertain boundaries. Their increasing complexity derives also from the company they keep, whether this is in terms of what Bhatia has called 'colonies' or systems of genre, or in terms of the chaining of genres. As an example of the latter, we notice in the healthcare context in hospitals, how registration forms are linked to patient notes, to requests for specialist treatment or analysis, all tightly linked institutionally in a well-defined process of what one might call organizational sequencing. It is worth remembering that this complexity also derives from the now pervasive multi-modality of genres – while in the early days there may have been a natural concentration on the written (usually printed) text – this is, and can no longer be, the case. As Scollon (1998) points out in his work on news discourses, and quite generally in the work of Kress and van Leeuwen (1996), as genres are multi-modal in practice they need also to be so in their analysis.

It is against this background of intense intertextuality and interdiscursivity that Bhatia's present book makes an important and original contribution. He begins from variation, hybridity and dynamism in the accounting for genres, and focuses on how such complexity can now be recognized as co-occurring with increasing hybridization of organizational life, and how to analyse such hybrid genres with view to their application potential. In this sense, his book is much more than an exercise in specialized text or discourse analysis. Indeed, it is very much more than a book about genres. The main title *Worlds of Written Discourse* is an invitation to recognize that shift in genre studies we have alluded to above. There is also another shift to be discerned: one away from the overwhelmingly pedagogic orientation of earlier work on genre, concerned with, and indeed driven by, practices in the field of teaching foreign languages for specific purposes, towards one engaged with new audiences concerned with the exploitation of genres in their social and institutional space.

We envisage that new fields of applied linguistic endeavour, for example in professional and organizational communication, will find much in this book to underpin their field research and analytic gaze, as well as their own applications to practice. At the same time, we believe the book will sit well with current engagements with discourse in the sociology of work, especially in exploring orders of discourse in the workplace, as with the critical analysis of, say, how genres can be deliberately designed as obligatory performance targets as a way of apprenticing workers into conforming to organizational objectives. That such processes are not unproblematic is evidenced by internal struggles over ideology which are in themselves prime motivators for precisely the generic hybridity and instability that Bhatia identifies and illustrates here. As just three examples, we might point to current research and publication over the issue of GM (genetically modified) foods where scientific, political, and plain consumer-persuasion genres are inextricably and deliberately confounded in public presentation; or in the field of alternate dispute resolution, where more therapeutically grounded genres have been melded with the more adjudicatory, as mediation specialists construct a novel professional identity from the fields of counselling and law (Candlin & Maley 1997); or in Swales' genial study of the genres within an academic building in terms of what he calls its 'textography' (Swales 1998). We have, then, an increasingly rich store of data on just such generically evidenced contestation and hybridity. It is against this background that this book presents a critical and explanatory, as well as a descriptive and interpretive dimension.

There are two other areas which warrant identifying, however, from the arguments in this book. One has to do with the increasing interest in *creativity* in discourse (Carter 2004), where the argument that demotic creativity as a property of everyday talk (and writing) is gaining considerable applied linguistic interest over the study of more canonical forms of literary and artistic creativity, the property of stylistics. If, as Carter argues, we are all in some sense creative artists, then it is our manipulation and dynamic utilization of the construct of genre which enables us to warrant this creativity. As all artists work within certain frames, if only to fracture them, so there is value in genre studies in establishing by all manner of descriptive means what those boundaries might be, however metaphysical, as much as there is value in exploring how they are creatively contravened and breached. Bhatia's book has much to contribute here in his discussion of what he calls *tactical space*. Secondly, we may point to the preponderance of genre analyses in the past which have focused on performance and production. Of equal interest, as Sarangi (2004) indicates, is the interpretative potential of genres. What interpretations do they evoke, which are in fact taken up, and which constrained? Here, of course, we return to that socio-cognitive perspective on genre we referred to earlier, but with a twist. The socio-cognition here is not merely psychological, it is tightly connected to the exigencies of the social, once more reinforcing the social and critical perspective of this innovative contribution to the *Advances in Applied Linguistics* series, and widening considerably its audiences. Although the Series ceases to exist under this label, we are confident that the philosophy and principles underlying the Series will continually inform future scholarship in the field of applied linguistics.

References

Bhatia, V. K. (1993) *Analysing Genre: Language Use in Professional Settings.* London: Longman.

Candlin, C. N. and Maley, Y. (1997) Intertextuality and interdiscursivity in the discourse of alternative dispute resolution, in B-L. Gunnarsson, P. Linell and B. Nordberg (eds), *The Construction of Professional Discourse.* London: Longman, 201–222.

Carter, R. (2004) *Language and Creativity: The Art of Common Talk.* London: Routledge.

Fairclough, N. (1993) Critical discourse analysis and the marketization of public discourse: the universities. *Discourse & Society* 4, 2, 193–217.

Kress, G. and van Leeuwen, T. (1996) *Reading Images.* London: Routledge.

Martin, J. R. (1985) Process and text: two aspects of human semiosis, in J. D. Benson and W. S. Greaves (eds) *Systemic Perspectives on Discourse. Volume 1.* Norwood, N.J. Ablex 248–274.

Miller, C. R. (1984) Genre as social action. *Quarterly Journal of Speech* 70, 151–167.

Sarangi, S. (2004) Mediated interpretation of hybrid textual environments. Editorial. *Text* 24/3.

Scollon, R. (1998) *Mediated Discourse as Social Interaction: A Study of News Discourse.* London: Longman.

Swales, J. (1990) *Genre Analysis: English in Academic and Research Settings.* Cambridge: Cambridge University Press.

Swales, J. (1998) *Other Floors, Other Voices: A Textography of a Small University Building.* Mahwah, N.J.: Lawrence Erlbaum.

Christopher N Candlin
Srikant Sarangi
General Editors

Introduction

Genre theory in the past few years has contributed immensely to our understanding of the way discourse is used in academic, professional and a variety of other institutional contexts; however, its development has been quite understandably constrained by the nature and design of its applications, which have invariably focused on language teaching and learning, or communication training and consultation. In such narrowly identified and restricted contexts, one often tends to use simplified and idealized genres. The real world of discourse, in contrast to this, is complex, dynamic, versatile and unpredictable, and often appears to be confusing and chaotic. These aspects of the real world have been underplayed in the existing literature on genre theory and practice. As a consequence, we often find a wide gap between genre analyses of texts in published literature, emphasizing the integrity and purity of individual genres, and the variety of rather complex and dynamic instances of hybridized genres that one tends to find in the real world. This tension between the real world of written discourse and its representation in applied genre-based literature, especially in the context of the present-day academic, professional and institutional world, is the main theme of this book.

The book addresses this theme from the perspectives of four rather different worlds: the *world of reality*, which is complex, ever changing and problematic; the *world of private intentions*, where established writers appropriate and exploit generic resources across genres and domains to create hybrid (mixed or embedded) forms, or to bend genres; the *world of analysis*, which proposes a multidimensional and multi-perspective framework to explore different aspects of genre construction, interpretation and exploitation; and finally the *world of applications*, where we focus on the implications of this view of genre theory, interpreting applied linguistics rather broadly in areas other than ESP and language teaching. Each of these worlds forms the basis of each of four sections of the book. In addition, there is the introductory section, which consists of the first chapter, which provides an overview of the field and proposes a four-space genre-based model of analysis of written discourse.

The overview in Chapter 1 claims that the present work in genre analysis has been the result of a systematic development of discourse analysis, which has gone through three main stages of 'textualization of lexico-grammar', 'organization of discourse' and 'contextualization of discourse'. Based on this historical development of genre theory, the chapter then proposes a four-space model of genre analysis, which looks at language as text, language as genre, language as professional practice and language as social practice.

The following two chapters then look at the real world of written discourse. The main argument is that the complexity of the real world can be viewed in terms of two rather different but related views of the world; one looks at genres within specific disciplinary domains, highlighting disciplinary differences within specific genres, whereas the other considers genre relationships across disciplinary domains, highlighting similarities across disciplines. The first one thus focuses on individual genres within disciplines, whereas the second one considers constellations of genres, which can be seen as 'genre colonies' across disciplinary boundaries. Both these views of the real world of discourse are useful for a more comprehensive understanding of the complexities of the real world of written discourse.

Section three incorporates Chapters 4 and 5. Chapter 4 explores a further dimension of written discourse which distinguishes genre construction, interpretation and use based on 'socially recognized' conventions from a careful 'exploitation' or 'manipulation' of shared genre conventions. Taking this view, on the one hand we find a range of genres in a variety of interacting relationships with one another, unfolding rich and often complex patterns of interdiscursivity, whereas on the other hand we find expert members of professional cultures exploiting this richness to create new forms of discourse, often to serve their 'private intentions' within the constructs of socially recognized communicative purposes as realized through specific genres. The chapter also takes a closer look at two of the many interesting examples of generic appropriation and conflicts, the first from the context of fundraising, where generic resources are appropriated from the discourse of marketing, creating conflicts between the corporate and the philanthropic cultures, and the second from legislative writing from two rather distinct legal systems, where two different socio-legal contexts coming in contact with each other create potential conflicts in the interpretation of similar genres. The chapter thus introduces greater complexity within the tactical space, leading to the appropriation of linguistic resources across genres, often encouraging expert writers to exploit conventions to 'bend' genres to their own advantage, sometimes giving rise to conflicts in generic interpretation. This also results in the creation of hybrid genres (both mixed and embedded).

These manipulations of established conventions raise legitimate questions about the integrity of genres and the extent of freedom that professional writers have when they choose to bend generic norms and conventions in order to create new forms. This brings into focus the underlying tension between 'generic integrity', 'generic appropriation' and 'generic creativity', which lies at the very centre of applied genre theory. Chapter 5 highlights the fact that 'generic integrity' is not something which is static or 'given', but something which is often contestable, negotiable and developing, depending upon the communicative objectives, nature of participation, and expected or anticipated outcome of the generic event. The chapter also focuses on two other related aspects of genre theory, the relationship between professional genres and expertise in particular professional fields, and how expert professionals acquire such expertise in their specialist fields and what role genre knowledge plays in this acquisition.

The emerging picture thus looks very much more complex and dynamic than what we had been familiar with in typical genre-based analyses of professional discourse. To investigate such a world, we need to have an equally complex, multidimensional and multi-perspective model of genre analysis. The next section, incorporating Chapter 6, is an attempt to provide a possible answer to the issues raised and proposes a multi-perspective and multidimensional framework for extending the theory and scope of genre analysis in an attempt to see 'the whole of the elephant', as they say, rather than approaching it from any specific point of view for a partial view. The chapter also illustrates the use of such a framework by undertaking analysis of a real text, highlighting some of the advances that the proposed framework claims.

The final section of the book takes up some of the implications of genre theory and identifies specific areas of application. In the context of applications, there is an attempt to give applied linguistics a much broader interpretation than language teaching and learning. In a similar manner, ESP is interpreted to cover language learning at work, either as part of what Lave and Wenger (1991) called *Legitimate Peripheral Participation*, or as communication training in the context of specific workplace practices.

With the rapid pace of economic development in recent years, the world has become a much smaller place; socio-political boundaries are being consistently undermined in an attempt to create global markets, which have created opportunities for interaction across linguistic boundaries. This development has created contexts where translation and new forms of information and document design have assumed a much greater importance than at any time in the history of our civilization. Genre theory, as part of its objective to understand language use, has a valid contribution to make in this area as well. Thus teaching of language is no longer seen as an end in itself; it is increasingly seen as a means of acquiring professional expertise associated and integrated with the discursive practices of the work-place and professional cultures, whether they relate to the construction and interpretation of professional documents, designing of information through the new media, or translation across languages and cultures. In this sense, genre theory has become increasingly popular and powerful in the last few years.

In order to cope with these demands in broadly interpreted applied linguistics, the tools for analysing language are also becoming much more comprehensive and hence powerful in two ways at least. On the one hand, advancement in the field of computational linguistics has made it possible to process large corpora of language use and draw more reliable conclusions. On the other hand, interdisciplinary interests in the use of language have encouraged analysts to look for more meaningful relationships between language descriptions and institutional, professional and socio-cultural processes that shape the use of language in society, giving immense power to expert professionals and writers. If genre brings power, can we afford to ignore the politics of genre? Genre theory has significant implications for the politics of language use, and therefore the final chapter pays some attention to the exploitation of genres in the maintenance of power and the politics of language use in professional contexts.

In this book I have made an attempt to take my understanding of genre beyond my earlier concept of genre, which was restricted by my pedagogic concerns of the classroom. I have deliberately and consciously tried to turn my back on the classroom to face the world of discourse as it really is: complex, dynamic, changing, unpredictable and sometimes chaotic. I have tried to develop a model of genre analysis which adds to my earlier work and also to that of a number of other researchers. I see this as an attempt to integrate various frameworks and views of genre theory, rather than as an entirely new development.

Vijay K. Bhatia

OVERVIEW

1 Perspectives on written discourse

I am using the term *discourse* in a general sense to refer to *language use* in institutional, professional or more general social contexts. It includes both the written as well as the spoken forms, though I will be mainly concerned with written discourse in this book. Discourse analysis refers to the study of naturally occurring written discourse focusing in particular on its analysis beyond the sentence level. As a general term, discourse analysis therefore can focus on lexico-grammatical and other textual properties, on regularities of organization of language use, on situated language use in institutional, professional or organizational contexts, or on language use in a variety of broadly configured social contexts, often highlighting social relations and identities, power asymmetry and social struggle.

1.1 History and development

In this opening chapter, I would like to give some indication of the way analysis of written discourse has developed in the last few decades. There are a number of ways one can see the historical development of this field. Viewing primarily in terms of different perspectives on the analysis of written discourse in academic, professional and other institutionalized contexts, one can identify a number of rather distinct traditions in the analysis of written discourse, some of which may be recognized as *discourse as text, discourse as genre, discourse as professional practice* and *discourse as social practice*. On the other hand, it is also possible to view the chronological development of the field in terms of three main phases, each one highlighting at least one major concern in the analysis of written discourse. The first phase can be seen as focusing on the *textualization* of lexico-grammatical resources and the second one on the regularities of *organization*, with the final one highlighting *contextualization* of discourse.

There is some value attached to both the views, and therefore I would like to highlight some aspects of the field based on the chronological development first, and then make an attempt to integrate them into a coherent argument for treating the field of written discourse analysis as a gradual development in the direction of a number of specific perspectives on the analysis of written discourse. The chapter therefore represents historical development of the field on the one hand, and increasingly thicker descriptions of language use on the other.

The three phases that I have referred to above in the historical development of analysis of written discourse thus are:

- Textualization of lexico-grammar
- Organization of discourse
- Contextualization of discourse

In discussing these three rather distinct phases in the development of analysis of written discourse, I would like to further distinguish them in terms of various stages, some of which will show occasional overlaps; however, the purpose of the discussion is to highlight the nature of the development of the field, and more importantly the influence of relevant insights from disciplines other than descriptive linguistics, which was the main influence in the early descriptions of language use. Let me discuss some of the important aspects of what I have referred to as the chronological development of the field.

Textualization of lexico-grammar

The analyses of language use in early days, especially in the 1960s and the early 1970s, were overly influenced by frameworks in formal linguistics, and hence remained increasingly confined to surface-level features of language. These analyses were also influenced by variation studies due to the interest of many linguists in applied linguistics and language teaching (Halliday, McIntosh and Strevens 1964). Without getting into a detailed history of language variation and description, I would like to highlight some of the important stages of such a gradual development.

As part of the study of language variation as 'register' (Halliday, McIntosh and Strevens 1964), the early analyses of written discourse focused on statistically significant features of lexico-grammar used in a particular subset of texts associated with a particular discipline. Barber (1962) was probably one of the earliest studies identifying significant grammatical features in a corpus of scientific texts. Computational analytical procedures were not developed at that time, and hence the analytical findings were confined to only some of the significant features rather than a complete analysis of the corpus as such. Similarly, Gustaffsson (1975) focused on only one syntactic feature of legal discourse, i.e. binomials and multinomials. In a similar manner

4

Spencer (1975) identified yet another typical feature of legal discourse, *noun–verb combinations*. The trend continued with Bhatia and Swales (1983) who identified nominalizations in legislative discourse as their object of study. In all these preliminary attempts, one may notice two concerns: an effort to focus on the surface level of specialized texts, and an interest in the description of functional variation in discourse by focusing on statistically significant features of lexis and grammar. Both these concerns seemed to serve well the cause of applied linguistics for language teaching, especially the teaching and learning of English for Specific Purposes (ESP). There was very little attention paid to any significant comparisons of different varieties, perhaps because of the focus on ESP, which often concerned a well-defined group of learners from a specific discipline.

Some of the early analyses of lexico-grammar in specialized texts used in language teaching and learning gave an incentive to investigations of functional values that features of lexico-grammar in specialized texts represent, though often within clause boundaries without much reference to discourse organization. Functional characterization of lexico-grammar or textualization in terms of discoursal values within the rhetoric of scientific discourse was investigated in Selinker, Lackstrom and Trimble (1973). During this phase there was a clear emphasis on the characterization of functional values that features of lexico-grammar take in written discourse. Swales (1974) investigated the function of en – participles in chemistry texts; Oster (1981) focused on patterns of tense usage in reporting past literature in scientific discourse; and Dubois (1982) analysed the discoursal values assigned to noun phrases in biomedical journal articles. Swales (1974) documents one of the most insightful analyses of functional values of 'bare' attributive en-participles in single-noun NPs, both in the pre- and post-modifying positions, in a corpus of chemistry textbooks. He assigns two kinds of functional values to pre-posed uses of *given*, that of clarification of the 'status' of the sentence or that of exemplification by the author. The following text (Swales 1974: 18) contains the use of an en-participle for clarification:

> A given bottle contains a compound which upon analysis is shown
> to contain 0.600 gram-atom of phosphorous and 1.500 gram-atom
> of oxygen.

He explains that the function of given is to prevent unnecessary and irrelevant enquiries of the following kind:

- Is this a typical experiment?
- Who did the experiment?

● How large was the bottle?

Since attribution is an important convention in science, the role of given here is to signal unmistakably that the convention is being suspended. On the other hand, <u>given</u> in the following sentence is used as a crypto-determiner to assign a very specific meaning to the noun:

> Figure 9.5 shows how the vapour pressure of <u>a given</u> substance changes with temperature.
>
> (Swales 1974)

Swales (1974: 19) rightly claims that any of the ordinary language substitutions for <u>a given</u>, such as <u>a certain</u> or <u>a particular</u>, in a case like this will make the reading 'insufficiently generalized', whereas a substitution such as <u>any</u> or <u>every</u> will lead to over-generalization. This leads Swales to conclude that this particular en-participle performs a very specific rhetorical function, which is unique to scientific discourse.

It is possible to extend such a study of textualization of lexico-grammatical features to other genres, often comparing their use across different genres. In an earlier study (Bhatia 1991), while investigating the use of nominals in professional genres such as advertisements, scientific research reports and legislative provisions, I discovered that although nominals were used overwhelmingly in all these genres, they were markedly different not only in their syntactic form, but also in their rhetorical function. In advertising, nominals typically take the form *(Modifier) Head (Qualifier)*, where modifiers are realized primarily in terms of a series of linearly arranged attributes as follows:

(Determiner) (Adjective) (Adjective) (Adjective) ... Head (Qualifier)

Since one of the main concerns in advertising is to offer a positive evaluation of products or services being promoted, and nominals, in particular noun phrases, are seen as carriers of adjectives, we are likely to find an above-average incidence of nominals in such genres. The following is a typical example of this:

> The world's smallest and lightest digital camcorder
> that's also a digital still camera

On the other hand, nominals in academic research genres, especially in the sciences, are used to create and develop technical concepts. These nominals take the form of nominal compounds that have the following structure:

(Modifier) (Modifier) (Modifier) ... Head (Qualifier)

where modifiers are typically realized in terms of a series of linearly arranged nouns functioning as classifiers and occasionally incorporating an adjective. The following is a typical example of this phenomenon (Bhatia 1993: 149):

> Nozzle gas ejection space ship attitude control

In the case of legislative discourse, nominals are typically realized in the form of nominalizations as these syntactic forms allow draftsmen to condense clauses for subsequent references in the same sentence, adding precision and unambiguity to legislative provisions (Bhatia 1982, 1993). The following is a typical example of such a process of nominalizations (underlined):

> If the debtor fails without reasonable cause to attend on the Official Receiver as aforesaid or to furnish him with such <u>information</u> as aforesaid, or if the debtor obstructs the search of the premises or the <u>production</u> of any book or <u>document</u> required in connection therewith, or authorizes or permits any such <u>obstruction</u>, the debtor shall be liable on summary <u>conviction</u> to <u>imprisonment</u> for any term not exceeding 6 months, and every person who takes any part in any such <u>obstruction</u>, whether authorized or permitted by the debtor or not, shall be liable to the like <u>penalty</u>.
> (Section 8.3 of the Bankruptcy Ordinance 1997, HKSAR)

Almost at the same time one could see attempts towards a conceptualization of text and discourse through semantics and pragmatics by van Dijk (1977, 1985), Beaugrande and Dressler (1981), Brown and Yule (1983) and several others who focused on developing a relationship between the choice of lexico-grammar and specific forms of discourse organization that can be viewed as an extension of linguistic description. Although the terms used were text and discourse organization, the emphasis clearly was on cohesion and coherence, macro-structures and information structures of discourse. Beaugrande and Dressler (1981) and van Dijk (1985) relied more on linguistics and psycholinguistics to focus on what became popular as text-linguistics, which was developed as a reaction to the study of ideal language within sentence boundaries in much of descriptive linguistics. It was an attempt to focus on authentic texts seen as instances of language use in real contexts. Text-linguistics marked an interesting departure from descriptive linguistics in that it firmly believed that one must investigate as many texts as possible in order to see what is more typical, more frequent and more often done in certain contexts, and so on, even though it may not apply to the language as a whole. So this departure from language as a whole to specific instances of language use was a significant step in the development of discourse analysis. However, one of the common denominators in these studies was a relative lack of attention to functional variation in various discourse forms, which encouraged them to look for patterns of connectivity explored through cohesion and coherence in texts, sometimes leading to the identification of global discourse structures, which included macro-structures, as in van Dijk (1985), schematic structures, as in Beaugrande and Dressler (1981), or information structures, as in Brown and Yule (1983). All these aspects of discourse organization, however, were applicable to discourse in general rather than to specific genres.

Almost at the same time, drawing on disciplines such as philosophy, anthropology, sociology, psychology and linguistics, in particular seeking insights from speech act theory (Searle 1969), conversational maxims (Grice 1975), ethnography of communication (Hymes 1964) and conversational analysis, Coulthard (1977) proposed a multidisciplinary approach to discourse analysis that marked yet another significant departure from a linguistics-based description of language use.

One of the common characteristics of the studies of textualization of lexico-grammar in this phase was that, although most of these functional values were invariably investigated within the framework of a set of restricted aspects of specialist discourse, they certainly prompted analyses of broader rhetorical patterns leading to the identification of macro-structures, thus extending the scope of textualization from clause-level units to larger rhetorical structures such as extended clause-relations, as in Winter (1977), macro-structures in text-linguistics (van Dijk 1977 and others), information structures as in Hoey (1983), 'predictive structures' as in Tadros (1985) and rhetorical structures, as in Trimble (1985), some of which we now turn to in the next phase of development.

Organization of discourse

Focus on patterns of organization in written discourse triggered a more serious interest in the analysis of larger stretches of discourse, which also led to the identification of more global structures in various discourse types, encouraging analysts to study the immediate contexts in which such discourses are often embedded.

The next stage thus can be viewed as a continuation of exploration in textual organization, and is marked by attempts to identify patterns of discourse organization either in terms of problem-solution structures, as in Hoey (1983), rhetorical structures, as in

Widdowson (1973), or schematic structures, as in van Dijk (1988). Studies such as these established the development of discourse analysis because of the strong emphasis on regularities of organization in discourse. One can see this development in terms of three rather distinct stages: the first with focus on patterns of organization of information, specifically targeting specialized areas of discourse, the second with focus on general discourse organization patterns without any reference to functional variation, and the third with focus on discourse patterns across academic and professional genres. Widdowson (1973) mostly focused on rhetorical structures in scientific discourse, whereas van Dijk (1988) used schematic structures to analyse news reports. Coulthard (1977), van Dijk (1977) and Hoey (1983), on the other hand, focused on more global patterns of organization that applied to several forms of discourse across discourse types and genres. However, the emphasis in both of them was on regularities of discourse organization in terms of structural elements, which were often broadly explained by reference to the rhetorical processes involved in the construction of such texts.

This kind of engagement with the structuring of discourse was taken further by those involved in the analysis of text as genre, relating discourse structures to communicative purposes the genres in question served. They interpreted such structures not simply in terms of schematic patterns of individual readers, but more narrowly in terms of the socio-cognitive patterns that most members of a professional community use to construct and interpret discourses specific to their professional cultures. Quite appropriately, these regularities were seen in terms of 'moves', rather than schematic structures, as proposed in Swales (1981a, 1990) and Bhatia (1982, 1993).

As a result of this continual quest for more detailed and grounded descriptions of language use, discourse analysts in the next phase of development started taking context of language use in a more serious way: context, both the immediate context in the form of what surrounds a particular text, and also context in a much broader sense in the form of 'what makes a particular text possible' and 'why most of the professionals from the same disciplinary culture construct, interpret and use language more or less the same way in specific rhetorical situations'. However, during this initial phase we continue to see central interest in the organization of discourse as genre in the form of move structures, which were seen as cognitive structures that professionals often use to make sense of the genres they habitually used. The monograph by Swales (1981a) on 'Aspects of Article Introductions' was probably the most significant contribution to the development of genre theory in this direction, followed by his more

9

comprehensive version in Swales (1990). Bhatia (1993) extended the study of move structures in two ways, firstly by applying it more generally to a number of other professional genres, most significantly from legal and business domains, and secondly by extending the role of context to bring in a number of other factors, particularly socio-cognitive. Although the analysis of generic moves was motivated by issues related to the rationale for genres, the emphasis in practice at this stage continued to be on regularities of organization.

The most significant development in this phase was the emergence of genre theory for the analysis of written discourse. One may identify three rather distinct frameworks developed and used for analysing genre. These are popularly known as the American school of genre studies, as represented in the works of Miller (1984, 1994), Bazerman (1994) and Berkenkotter and Huckin (1995); the Sydney school of systemic-functional approach to genre, as developed by Martin, Christy and Rothery (1987) and Martin (1993); and the British ESP school, as represented in the works of Swales (1981a, 1990) and Bhatia (1982, 1993). Several accounts of these developments based on variations in frameworks are available in literature (Bhatia 1996a, 1997c; Hyon 1996; Johns 2002; Yunick 1997).

Analysing discourse as genre in this phase rapidly became a popular framework for the investigation of conventionalized or institutionalized genres in the context of specific institutional and disciplinary practices, procedures and cultures in order to understand how members of specific discourse communities construct, interpret and use these genres to achieve their community goals and why they write them the way they do. At the same time one can see greater importance given to the role of context in a wider sense to incorporate the real world, especially the academic world and the world of the professions, to give greater validity to analytical findings. This saw a movement in two somewhat overlapping directions: one towards analysing the real world of discourse, which was complex, dynamic and continually developing, and the other towards the role of broader social factors such as power and ideology, social structures, social identities, etc. (in addition to narrowly identified professional or institutional factors such as disciplinary cultures, discursive practices and discursive procedures) that were seen to contribute in a significant way to the construction and interpretation of discourse. The first one saw the emergence of a whole body of literature on hybridization in discourse, both in the form of mixed and embedded genres (Bhatia 1995, 1997a, 1998a), development and change in genres (Berkenkotter and Huckin 1995), and historical development of genres and systems of genres (Bazerman 1988, 1994). The other concern to assign a greater role to social context developed into an area of discourse analysis popularly known as critical discourse analysis, on the one hand, and multidimensional and multi-perspective analysis of professional genres on the other. Analyses of discourse in the 1990s thus can also be seen as analyses of social context.

Contextualization of discourse

Once again it is possible to see three rather distinct concerns, though overlapping in a number of other ways, in handling social context. The first kind could be seen as an extension of the previous phase to look at genres in more detail, focusing on what makes these professional and institutionalized genres possible, particularly looking at most of the external aspects of genre construction, such as the following:

Purposes: Institutionalized community goals and communicative purposes
Products: Textual artefacts or genres
Practices: Discursive practices, procedures and processes
Players: Discourse and professional community membership
(Bhatia 1999a)

This concern to look more widely at disciplinary and institutional context also gave rise to a number of studies that looked at disciplinary variations (Bhatia 1999c; Hewings 1999; Hyland 2000), and in a number of cases, potential conflicts (Bhatia 1998b, 2000). While specialists in genre studies were extending their involvement with professional and disciplinary contexts, other discourse analysts were widening the role of context in a much broader sense, to include social context, in an attempt to investigate how discourse is used as a powerful instrument of social control (Sarangi and Slembrouck 1994), to establish identities, to communicate ideology, or to influence and maintain social processes, social structures and social relations. All these concerns became central to what in present-day literature is popularly identified as critical discourse analysis (Fairclough 1985, 1989, 1993, 1995; van Dijk 1993; Wodak 1994, 1996; Wodak *et al.* 1999). In this phase it is possible to distinguish yet another development, which overlaps considerably with genre and critical discourse analysis, which is known as analysis of (mediated) discourse as social interaction, represented by the works of Scollon (1998) and Gee (1999). These three states have been visually represented in Diagram 1.1, which has been inspired by a very early version of a similar display by Swales (unpublished notes).

STAGE	ANALYSIS	FINDINGS	EXAMPLES
T E X T U A L I Z A T I O N	Statistical significance of lexico-grammar	Passives in EST; Nominalizations in legal English; Noun-verb combinations in legal texts	Halliday *et al.* (1964); Barber (1962); Crystal and Davy (1969); Spencer (1975)
	Textualization of distinctive lexico-grammatical resources	Tenses in the rhetoric of science; En-participles in chemistry texts; Tenses in reporting past literature; Nominals in academic writing	Swales (1974); Oster (1981); Dubois (1982); Trimble (1985)
	From textualization to text and discourse	Relationship between semantics and pragmatics of text; Coherence in text interpretation; Intertextuality	van Dijk (1977); de Beaugrande and Dressler (1981); Brown and Yule (1983)
O R G A N I Z A T I O N	Textual patterns leading to text types, highlighting rhetorical patterns	Rhetorical structures; Rhetorical-grammatical structures in science texts; Predictive structures in economics textbooks	Widdowson (1973); Selinker *et al.* (1973); Tadros (1985); Candlin *et al.* (1980)
	General global patterns of discourse organization	Rhetorical patterns; Problem-solution patterns; Schematic structures; Macro-structures	Coulthard (1977); Hoey (1983); van Dijk (1988)
	Cognitive structures and rationale in genres	Move structures in genres; Qualificational patterns; Generic structure potential	Swales (1981a, 1990); Bhatia (1982, 1993); Hasan (1985)
C O N T E X T U A L I Z A T I O N	Socio-cognitive aspects of genres; development and exploitation of generic resources	Genre development and change; Genre mixing, embedding; Appropriation of generic resources; Systems of genres	Berkenkotter and Huckin (1995); Bazerman (1994); Bhatia (1997a, 1998a)
	Multidimensional, and multi-perspective analyses of professional and institutional genres	Why do professionals use language the way they do?; Disciplinary variation and conflicts in genres	Swales (1998); Bhatia (1999c, 2000); Hyland (2000); Candlin and Hyland (1999)
	Language as critical discourse; Language as social control; Language in and as social interaction	Discourse, change and hegemony; Social control in institutionalized discourses; Language and ideology; Language as mediated discourse	Fairclough (1992, 1993, 1995); Sarangi and Slembrouck (1994); Scollon (1998)

Diagram 1.1: *Historical development of written discourse analysis*

From this rather brief journey through the history of discourse analysis, especially in applied linguistics, it is possible to visualize that the field of discourse and genre analysis has developed gradually, and somewhat consistently. However, it must be pointed out at this stage that if one were to consider developments in discourse analysis, with a particular focus on spoken discourse in broadly identified social contexts, one could view this movement in somewhat the opposite direction, i.e. from contextualization to textualization. In the present context, since I am focusing on the historical development of institutional and disciplinary variation in written discourse, I would prefer to take the movement from textualization to textual organization, and then to contextualization, rather than the other way round. Let me illustrate these three aspects of the development, i.e. textualization, text organization and contextualization, by taking an example from a specific field of discourse, that is a letter from the chairman of a public listed company to its shareholders, shown in Figure 1.1.

A text like this in the 1960s and early 1970s was invariably analysed in terms of its statistically significant features of lexis and grammar. Two of the important aspects that become immediately obvious for lexico-grammatical attention are the patterns of verb tense and nominals. The text contains a very high incidence of present perfect tenses, such as the following:

- have made
- have concentrated
- (have) pursued
- have responded
- have increased
- (have) reduced
- extended
- reduced
- have brought together

There are other verb forms that project future expectations:

- has been positioned to prosper
- will be able to exploit

The text also contains a very high incidence of three kinds of nominals. The first kind consists of the following instances:

- the progress
- the challenges
- the merger
- objectives
- economic environment
- intense competition

Dear fellow shareholders,

I am pleased to present our interim results for the six months ended [date] on behalf of my fellow directors.

It is now two years since the merger of [Name of Company 1] and [Name of Company 2], and it is appropriate to address the progress we have made and the challenges ahead. Since the merger, we have concentrated on and successfully pursued three objectives.

First, we have responded to the poor economic environment and intense competition in our industry by driving operating efficiencies within our Company. Secondly, we have increased our financial flexibility, successfully reduced debt to a prudent level, extended the maturity of our remaining debt and reduced significantly our overall funding costs. Thirdly, we have brought together a world-class management team with broad industry experience and strong leadership qualities. Increased operating efficiencies and reduced funding costs are, in turn, driving strong and accelerating free cash flows to give the Company unprecedented flexibility going forward. Without diminishing our commitment to the objectives set during our first two years and, in particular, our commitment to find greater productivity gains and to reduce debt further, our management team is now concentrated on forming strategies to deliver sustained growth over the coming years.

Since the merger, [Name of Company 1] has been positioned to prosper in extraordinarily difficult economic and operating conditions.

Accordingly, when our economy and operating environment turns round, [Name of Company 1] will be able to exploit opportunities to the benefit of our shareholders, customers and employees.

[Name]

Chairman   [Date]

Figure 1.1 *Letter from the chairman of a public listed company to its shareholders*

The second kind contains a number of other nominals that express business concepts:

- operating efficiencies
- financial flexibility
- prudent level

- the maturity of our remaining debt
- overall funding costs
- free cash flows
- productivity gains

The third kind has a number of other nominals that are associated with positive expectations regarding future business performance:

- a world-class management team
- broad industry experience
- strong leadership qualities
- increased operating efficiencies
- reduced funding costs
- strong and accelerating free cash flows
- unprecedented flexibility
- commitment to the objectives
- commitment to find greater productivity gains

An overwhelmingly typical incidence of these two features of lexico-grammar, i.e. three types of nominals and the use of perfect and future tense forms, is interesting. The features interestingly cooperate in this context to indicate that the text is embedded in a specific business context (note specifically the use of *economic environment, intense competition, financial flexibility*, etc.), and that it strongly projects a positive and forward-looking image of the achievements of the specific organization in question (see the use of *has been positioned to prosper, will be able to exploit*, and *have responded*, etc.). Going a little further one may also interpret this as being very typical of business activity, which always thrives on building positive relations between various participants, in this case the organization, the employees and the shareholders. However, one may like to go still further to explore the relationship between some of these features and the discourse action that is intended through this text, and in order to investigate this, one may need to go beyond the typical use of these individual linguistic resources to see the whole text as a unit of discourse, its organization and purpose. In particular, one may notice the use of statements like '[Name of Company 1] has been positioned to prosper in extraordinarily difficult economic and operating conditions', which may indicate a relatively more depressing business scenario than has otherwise been projected in earlier sections. The text, on the surface, may give a very positive image, but underneath it has a rather more cautious and to some extent more negative interpretation.

That is where one may invariably move to organization of discourse, and may notice that the text is a letter from the chairman of the company to its shareholders. It contains a number of conventional indicators that go with such a genre. As an example of a letter, it has all the typical signals such as the opening address, the closing, and of course the body of the letter. Moving more towards treating this as a genre one may claim that the communicative purpose of this letter is to inform the readers, who are the stakeholders in the company, about the performance of the company in the past year. The rationale for writing this letter the way it has been written in such a positive tone is that businesses often downplay any indications of negative performance to highlight positive aspects for future growth. Letters like these are often accompanied by annual reports which are supposed to contain more realistic and objective performance indicators, such as the facts and figures of growth and achievement, profit or loss, past weaknesses and future strengths of the company in question. In order to get the real picture, the stakeholders often need to go beyond the rhetoric and interpret the results carefully. All these factors, when analysed closely in the context of the rationale for the genre, the lexico-grammatical features of the text and also the nature of participant relationship, will disclose a number of interesting interpretations of the genre.

In addition, one may find it more useful to go beyond this analysis of the surface of the text and may look at other accompanying or related texts, one of which may be what is popularly known as the disclaimer. Let us go beyond the present text and look at part of the disclaimer, in Figure 1.2.

The disclaimer forms an interesting part of the genre. In the absence of such a disclaimer, one is likely to have only a misleading interpretation of the letter. If the letter is a claimer, in that it was designed to claim a positive and reassuring picture, the disclaimer makes it complete, in that it is meant to remedy any misleading impression it might have given about the future promises. This process of going beyond the surface of discourse to what makes a particular text or its interpretation possible is very much central to genre analysis.

It is also possible, and indeed desirable in some contexts, to explore other issues connected with broad contextualization, which will require a deeper understanding of context in addition to textualization, textual organization and the immediate context, including other relevant texts. Especially important is the asymmetry in the role relationship between the participants, accompanied by the power distance between the company chairman and the shareholders, on the one hand, and social proximity between the chairman and the

[NAME OF THE COMPANY]
Disclaimer
FORWARD-LOOKING STATEMENTS

This annual report contains forward-looking statements ... These forward-looking statements are not historical facts. Rather, the forward-looking statements are based on the current beliefs, assumptions, expectations, estimates and projections of the directors and management of [Name of the Company] ('the Company') about its business and the industry and markets in which it operates.

These forward-looking statements include, without limitation, statements relating to revenues and earnings. The words 'believe', 'intend', 'expect', 'anticipate', 'project', 'estimate', 'predict' and similar expressions are also intended to identify forward-looking statements. These statements are not guarantees of future performance and are subject to risks, uncertainties and other factors, some of which are beyond the Company's control and are difficult to predict. Consequently, actual results could differ materially from those expressed or forecast in the forward-looking statements.

Reliance should not be placed on these forward-looking statements, which reflect the view of the Company's directors and management as of the date of this report only. The Company undertakes no obligation to publicly revise these forward-looking statements to reflect events or circumstances that arise after publication.

Figure 1.2 *Part of the disclaimer*

fellow directors, on the other. One may also notice the indications of one-way unequal interaction, with the writer providing general information to recipients who may not share the same awareness about the company's past performance. The social or professional context in which this text or genre plays an important role, the social action that this particular example of text represents, and the institutional, social or professional culture it invokes when it is constructed and interpreted, are some of the important issues that need to be investigated. It is not simply that a professional genre is constructed and used for a specific professional purpose; it may be that a specific genre is deliberately and consciously bent to achieve something more than just a socially accepted and shared professional objective. One may need to investigate how and to what extent this seemingly harmless genre can be used to disinform, if not deliberately misinform, minority shareholders and other stakeholders of the company about the real performance of the company. One may need to develop a much broader understanding of context to answer some of

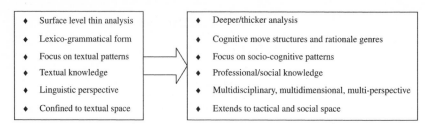

Diagram 1.2: *Discourse variation studies in disciplinary contexts*

these questions, which leads us to the third phase of the development as represented in Diagram 1.1. The movement from textualization to contextualization indicates explorations from textual space to social space, through socio-cognitive and professional space, which incorporates a gradual development as set out in Diagram 1.2.

1.2 Multi-perspective model of discourse

The story of written discourse analysis presented here has been a journey through several conceptualizations of space: beginning in the early 1960s with the textual space; and then, under the influence of speech act theory, ethnography of communication, conversational analysis, pragmatics and cognitive psychology, and also because of interest in the teaching and learning of English for Specific Purposes (ESP) and professional communication, moving into what could be identified broadly as socio-cognitive (tactical as well as professional) space; and finally, because of the increasing influence of socio-critical concerns, moving into social space. The various frameworks used for discourse analysis therefore are reflections of these concerns, and can be identified as discourse as text, discourse as genre, discourse as professional practice, and discourse as social practice, which can be combined into a multi-perspective four-space model of discourse analysis as represented in Diagram 1.3.

The four-space model outlined in this chapter, which forms the basis of the present theoretical framework for analysing written discourse, will be explored in greater detail in later chapters of the book through investigations into what could be identified as the four worlds of discourse: the world of reality (i.e. the world of discourse in action), the world of private intentions (i.e. exploitations of discourse by expert and established writers), the world of analysis (i.e. the role of analytical tools) and the world of applications. However, before we go to these chapters, some further elaboration is necessary here. As mentioned at the outset, I am using 'discourse' as a general term to

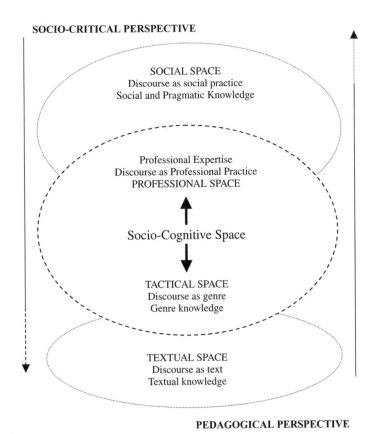

SOCIO-CRITICAL PERSPECTIVE

SOCIAL SPACE
Discourse as social practice
Social and Pragmatic Knowledge

Professional Expertise
Discourse as Professional Practice
PROFESSIONAL SPACE

Socio-Cognitive Space

TACTICAL SPACE
Discourse as genre
Genre knowledge

TEXTUAL SPACE
Discourse as text
Textual knowledge

PEDAGOGICAL PERSPECTIVE

Diagram 1.3 *Perspectives on written discourse analysis*

refer to any instance of the use of written language to communicate meaning in a particular context, irrespective of any particular framework for analysis. The analysis of discourse, however, can be viewed in different ways, as text, genre, professional practice or social practice. Let me give more substance to this view.

I am using *discourse as text* to refer to the analysis of language use that is confined to the surface-level properties of discourse, which include formal as well as functional aspects of discourse, that is phonological, lexico-grammatical, semantic, organizational (including intersentential cohesion) and other aspects of text structure (such as 'given' and 'new', 'theme' and 'rheme') or information structures (such as 'general-particular', problem-solution, etc.) not necessarily having interaction with *context* in a broad sense but merely taking into account what is known as co-text. Although as indicated earlier,

19

discourse is essentially embedded in context, *discourse as text* often excludes any significant engagement with context, except in a narrow sense of intertextuality to include interactions with surrounding texts. *Discourse as text* thus operates essentially within a *textual space* where the knowledge about language structure and its function, which may include the knowledge of intertextuality, is exploited to make sense of it. The emphasis at this level of analysis is essentially on the properties associated with the construction of the textual product, rather than on the interpretation or use of such a product. It largely ignores the contribution often made by the reader on the basis of what he or she brings to the interpretation of the textual output, especially in terms of the knowledge of the world, including the professional, socio-cultural and institutional knowledge as well as experience that one is likely to use to interpret, use and exploit such a discourse.

Discourse as genre, in contrast, extends the analysis beyond the textual product to incorporate context in a broader sense to account for not only the way text is constructed, but also for the way it is often interpreted, used and exploited in specific institutional or more narrowly professional contexts to achieve specific disciplinary goals. The nature of the questions addressed in this kind of analysis may often include not only the linguistic, but also the socio-cognitive and the ethnographic. This kind of grounded analysis of the textual output is very typical of any framework within genre-based theory. Genre knowledge that makes sense of the text at this level includes, in addition to textual knowledge, the awareness and understanding of the shared practices of professional and discourse communities (Swales 1990) and their choice of genres in order to perform their everyday tasks. Genres often operate in what might be viewed as *tactical space* that allows established members of discourse communities to exploit generic resources to respond to recurring or often novel situational contexts. Closely related to this, one may find the concept of *discourse as professional practice*, which essentially extends the notion of genre use to relate it to professional practice. In order to operate effectively at this stage, one may require professional knowledge and experience of professional practice, in addition to genre knowledge. It operates in what could be regarded as *professional space*.

Discourse as social practice takes this interaction with the *context* much further in the direction of broader social context, where the focus shifts significantly from the textual output to the features of context, such as the changing identities of the participants, the social structures or professional relationships the genres are likely to maintain or change, and the advantages or disadvantages such genres are likely to bring to a particular set of readers. *Discourse as social practice* thus functions within a much broader *social space*, where one may essentially need social and pragmatic knowledge in order to operate effectively.

It is important to note that the three interacting views of discourse are not mutually exclusive, but are essentially complementary to each other. It is possible to use the proposed framework in a number of ways, depending upon the objective one may decide to pursue. A typical socio-linguist interested in discourse analysis will perhaps begin from the top end, looking deeply and exhaustively into the social context, working his way downward, but not often getting seriously engaged in the textual space. An applied linguist, on the other hand, would find it more profitable to begin at the bottom end, exploring the textual space exhaustively, working toward social space, often using social context as the explanation for the analysis of textualization of lexico-grammatical and discoursal resources. However, most users of the framework, whether interested in socio-cultural issues or pedagogical ones, at some stage or other will necessarily pay some attention to the socio-cognitive domain in order to consider socio-cognitive aspects of genre construction, interpretation and use or the exploitation of generic resources.

One can also see the prominence of the socio-cognitive space, which again incorporates two rather overlapping conceptualizations of tactical space and professional space in the proposed framework. These concepts seem to have a large degree of overlap because both of them work within the same socio-cognitive space, and also because genres are an integral part of professional practice, and hence both are closely related to each other in the context of professional cultures. We will explore this relationship between genre (tactical space) and professional practice (professional space) in more detail in Chapter 5, when we will focus on the acquisition of professional competence. At this stage it is sufficient to keep in mind that it is through genres that professional objectives are achieved, and it is through shared generic knowledge that professional solidarity is maintained.

The four-space model as outlined in Diagram 1.3 indicates two major perspectives on the analysis of written discourse, an essentially pedagogic perspective and a socio-critical perspective; however, there can be a third perspective as well, that is a generic perspective. This will look at discourse essentially as genre within a socio-cognitive space, and will pay some attention to textual features of language use, especially to textualization of some specific features of lexico-grammar, and textual organization, on the one hand, and to certain features of social practices, especially those related to professional practices, on the other. The strength of this perspective on language use is that although it specifically focuses on the construction and use of written discourse, especially the way it is done in professional practice, it does not ignore textual features completely. In fact, it pays all the necessary attention to the relevant features of textual form, without getting completely absorbed by formal properties of textual space. Similarly, on the other hand, although this view of discourse more centrally focuses on professional practice, it does not ignore issues within the social space. It views specific professional practices within a broader context of social practices, processes and procedures, without getting lost in broadly configured socio-cultural realities. Let me explain this genre-based view of discourse in some more detail.

1.3 Genre-based view of discourse

Many of the developments mentioned in the preceding discussion can be characterized in terms of a quest for thicker descriptions of language use, incorporating, and often going beyond, the immediate context of situation. This quest for thicker descriptions of language use has become popular as genre analysis, where an attempt is made to offer a grounded description of language use in educational, academic or professional settings. We can also see how linguistic analyses have become much more than mere descriptions, often attempting to offer an explanation for a specific use of language in conventionalized and institutionalized settings. These analyses, offering more explanatory linguistic descriptions, often attempt to answer the question: *why does a particular use of language take the shape it does*? In more recent years, genre analysis has developed further in the direction of a more comprehensive exploration of social space to raise a number of other interesting issues, in particular those that question some of the basic assumptions about the integrity of generic descriptions. But before we identify and discuss some of these issues, let us have a brief look at the assumptions first.

Genre analysis is the study of situated linguistic behaviour in institutionalized academic or professional settings, whether defined in terms of *typification of rhetorical action*, as in Miller (1984), Bazerman (1994) and Berkenkotter and Huckin (1995), *regularities of staged, goal-oriented social processes*, as in Martin, Christie and Rothery (1987) and Martin (1993), or *consistency of communicative purposes*, as in Swales (1990) and Bhatia (1993). Genre theory, in spite of these seemingly different orientations, covers a lot of common ground, some of which may be summarized on the basis of the analysis of these studies.

22

1. Genres are recognizable communicative events, characterized by a set of communicative purposes identified and mutually understood by members of the professional or academic community in which they regularly occur.
2. Genres are highly structured and conventionalized constructs, with constraints on allowable contributions not only in terms of the intentions one would like to give expression to and the shape they often take, but also in terms of the lexico-grammatical resources one can employ to give discoursal values to such formal features.
3. Established members of a particular professional community will have a much greater knowledge and understanding of the use and exploitation of genres than those who are apprentices, new members or outsiders.
4. Although genres are viewed as conventionalized constructs, expert members of the disciplinary and professional communities often exploit generic resources to express not only 'private' but also organizational intentions within the constructs of 'socially recognized communicative purposes'.
5. Genres are reflections of disciplinary and organizational cultures, and in that sense, they focus on social actions embedded within disciplinary, professional and other institutional practices.
6. All disciplinary and professional genres have integrity of their own, which is often identified with reference to a combination of textual, discursive and contextual factors.

As we can see, the most important feature of this view of language use is the emphasis on conventions that all the three manifestations of genre theory consider very central to any form of generic description. Genre essentially refers to language use in a conventionalized communicative setting in order to give expression to a specific set of communicative goals of a disciplinary or social institution, which give rise to stable structural forms by imposing constrains on the use of lexico-grammatical as well as discoursal resources. Some of these constraints can also be attributed to variations in disciplinary practices.

The second important aspect of genre theory is that although genres are typically associated with recurring rhetorical contexts, and are identified on the basis of a shared set of communicative purposes with constraints on allowable contributions in the use of lexico-grammatical and discoursal forms, they are not static. As Berkenkotter and Huckin (1995: 6) point out,

> ... genres are inherently dynamic rhetorical structures that can be manipulated according to conditions of use, and that genre knowledge is therefore best conceptualized as a form of situated cognition embedded in disciplinary cultures.

Emphasis on conventions and propensity for innovation, these two features of genre theory, may appear to be contradictory in character. One tends to view genre as a rhetorically situated and highly institutionalized textual activity, having its own generic integrity, whereas the other assigns genre a natural propensity for innovation and change, which is often exploited by the expert members of the specialist community to create new forms in order to respond to novel rhetorical contexts or to convey 'private intentions within the socially recognized communicative purposes' (Bhatia 1993). How do we react to this contradiction?

Although genres are associated with typical socio-rhetorical situations and in turn shape future responses to similar situations, they have always been 'sites of contention between stability and change' (Berkenkotter and Huckin 1995: 6). However, we know that situations, and more importantly rhetorical contexts, may not always recur exactly in the same way, though they may still have a considerable overlap. It may be that a person is required to respond to a somewhat changing socio-cognitive need, encouraging him to negotiate his response in the light of recognizable or established conventions. It may also be that he or she may decide to communicate 'private intentions' within the rhetorical context of a 'socially recognized communicative purpose' (Bhatia 1993). The example of text in Section 1.1, i.e. the letter from a company chairman to the shareholders, is a good example of expert manipulation of generic resources to convey a positive image about a company's somewhat negative performance. In contexts like these, it is often possible for established members of a professional community to manipulate institutionalized generic forms. Their experience and long association with the professional community give them 'tactical freedom' to exploit generic resources to negotiate individual responses to recurring and novel rhetorical situations. However, such liberties, innovations, creativities, exploitations, whatever one may choose to call them, are invariably realized within rather than outside the generic boundaries, whichever way one may draw them, in terms of recurrence of rhetorical situations (Miller 1984), consistency of communicative purposes (Swales 1990) and existence and arrangement of obligatory structured elements (Hasan 1985). It is never a free-for-all kind of activity. The nature of genre manipulation is invariably realized within the broad limits of specific genres and is often very subtle. A serious disregard for these generic conventions leads to opting out of the genre and is noticed by the specialist community as odd.

However, we also know that people, especially those who have the expertise and the power, do not hesitate to exploit some of these conventions to create new forms, in turn making this world of discourse much more complex and dynamic. Their communicative behaviour in such conventionalized contexts often gives rise to a number of issues based on tensions of the following kind:

1. Although genres are identified on the basis of conventiona-lized features, they continually develop and change.
2. Genres are associated with typical textualization patterns, yet expert members of professional communities exploit them to create new patterns.
3. Genres serve typical socially recognized communicative purposes; however, they can be exploited or appropriated to convey private or organizational intentions.
4. Although we often identify and conceptualize genres in pure forms, in the real world they are often seen in hybrid, mixed and embedded forms.
5. Genres are given typical names, yet different members of discourse communities have varying perspectives on and interpretations of them.
6. Genres, in general, cut across disciplinary boundaries, yet we often find disciplinary variations in many of them, especially in those used in academic contexts.
7. Genre analysis is typically viewed as a textual investigation, yet comprehensive analyses tend to employ a variety of tools, including textual analyses, ethnographic techniques, cogni-tive procedures, computational analysis and critical aware-ness, to name only a few.

These are all relevant issues for genre theory, and hence will be the focus of this book in the following sections. In many of the existing analyses of genre one tends to focus on typically identifiable and largely ideal instances of genres; in this volume, I would like to turn my back on the ideal world, as it were, and try to face the real world of discourse, which is complex, dynamic, constantly developing and often less predictable. There are regularities of various kinds, in the use of lexico-grammatical, discoursal and generic resources; there are rhetorical situations, which often recur, though not exactly in the same form or manner; there are expert and well-established users of language in specific disciplinary cultures who try to exploit, appropriate and even bend generic expectations in order to be innovative and effective in their use of language. All these factors make the real world of discourse complex and yet interesting. How do we handle a world of this kind, which is not entirely systematic, predictable and disciplined? How do these complexities create problems for genre theory and how do we use genre theory to account for the realities of the world of discourse? These are some of the challenges for this book.

THE WORLD OF REALITY

2 Genres within specific domains

The real world of discourse challenges the present-day theory and practice of genre in a number of ways. Firstly, the real world of discourse displays a degree of complexity in terms of 'genre sets' (Devitt 1991), 'systems of genres' (Bazerman 1994), 'disciplinary genres' (Bhatia 1998b, 1999c; Hyland 2000), registers (Halliday *et al.* 1964) and colonies of genres within and across disciplinary boundaries (Bhatia 1997b, 1998a; Bargiela-Chiappini and Nickerson 1999), which has not been fully accounted for in available literature. Genres have so far been individually and independently viewed as clearly distinct entities. Although it is true that most genres have an identifiable 'integrity' of their own (Bhatia 1993, 1994), it may often be seen as unstable, even 'contested' sometimes (Candlin and Plum 1999; Sarangi and Roberts 1999). Genres in the real world are often seen in relation to other genres with a certain degree of overlap or, sometimes, even conflict (Bhatia 1998a). Interestingly enough, on the one hand we find colonies of reporting genres, promotional genres, academic introductions, and I am sure many others, which often transcend disciplinary boundaries; on the other hand we find systems of genres which are often confined to specific disciplinary cultures, e.g. legislation, cases, judgements, discussion notes, briefs, etc., which are often largely associated with legal culture alone.

The second important aspect of variation in genres is sometimes associated with the evolution and development of genres (Berkenkotter and Huckin 1995). Although genres are often identified on the basis of their integrity, which is a reflection of their conventionalized characteristics, they are far from static. Most of them are dynamic, in the sense that they can be exploited to respond to novel rhetorical contexts, and thus have propensity for innovation and further development (Berkenkotter and Huckin 1995; Bhatia 1997a). The only problem is that one needs to have a certain degree of expertise, recognition and status in the professional community to be able to identify and exploit some of these conventionalized aspects of genre expectations (Kress 1987).

The third challenge to genre theory comes from disciplinary overlaps and conflicts within and across genres. Genre analysis has been conventionally viewed as the study of situated linguistic behaviour in institutionalized, academic or professional settings, where one often gets the impression that disciplinary distinctions do not play a significant role. As a result, disciplinary characteristics have often been ignored in most of the analyses of genres. However, in recent studies of professional discourses (Hyland 2000; Bhatia 1999b, 1999c; Hewings and Nickerson 1999), disciplinary distinctions have been found to play a significant role, especially in professional and workplace practices, where disciplinary boundaries are being renegotiated, giving rise to interdisciplinary discourses. Therefore, genre theory cannot afford to ignore the disciplinary conflicts any longer, and must come to terms with this aspect of discourse construction, interpretation and use. Let me discuss some of these terms in detail.

2.1 Registers, genres and disciplines

Discourse has been configured, analysed and understood in various ways, some times as *register* and more recently as *genre*, and often interacting with these two is the concept of *disciplinary discourses* (Hyland 2000). As one can see, these three ways of looking at discourse have a number of distinctive as well as overlapping features. In addition, there may be other ways of looking at discourse, especially as action, culture, power, etc., but I would like to restrict the discussion at this stage to registers, genres and disciplines only.

Discourse variation in academic, professional or workplace contexts has been popularly analysed first in terms of registers, and then more recently as genres, but both of them take into account some aspects of disciplinary variation. Registers have been variously identified, often on the basis of a specific configuration of three contextual factors: *field of discourse, mode of discourse* and *tenor of discourse* (Halliday *et al.* 1964). Closely related to registers we find *disciplines*, which invariably display predominant characteristics of the subject matter that they represent. However, the two are not synonymous. One represents the content, whereas the other represents the language associated with it. In the early years of ESP work, we often found these two terms considerably overlapping. Genres, on the other hand, cut across disciplines in an interesting manner. We often find textbooks displaying typical generic characteristics across a wide range of disciplines, which may include a number of disciplines in humanities, natural sciences or social sciences. They all seem to be driven by their communicative purpose of making established disciplinary knowledge accessible to large sections of uninitiated novice readers, and often displaying what could be regarded as the 'textbook competence' of knowledgeable and expert authors. As a consequence, in spite of their specific disciplinary characteristics, textbooks often display the use of overlapping generic resources, which may include typical features of lexico-grammar, rhetorical organization and the use of multiple modalities to make disciplinary knowledge accessible to an uninitiated readership. The work of Kress and Van Leeuwen (1996), specifically focusing on how people use communicative modes and media in actual, interactive instances of communicative practice, is particularly interesting.

The interrelationship between registers, genres and disciplines can be represented visually as shown in Diagram 2.1.

Although registers are seen as typical configurations of field, mode and tenor of discourse, disciplinary specificity does play a significant role in their identification (Hasan 1973). Disciplines, unlike registers, tend to be identified more in terms of their content, and in part by the field of discourse, rather than any typical configuration of all the three contextual factors of field, mode and tenor. However, it is sometimes possible to identify a register largely on the basis of one or

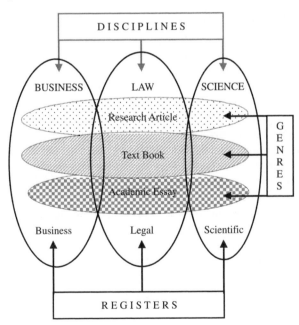

Diagram 2.1 Registers, genres and disciplines in academic discourse

two of these contextual factors only, and such registers are regarded as either primarily field-dominated registers, such as 'scientific register', or mainly mode-dominated register, as in the case of 'casual conversation', or tenor-dominated register like 'client consultation'. It was for this reason that in early ESP work, which primarily focused on field-dominated registers such as the registers of science or business, functional variation in them was seen primarily in terms of specialist lexis and some surface-level syntactic features alone. Disciplines, on the other hand, in spite of the overlap with registers, have their typical characteristics, and are primarily understood in terms of the specific knowledge, methodologies and shared practices of their community members, especially their ways of thinking, constructing and consuming knowledge, their specific norms and epistemologies and, above all, their typical goals and disciplinary practices to achieve those goals.

Genres cut across disciplines. Textbook as a genre, for instance, will certainly display a number of shared features across disciplinary boundaries. However, genres, at the same time, are sensitive to disciplinary variations as well. They display subtle variations in terms of specific disciplinary concerns, some of which are mutually exclusive. Textbooks in economics, for instance, will certainly display a number of similarities with textbooks in political science, because of their common concern with making disciplinary knowledge accessible to learners new to the disciplines. However, they will differ significantly in terms of their disciplinary characteristics, especially in the way they approach disciplinary knowledge, the way they present arguments, the kind of evidence they consider valid in that discipline, and also the strategies they find more useful to make difficult concepts accessible to learners. In relation to registers, genres are much more action-oriented than registers, which often indicate the general flavour of lexico-grammatical choices. Also, genres have certain socio-cognitive realities, in that they invariably display typical cognitive structuring realizing communicative purposes (move structures in Swales 1990 and Bhatia 1993), whereas registers are restricted to typical configurations of contextual features as realized through different aspects of the grammatical system.

The general picture thus tends to be a lot more complex than what may appear to be the case on the surface. There are variations of several kinds, interacting with one another in a number of interesting ways. The relationship between registers and specialist disciplines is more difficult to specify than the one between genres and disciplines. If disciplinary discourses display large areas of overlap with registers, they display significant areas of contrast with genres. Let me give more substance to this by considering disciplinary variations in some of the typical genres associated with academic context.

2.2 Disciplinary variation in genres within academic domains

(A) Disciplinary variation in textbooks

The textbook genre, irrespective of the discipline it is associated with, serves a common purpose in academic contexts, which is reflected in a number of typical features of textbook genres. As Hyland (2000: 104) points out:

> Textbooks are indispensable to academic life, facilitating the professional's role as a teacher and constituting one of the primary means by which the concepts and analytical methods of a discipline are acquired. They play a major role in the learners' experience and understanding of a subject by providing a coherently ordered epistemological map of the disciplinary land-scape and, through their textual practices, can help to convey the values and ideological assumptions of a particular academic culture.

Textbooks thus disseminate discipline-based knowledge and, at the same time, display a somewhat unequal writer–reader relationship, with the writer as the specialist and the reader as the non-initiated apprentice in the discipline, or the writer as the transmitter and the reader as the recipient of established knowledge. However, this effort to disseminate introductory uncontested knowledge is sometimes compromised by an attempt to offer what Love (2002: 76), on the basis of her analysis of sociology (Giddens 1993), claims to be the 'cutting edge' theories. Textbooks nevertheless are seen as 'repositories of codified knowledge' (Hyland 2000: 105) made accessible to large audiences by the frequent use of a variety of rhetorical devices. Some of these have been variously identified and named in applied linguistics literature as 'rhetorical structures' (description, definition, classification, etc.) in Trimble 1985 or Widdowson 1978, 'predictive structures' in Tadros 1989, 'access structure' in Waller 1977, or 'easification procedures' in Bhatia 1983. Tadros (1989) proposed an elaborate model of discourse prediction based on her analysis of data from textbooks in economics, and proposed a number of categories of predictive rhetorical structures, some of which included *reporting, question, advance labelling, enumeration, recapitulation* and *hypotheticality*. Later she applied the same model to law, and found that it worked well for this discipline too. These devices also include rhetorical questions as section headings to guide learners through the intricacies of discipline-based understanding, non-linear rhetorical devices like charts, diagrams, figures, pictures, etc. to express complex materials (Bhatia 1984; Trimble 1985), metadiscourse, especially lexical familiarizations or word glosses (Williams 1985) to explain difficult concepts, and a number of others such as box items, page-margin glosses, summaries, end-of-the-chapter exercises, suggestions for further reading, etc., and it is true that they are often used across a range of disciplines to make textbook knowledge accessible to non-initiated student populations.

However, in spite of these shared characteristics of textbooks across disciplines, we find that disciplinary cultures differ on several dimensions, some of which include constraints on patterns of membership and initiation into disciplinary communities, variation in knowledge structures and norms of inquiry in different disciplines, typical patterns of rhetorical intimacy associated with typical modes of expression, specialist lexis and discourses associated with different academic disciplines, and distinct approaches to the teaching of these disciplines.

Let me begin with two disciplines, i.e. those of economics and law, in an attempt to compare the way disciplinary knowledge is structured and communicated in instructional contexts. On the face of it, the two disciplines appear to be similar in that both of them tend to reinforce the relationship between theoretical aspects, processes and outcomes. Similarly, they may also create and formulate a complexity of integrated concepts and use what Halliday (1994) refers to as 'grammatical metaphor' to pack disciplinary knowledge for their specific audiences. The two disciplines may also share the way they need to explain the interrelationship between various concepts by referring to facts and figures, though it is quite likely that in business such facts and figures will have numerical values, whereas in law they will consist of human acts entangled in socio-legal relations.

In a number of other ways, the two disciplines appear to be very different, especially in terms of the rhetorical strategies they employ to construct knowledge. Business studies, in general, depends on aggressive innovation in the way it constructs its discourses. In fact, much of innovation in communicative practices in many other professional contexts has, in the last few decades, been inspired by changes in communicative patterns in the field of business, which is also reflected in economics textbooks. Law, on the other hand, relies on extreme conservatism in the way it constructs its discourses. Legislative and other statutory forms of writing, which are some of the most important genres in law, have not changed much in the last few decades. This has also influenced other forms of expression in the field. Textbook writing in law is no exception in this respect (see Bhatia 1998b, 1999c; Bhatia and Candlin 2001; Candlin *et al.* 2002).

The two disciplines also vary in terms of instructional strategies used in textbook materials. In economics textbooks, knowledge is often structured in the form of smaller units for greater understanding of ideas and information, and there is a constant effort to check that these units are accessible to learners. In law, on the other hand, information is more holistically structured, so that the learners do not misunderstand any idea or concept out of context. That is also one of the reasons why there is an extremely high degree of intertextuality and interdiscursivity in legal discourse, whether it is the case of textbooks, cases, judgements or legislation. In the case of textbook writing, in particular, one is often amazed at the number of footnotes one often finds in the discourses of law, although such rhetorical forms have become almost extinct in other disciplines. We also find significant variations in the nature and development of argumentation in the two disciplines, especially the way evidence is used to make claims, e.g. the way cases and legislation are used to make claims and to argue for them in the discourse of law, and the way numerical data is used to construct, formulate and support argumentation in economics.

Some of these disciplinary differences are reinforced in the advice that textbook writers often give as part of the introduction to their effort. Here is an extract from an economics textbook.

The main emphasis in *A Textbook of Economics* is on:

- incorporation of quantitative data in the teaching of economics without confusing it with a move towards mathematical economics,
- integration of this data with the theoretical arguments, and
- presentation of materials relating to actual economic events and processes, and how they relate to political economy in order to recognise the fact that the economic actions of individuals, firms and governments are often influenced by a range of motives, some of which may be political.

(Livesey 1982, emphasis added)

In the case of law, Gold (1982: 35), using Bloom's taxonomy of six constituent elements, points out:

The competent lawyer must not only know rules, theories, practices and procedures; he or she must most often also understand their meaning and their derivation. She or he must also be able to apply her or his knowledge to new similar or analogous situations. The lawyer must be able to analyze problems, doctrine, theory, and concepts and reduce them into their individual elements, and see patterns and structure apparent only after the analysis is complete. He or she must also be able to carry out the reverse process so that he or she can combine individual elements in such a way so as to be able to create a pattern not clearly visible before. Finally, the lawyer must exercise effective evaluation powers. This includes making judgments about the usefulness of certain rules, practices or procedures. It also includes being able to test the logic of arguments and reasons for judgment. The lawyer must be able to compare alternative approaches and choose among them.

The above extracts on the nature of learning in economics and law clearly indicate that although there is a strong emphasis on dissemination of theoretical concepts in law, their development is necessarily supported by and integrated with quantitative data from the economic actions of individual firms and governments. In order to do this, economists frequently use tables, graphs and equations as tools to show the relationships between variables or factors which bring about changes in patterns of production, distribution and consumptions of goods and services (Gordon and Dawson 1991). In the field of law, on the other hand, although there is a strong emphasis on deriving principles of law from the material facts of life, there is an equally strong emphasis on applying legal principles to specific material facts of life. The principles are often treated as given in the form of legislative provisions, and the main tasks are to understand, analyse, synthesize, evaluate and apply them to real data from human actions and their problematic legal relations (certainly not quantitative, in this case). The main objective in legal textbooks is to encourage legal reasoning, to think as a lawyer in order to understand and reflect on the nature of law, its functions and applications, all at the same time.

Demarcations between these broad subject areas thus appear not only to reflect differences in the structure of knowledge systems, but also to embody quite different assumptions about discourse and communication (Berkenkotter and Huckin 1995). These differences influence both the preferred modes of communication in different disciplines and the rhetorical characteristics of genres that students are expected to manage in becoming competent members of the discourse community. It would be interesting to see how these disciplines use rhetorical strategies to make knowledge accessible to student readers. Learning encounters with the disciplinary discourses for new entrants to specialist disciplinary cultures can hardly be more than what Lave and Wenger (1991) call a 'peripheral participation'.

In order to investigate this further, I would like to focus, though briefly, on the nature of discursive practices in different disciplines, and see the kind of rhetorical strategies that are typically favoured in these disciplinary instructional discourses. Instructional strategies used in present-day business education are becoming increasingly interactive and innovative. Many professionals and textbook writers in the discipline quite appropriately use the metaphor 'making learning a game' to refer to this kind of new approach to business and management studies. The nature of innovative and reader-friendly rhetorical strategies used in business and management textbooks, especially in those published in the USA, can be compared with the use of similar strategies in advertising. This may be attributed to several factors, which may include recent innovative practices very much characteristic of the discipline, intensity of competition in the textbook market, and the applied nature of the discipline. Whatever the motivation, it is true that business and management textbook writers have been able to exploit the full potential of the new technological resources and communicative media, which have become a characteristic feature of the business world. The use of specially designed sections on learning goals, opening profiles, progress checks, interactive summaries, reader involvement in learn-ing activities, practice cases, with colourful and attractive visuals and illustrations, as well as test banks, computer simulation exercises, stock market games, etc. is significantly more common in this discipline than in any other.

Law, on the other hand, in spite of intense competition in the textbook market, relies heavily on tried and tested modes of communication. The main objectives are to encourage legal reasoning to reflect on the nature of law and to pursue legal issues through research. The emphasis is on deriving principles of law from facts of life and also on applying principles to facts of life. Unlike textbooks in economics and business studies, strategies in law textbooks to promote learning are deeply rooted in the discourse of law and have remained unchanged for as long as one can think. Let me give some more substance to this claim by taking some examples of textbook discourses from different disciplines.

Gross National Product

Gross national product (GNP) is the total value of a country's output of goods and services in a given year. It is a measure of economic growth or decline. When people discuss what share of the 'economic pie' should go to the government, they mean what percent of GNP should be spent on defense, welfare, education, and other government programs. Also, GNP gives business owners some measure of how the economy is functioning. If the GNP is rising rapidly, the economy is said to be relatively strong. If the GNP is stable or falling, the economy is said to be relatively weak.

(Nickels 1987: 71)

Economics, like any other discipline, is concerned with defining and clarifying technical concepts, such as Gross National Product (GNP); however, another important aspect of this kind of conceptualization is also the need to create and formulate a complexity of integrated concepts and to work out their interrelatedness by referring to facts and figures in numerical terms. One such set of integrated concepts consists of the following:

- *Gross National Product*
- *Gross Domestic Product*
- *Gross Domestic Product at market prices*
- *Gross Domestic Product at factor cost*
- *Gross Domestic Fixed Capital Formation*
- *Gross National Disposable Income*
- *Gross Fixed Investment*

It is interesting to note how some of these interrelated concepts are dealt with in the discourse that follows, which seems to be rather typical of the discipline.

Total Final Expenditure and Gross Domestic Product

The sum of the above items gives total final expenditure at market prices which, as shown in Table 3.1, amounted in 1980 to £283 billions. However not all of this expenditure resulted in the utilization of domestic resources. To obtain a measure of resource utilization we have to subtract two items, imports and expenditure taxes.

One may notice two very important aspects of this kind of conceptualization in economics. There is no attempt to define the term in conventional linguistic forms, some of which have long been the focus of attention in many successful and not so successful ESP textbooks. Even if there are definitions in this discipline, their form,

Table 3.1 *Gross Domestic Product, U.K. (1979)*

	£billions
(1) Consumers' expenditure	135,403
(2) General government consumption	48,337
(3) Gross domestic fixed capital formation	40,050
(4) Value of physical increase in stocks and work in progress	−3,596
(5) Exports of goods and services	63,198
Final expenditure on goods and services at market prices	283,392
(6) *Minus* Imports of goods and services	−57,832
Gross domestic product at market prices	25,560
(7) *Minus* Taxes on expenditure (net of subsidies)	−32,072
Gross domestic product at factor cost (G.D.P.)	193,488

Source: National Income and Expenditure (Livesey 1982: 30–1)

distribution and functional values are very different from those in law (see Swales 1981b, 1982) and, indeed, in many other disciplines. In this case, the concept is explained through reference to worked-out examples of the analysis of numerical data. The importance of relating theoretical concepts to numbers is also underlined by the fact that a similar process is repeated in the end-of-the chapter exercises, as indicated in the following extract. The importance of these concepts is further reinforced in the True/False task set up for revision purposes, as illustrated in the following:

EXERCISES
3.1 Calculate from Table 3.7 each of the following: (a) gross domestic product at market prices, (b) gross domestic product at factor cost, (c) gross national product at factor cost, (d) (net) national income.

True/False
- Gross domestic product at market prices must always exceed gross domestic product at factor cost.
- Gross national product at market prices must always exceed gross domestic product at market prices.
- National income can never exceed gross national product.
- Gross national product can never exceed gross national disposable income.

(Livesey 1982: 38)

Table 3.7 The National Accounts of Britannica

	£billions
Consumers' expenditure	70
General government final consumption	10
Gross domestic fixed capital formation	15
Value of physical increase in stocks and works in progress	5
Exports of goods and services	9
Imports of goods and services	11
Taxes on expenditure	6
Subsidies	2
Net property income from abroad	3
Capital consumption	5

In order to investigate disciplinary variation further, I would like to take an example from law now, a discipline which may appear to be very different from business, but which is being increasingly integrated into most interdisciplinary curricula. In order to make a valid comparison with the section on the discussion of terminology in law discussed earlier, I will focus on the definition and explanation of *tort and crime* from a typical undergraduate law textbook, in particular focusing on the nature of legal knowledge disseminated in this discipline and the kind of rhetorical strategies used in achieving this objective.

Tort and crime

The idea of taking revenge and inflicting deterrent punishment underlies the development of the laws of tort and of crime.[17] Early English law did not distinguish between criminal and tortuous acts. Tort has its roots in criminal procedure. In fact, the writ of trespass so commonly used to support a tort action, was derived from a criminal type of proceedings.[18] Even today, the facts of many cases may disclose both a crime and a tort. Thus, where a person steals another's goods, he may be prosecuted for committing a theft or he may be sued in tort for trespass to goods and/or conversion. Again, both assault and battery are torts but they may also give rise to criminal prosecution. But despite common origin and some overlapping situations, tort and crime differ in several essential respects.

The object of criminal law is to punish the wrongdoer in order to protect society as a whole. Death, imprisonment and pecuniary fines are among the most important types of punishment. The essential characteristic of a tort action is not to seek punishment of the wrongdoer but to claim monetary compensation for the victim. On the other hand, a criminal court may order an offender to pay monetary compensation to the injured party[19] and a civil court may award exemplary damages in exceptional cases to punish the wrongdoer.[20] The most striking feature of modern tort law, however, is its attempt to allocate losses.[21]

(Srivastava and Tennekone 1995)

---

[17] See Holdsworth ii, pp 43–45.

[18] See infra pp 12–13.

[19] The Criminal Procedure Ordinance (Cap 221), s 73, provides:
  (1) Where a person is convicted of an offence, the court may, in addition to passing such sentence as may otherwise by law be passed or making an order under section 107(1), order the person so convicted to pay to any aggrieved person such compensation for–
    (a) personal injury;
    (b) loss of or damage to property; or
    (c) both such injury and loss or damage,
    as it thinks reasonable.
  (2) The amount ordered as compensation under subsection (1) shall be deemed a judgment debt due to the person entitled to receive the same from the person so convicted, and the order for payment of compensation may be enforced in such and the same manner as in the case of any costs or expenses ordered by the court to be paid under section 72.
    The Magistrates Ordinance (Cap 227), s 98 provides that a magistrate may in addition to other punishment, order an offender to pay to any aggrieved person compensation not exceeding $5,000. See Ashworth. 'Punishment and Compensation' (1986) 6 QJL 586, where the distinction between crime and compensation has been examined from a theoretical standpoint.

[20] See Rookes v Barnard [1964] AC 1192; Fridman, 'Punitive Damages in Tort', 48 Can B Rev (1970) 373: Stoll, 'Penal Purposes in the Law of Tort' (1970) 18 Am J Comp L3.

[21] See Fleming, *The Law of Torts* (8th edn. 1992) pp 8–9.

One of the most striking aspects of this text is that the treatment of terminological explanation seems to be based on historical development rather than on a clear and concise definition, as in the sciences, business studies or a number of other disciplines. As Swales (1981a, 1982) and Bhatia (1982, 1993, 1994) point out, legal definitions are expressed very precisely, clearly, unambiguously and all-inclusively in legislation, but that is an entirely different genre, where definitions are used 'to state the law' (Swales 1981b). Although it is true that one of the main functions of definitions in expository writings in most disciplines is what Williams (1985) calls 'lexical familiarization', there are more specialized and hence differently realized functions of definitions as well, which in many cases are discipline-specific. In the economics text that we considered earlier, for example, the main function of the text was to help the learner to explicate and develop GNP in the context of several other related concepts, without making any specific attempt at either lexical familiarization in the sense of general glossing or at establishing orientation within the field. In the case of the legal text, however, one can clearly see the attempt on the part of the textbook writers to interpret the textual material in the specific context of Hong Kong, analysing, synthesizing and evaluating legally constructed categories, almost in the same way as we saw in the economics text, except that in this case it is done on the basis of textual data, rather than numerical. The textual orientation in the legal text gives it a unique intertextual and interdiscursive quality, which is one of the main distinctive characteristics of most legal discourse.

To widen the disciplinary spectrum, let me take an example dealing with the introduction of new concepts in textbook writing from political science, which can be placed somewhere between economics and law. Although politics is one of the oldest human institutions, it is always in the process of change and development. Like political events that change over time, the perceptions and interpretations of political scientists also change with the changing socio-political circumstances. Therefore unlike the sciences and some areas of business, knowledge creation in political science depends more on the interpretation of events rather than on scientific research in a strict sense. It is more like knowledge creation, rather than scientific research. As such, illustrations are an important part of knowledge dissemination in political science, but the illustrations come from real socio-political events, rather than from quantitative data as in economics, rules and regulations as in law, new theoretical innovations as in the sciences, or manufactured examples of language use as in formal linguistics. I will now consider an extract from a textbook in political science.

> The term *government* is often used in two related but distinct senses. Sometimes it refers to a particular collection of *people*, each with individual idiosyncrasies, faults, and virtues, who are performing certain functions in a particular society at a particular time. And sometimes it refers to a particular set of *institutions*, that is, a series of accepted and regular procedures for performing those functions, procedures that persist over time regardless of who happens to be operating them.
>
> Both senses are incorporated in the definition of government we will use in this book: **Government** is *the body of people and*

institutions that make and enforce laws for a society.

Defined thus, government is undoubtedly one of the humanity's oldest and most nearly universal institutions. Some political philosophers, to be sure, have speculated about what life would be like in a state of **anarchy**–that is, in *a society with no government* ...

However, humanity's universal desire to government has by no means led all people at all times and in all societies to establish the same *kind* of government. Indeed, one of the most striking facts about actual governments, past and present, in their enormous variety ...

Evidently, then, different societies require different kinds of governments to satisfy their special needs ...

(Ranney 1990: 8)

It is interesting to note how the term *government* is introduced so tentatively as compared with what we saw in the extracts from economics and law. The idea is for the readers to become more generally aware of varying perceptions of different scholars and political thinkers in an attempt to create an understanding for themselves. The emphasis is not on the understanding and assimilation of a specific definition of a new concept, but on the process of arriving at a specific interpretation. This is further evidenced in the statement given below to help readers to develop such an understanding. Compared with numerical exercises in economics, the approach in political science seems to be very different.

... I have not attempted the impossible task of trying to tell readers everything they may ever want to know about politics and government ... What follows is a brief annotated list of some leading books on the topics we have covered ...

(Ranney 1990: 8)

In the preceding subsections, we noticed that in spite of some of the common characteristics of the textbook genre, different disciplines can be markedly different as a result of the conventions typically used in the construction, interpretation and dissemination of disciplinary knowledge, which, as Berkenkotter and Huckin (1995) point out, signal 'a discourse community's norms, epistemology, ideology, and social ontology'. Different disciplines have their own ways of constructing arguments, especially in respect of the nature and use of evidence, which is also interestingly reflected in patterns of intertextuality and interdiscursivity in such disciplinary discourses. To illustrate this point, let me now take up two examples, one each from applied linguistics and law.

> Catford (1965: 83) neatly expresses the point of view of translation theorists who have addressed themselves to the question of text context:
>
>> The concept of a 'whole language' is so vast and heterogeneous that it is not operationally useful for many linguistic purposes, descriptive, comparative, and pedagogical. It is therefore desirable to have a framework of categories for the classification of 'sub-languages' or varieties within a total language.
>
> So what determines variation in language use? We can approach this problem in terms of several different dimensions: the medium by which language is transmitted (phonic, graphic), formal patterning (lexico-grammatical arrangement), and situational significance (relevant extra-linguistic features).
>
> Halliday, McIntosh and Strevens (1964) recommend a framework for the description of language variation ... User-related varieties (Corder 1973) are called dialects. ... Use-related varieties are known as registers ... For example, the distinction between
>
>> (1) I hereby declare the meeting open.
>>   and
>> (2) Shall we make a start now?
>
> is use-related. On the other hand, the difference in voice quality or the way a particular vowel is pronounced when (1) and (2) are uttered by an Australian, an American or an Englishman is one of the phonic medium and is, therefore, user-related ...
>
> (Hatim and Mason 1990: 38)

The common law approach
At common law, contributory negligence on the part of the plaintiff, however slight, could have exculpated the defendant completely. In other words, it was a complete defence against the plaintiff's action in the tort of negligence. This rule was manifestly too harsh and the courts sought to mitigate its rigour by inventing a new rule, the last opportunity rule, which was equally unsatisfactory. In the leading case on this point, *Davies v. Mann* (1842) 10 M & W 546, the plaintiff had left his ass fettered by its forefeet on a highway. The defendant was driving his wagon and horses faster

than he should have done and collided with and killed the ass. The court held the defendant liable. Notwithstanding the plaintiff's negligence, the defendant could have avoided the consequence of the plaintiff's negligence had he only exercised ordinary care.[29] Neither in *Butterfield v Forrester* (1809) 103 ER 926 nor in *Davies v Mann* was the expression contributory negligence used though they were later relied on as stating the common law position on contributory negligence ...

Much of the law of contributory negligence relating to the apportionment of damages owes its origin to the rules of English maritime law. The Maritime Convention Act 1911, s 1, provides that:

(1) Where, by the fault of two or more vessels, damage or loss is caused to one or more of those vessels, to their cargoes or freight, or to any property on board, the liability to make good the damage or loss shall be in proportion to the degree in which each vessel was in fault:

Provided that –

(a) if, having regard to all the circumstances of the case, it is not possible to establish different degrees of fault, the liability shall be apportioned equally ...

[29] *Davies v Mann* was approved in *Rudley v London and North Western Rly Co.*

(Srivastava and Tennekone 1995: 226)

In the linguistics text, the argument for the variation in language is brought into focus by using other researchers' work as support for a particular point of view and also for the formulation and development of the argument. Catford (1965) provides the starting point to make a case for language variation. The use of rhetorical question (i.e. *So what determines variation in language use?*) develops the argument further, and then Halliday, McIntosh and Strevens (1964) and Corder (1973) are used as support in the development of further knowledge. The use of data in the form of appropriately chosen instances of language use (not necessarily naturally occurring instances from real life) for illustrative purposes is typical of the discipline. So the intertextuality heavily depends on the integration and use of published work by established researchers, and data from language use, as part of the argument. In the case of the legal text, on the other hand, the argument about contributory negligence is developed on the basis of historical development and the support for evidence and illustration comes from typical references to cases and precedents in a format that is very characteristic of the discipline. Even the way the whole reference is embedded within a prepositional locative (*In the leading case on this point*), and the way the reference is textualized (*Davies v. Mann (1842) 10 M & W 546*) and the way it then leads to the description of legally material facts (a form of narrative based on material facts: *the plaintiff had left his ass fettered by its forefeet on a highway*) has almost a formulaic expression very typical of the rhetoric of law. The argument is developed further by bringing in evidence from other cases and precedents and legal authority from *The Maritime Convention Act 1911, s 1*, a format which again must be followed in the way it is used here. Intertextual patterning takes a more complex shape with the introduction of yet another textual interaction, i.e. the *footnote*, which has become almost obsolete in textbook genre in most other disciplines. In legal textbooks, however, it has not only survived, but has become firmly established as one of the key indications of complete and comprehensive argumentation, so much so that in academic legal culture any lack or inadequate use of this rhetorical device in legal discourse is considered odd, if not entirely unacceptable. In linguistics and many other disciplines, on the other hand, the use of footnotes is becoming increasingly rare.

As is obvious from the discussion of these text examples, academic discourses in various disciplines do display variations in rhetorical strategies used, reflecting not only the nature of the discipline in question, but more importantly specifically favoured discursive practices, disciplinary methodologies and pedagogic practices considered effective for individual disciplines. It should be interesting to see if such variations are also part of other discourse forms, such as lectures and case studies, and we shall turn to these discursive forms in the next two sections.

(B) Disciplinary variation in lectures

Like textbooks, lectures can also vary significantly across disciplines. Olsen and Huckin (1990) argue for two different strategies which they call a 'point-driven' strategy and an 'information-driven' strategy for the comprehension of engineering lectures. Although they strongly recommend the teaching and learning of the 'discourse-level pragmatics of academic lectures', which they suggest can be useful in areas like humanities and social sciences, they caution that the learners must be given enough understanding to see 'how the organization of their discourse fits into larger goals, agendas', on the one hand, and 'contexts in their fields', on the other. Dudley-Evans (1994) takes the issues further to point out that frameworks for organizing lectures may vary significantly in different disciplines. Based on his study of lectures in two different disciplines, he concludes that although a problem-solution pattern is commonly used in highway engineering, it is not used at all in plant biology, where lecture organization draws heavily on a theoretical framework based on the work of various taxonomists who have developed systems of classification for plant genetic material.

Besides, one may find other disciplinary differences even in the organization of lectures based on *problem-solution* patterns. It is very likely that one may come across a straight solution in sciences and mathematics, but several variable ones in law, humanities and social sciences. Tauroza and Allison (1994), in their corpus of lectures drawn from engineering classes from Hong Kong, found a frequent use of what Hoey (1983) referred to as *problem-solution* structure. However, they found that it was not a simple *problem-solution*, but a more complex *situation cum problem-solution-evaluation* pattern, where students were always surprised by unexpected developments in discourse structures, causing difficulty in lecture discourse comprehension.

The lectures in different disciplines may also vary in terms of their use of patterns of intertextuality and interdiscursivity. As in the case of legal textbooks, law lectures are also likely to rely heavily on the use of intertextual material from cases, past judgements, statutes, ordinances and other legislative material, in addition to discussions from other legal specialists (Swales 1982). On the other hand, in most other disciplines, especially in the physical and natural sciences, intertextual elements are confined to claims by other specialists. The lecturing materials, and often the lecturing styles, may also be determined, to a large extent, by the nature of the disciplines. The handouts, so often used in present-day lectures, may be used for different purposes, once again depending upon, among other things, the discipline concerned. Some handouts are meant to give additional data or problems to learners, in order for them to work on their own as part of additional individual work outside the lecture hours, whereas others may be used to offer a straight summary of the main points covered as a supplement to learners' notes. The first kind is very often useful in sciences and mathematical studies, whereas the second kind is more useful in humanities and social sciences. Law, on the other hand, relies more heavily on the use of handouts for introducing legal problems, which is part of a standard methodology in academic legal studies. Disciplinary differences can also play a significant role in the development of lecturing stages. Discussion based on pre-selected illustrative texts forms a central part of any lecturing task on discourse analysis in linguistics, whereas in sciences, and more generally in mathematics, problem-solving is unfolded as a process in the presence of learners. The intervening stages in the unfolding of processes are crucial in these disciplines, whereas these aspects are less crucial in humanities and social sciences. Formal linguistics, in this sense, comes closer to mathematical sciences than social sciences. Similarly, the nature and procedures of note-taking may also vary across disciplines. In sciences, student notes often reflect a step-by-step close approximation of lecture development, whereas in social sciences they often incorporate considerable explanation and interpretation of the main points. The requirements in this respect are therefore very different in humanities and social sciences, in general, from those in physical sciences. Even the need to operate on different planes of discourse (Sinclair 1981) may not necessarily be universally applicable. And, on top of all this, one may need to take into account the individual variation in the delivery of lecturing material. In the case of an interdisciplinary programme, especially in business and law, it is interesting to note that students majoring in business are so used to Power Point presentations that they get thoroughly disappointed when they find the use of handouts as the accepted norm in law courses, often resulting in lower feedback for law teachers. They fail to realize that it is often the nature of the discipline and associated tasks that discourages teachers in law from following a similar practice. There is a similar problem in the treatment of cases in business and law, which often creates a problem for learners and teachers alike, and we shall turn to it in the next section.

(C) Disciplinary variation in cases

Cases form the most significant part of the repertoire of disciplinary discourses in at least two disciplines, business and law. In both these disciplines, this genre is viewed as a record of past events, leading to the identification of problematic issues, contextualization of opportunities for discussion and illustration of important disciplinary concepts, issues and decisions. In both these disciplines, the generic realizations begin with a characteristic narration and description of facts, leading to the identification of problems and discussion of issues at stake, and finally arriving at some form of solution or judgement based on disciplinary conventions. However, these surface similarities are unlikely to take one very far in the use of cases in the two disciplines.

In business studies, cases are often originally written for business students or sometimes for professionals for the identification and discussion of problems, leading to possible solutions of the identified problems, which eventually lead to more effective strategic planning (such as better marketing or sales strategies) or human resource management outcomes. In the academic contexts, cases are used for the development of professional business skills in somewhat realistic, though largely simulated, contexts. These skills include those of problem identification and analysis, critical thinking, communication, understanding group dynamics, data handling and decision-making. Cases in business contexts are meant to bring an element of realism to the classroom by simulating the roles of real-life executives and creating realistic business contexts for decision-making.

A law case, on the other hand, is essentially a report based on the judgement of a particular judge based on negotiation of justice in a court of law. These are public documents and are taken as records of court proceedings meant to be used as precedents for future judgements. In academic contexts, these are generally used to demonstrate the nature and logic of judicial reasoning in the negotiation of justice. As indicated in Bhatia (1993: 118):

> Legal cases are used in the law classroom, the lawyer's office and in the courtroom as well. They are essential tools used in the law classroom to train students in the skills of legal reasoning, argumentation and decision-making. Cases represent the complexity of relationship between the facts of the world outside, on the one hand, and the model world of rights and obligations, permissions and prohibitions, on the other.

Quoting Wisdom, Bhatia claims that 'the process of legal argumentation in cases' is

> ... not a 'chain' of demonstrative reasoning. It is a presenting and representing of those features of the case which 'severally co-operate' in favour of the conclusion, in favour of saying what the reasoner wishes said, in favour of calling the situation by the name by which he wishes to call it. The reasons are like the legs of a chair, not the links of a chain.
>
> (Wisdom 1964: 157)

In professional contexts, these cases serve as a guide to professional reasoning and use of appropriate authorities either in favour of or against a particular line of argument. In the courtroom, these cases serve as legal authorities along with legislative provisions. As Bhatia (1993: 175) points out:

> Legal cases and legislation are complementary to each other. If cases on the one hand attempt to interpret legal provisions in terms of the facts of the world, legislative provisions, on the other hand, are attempts to account for the unlimited facts of the world in terms of legal relations.

In order to fully understand the nature and function of argumentation in legal cases, it is important to understand the relationship between different forms of legal discourse, such as the legal judgment and legislative provision, on the one hand, and, on the other hand, the facts and events of the real world, and the value of socio-legal conventions and constraints, such as the role of precedence in a particular legal framework, without which it is impossible to construe legal interpretations. Some of these factors make legal argumentation rather complex in terms of intertextuality and interdiscursivity. Candlin and Maley (1997: 203) claim:

> Discourses are made internally viable by the incorporation of such *intertextual* and *interdiscursive* elements. Such evolving discourses are thus intertextual in that they manifest a plurality of text sources. However, in so far as any characteristic text evokes a particular discoursal value, in that it is associated with some institutional and social meaning, such evolving discourses are at the same time interdiscursive.

The two concepts of intertextuality and interdiscursivity form the very basis of the construction, interpretation and use of legal argumentation in legal cases, and are therefore important for our understanding of legal action. On the surface of the text past legal judgments, legislative provisions, annotations and legal interpretations by scholars etc. are used as relevant evidence to construct an argument by a judge, making the text in question rich in intertextuality; whereas at a deeper level of discourse, the conventions and principles of juridical interpretation grounded in specific legal practices are invoked as legally binding values to reconstruct legitimate legal interpretations of cases, which make legal arguments rich in interdiscursivity. These patterns of intertextuality and interdiscursivity can be visually represented as in Diagram 2.2.

In business education, on the other hand, cases are meant to provide a pedagogic context within which professional business skills are developed. The textualization of cases in the two disciplines, though superficially similar in a number of ways, have very different functions in the methodologies of the two disciplinary cultures and are differently textualized in the discourse of the two disciplines. This is reflected in the cognitive structuring in the two sets of cases. A

50

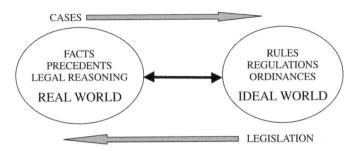

Diagram 2.2 *Cases and Legislation*

business case generally begins with a brief description of the company, which is seen as facing some difficulty, followed by a detailed description of facts, embedded in a situational context, eventually leading to a discussion of possible solutions, and sometimes a conclusion. A law case typically begins with the identification of the case, followed by establishing of facts, and then by the arguments of the judge, which also include deriving *ratio decidendi*, and always ends with the pronouncement of the judgment. Any surface level generic similarities across the two disciplines must be viewed with caution in this case. As Purves (1986: 39) rightly points out:

> Instruction into any discipline is acculturation, or the bringing of the student into the 'interpretive community' of the discipline. And there is evidence that each discipline is also a 'rhetorical community', that is to say a field with certain norms, expectations, and conventions with respect to writing.

One of the major differences in the handling of these two seemingly overlapping case-types in business and law is the way the decisions are arrived at and the kind of evidence that is considered crucial in each case. In business cases, most of the evidence comes from the interpretations and applications of business theories, often suggesting a novel and creative, but pragmatically successful business solution that is likely to 'work'. In law, on the other hand, the judgment (solution) is the result of a logical argument based on evidence from the interpretation of rules and regulations and precedents from earlier judgments, which seem to suggest that the solution is not only well argued but, more importantly, is consistent with earlier judgments. These significantly different disciplinary requirements are often overlooked by business students doing law as part of their inter-disciplinary programmes, which leads to frustrating experiences, both on the part of learners and teachers alike.

As part of a project on 'Teaching English to Meet the Needs of Business Education in Hong Kong' (see Bhatia and Candlin 2001: 33), I was surprised to find a law professor complaining about the misunderstanding her business students had about the requirements of problem question responses. After considerable discussion it was found that many of her students were genuinely puzzled by the conflicting disciplinary demands from the two disciplines. She speculated that her students found it difficult to grasp differences in problem-solving processes across the disciplines. To illustrate the point she mentioned a typical case where students were found to be suggesting solutions which she regarded as acceptable from a pragmatic (business studies) point of view, but legally problematic. Her experience was that students often went for a practical solution, which scored them next to nothing. But those who integrated practical and pragmatically successful solutions with relevant legal aspects (based on evidence from legislation and case precedents) got A+. Often weak answers used essay genre when a reporting genre was required.

In the preceding sections I have outlined some of the disciplinary perceptions of knowledge, which may influence generic boundaries within academic discourse. Although I have barely managed to scratch the surface of academic discourse, any understanding of academic discourse needs to be viewed in the light of interdisciplinary variations, which is likely to lead to a more realistic perception, understanding, construction, interpretation and use of academic discourses. Just as we need the sophistication and subtleties of disciplinary variations, we also need shared generic characterizations across disciplinary boundaries.

However, in order to deal with the complexity of generic patterns so commonly intertwined in academic discourses across disciplines, genre theory needs to be powerful enough to account for the intricacies of academic genres across disciplines and, at the same time, simple enough to be handled by practitioners and non-specialists with somewhat modest expertise in one linguistic framework or the other. In order to appreciate the dynamic complexity and variation within and across academic disciplines, genre theory needs to be developed in such a way that it accounts for discourse across generic boundaries, on the one hand, and is also sensitive to disciplinary variation, on the other.

In the foregoing I have considered the function of disciplinary knowledge in order to better understand genre-based variation in academic discourse, which underpins a strong argument in favour of looking at a range of genres within and across disciplinary domains, rather than individually. Let me now turn to generic variations within professional domains.

2.3 Variation in genres within professional domains

Domain-specific genres can be subcategorized in a number of ways. Devitt (1991) proposes the notion of *genre set* to refer to a range of text-genres that a particular professional group produces in the course of their daily routine. She discusses the case of *tax accountants*, who in their daily work produce a limited range of generic texts, some of which may include various kinds of letters such as an opinion letter to the client, a response letter to the client or a letter to tax authorities, all of which are distinct but at the same time intertextually linked to each other. In a similar fashion, one could consider the professional routine consultation involving a solicitor and a client, in the course of which a solicitor is typically required to complete a set of integrated tasks, which may include information gathering from a client, creating or updating the *client file* as a consequence of this, preparing a *legal brief* on the basis of legal research on the case, and finally writing a *letter of advice* to the client (see Candlin and Bhatia 1998). The typical set of products resulting from these tasks form a *genre set.* The genres comprising a set are individually distinct, but at the same time intertextually linked. The texts from a particular *genre set* also display typical patterns found in similarly produced texts by other fellow professionals in the same field. This rather limited set of generic texts resulting from a narrowly defined professional activity represents the participation of only one side of the professional output. The professional activity may involve a number of other participants from within or outside the profession, texts or other semiotic constructs, but the concept of *genre set* seems to include one side of the professional practice. As Bazerman (1994: 98–9) points out:

> The genre set represents ... only the work of one side of a multiple person interaction. That is, the tax accountants' letters usually refer to the tax code, the rulings of the tax department in this case, the client's information and interests, and these references are usually presented in highly anticipatable ways appropriate to the genre of the letter, but the genre set is only the tax accountant's participations, as intertextually linked to the participations of the parties.

To extend the concept of *genre set* in an attempt to account for the full set of genres, Bazerman (1994: 97) proposes the concept of *systems of genres*, which refer to all 'the interrelated genres that interact with each other in specific settings'. He points out:

> The system of genres would be the full set of genres that instantiate the participation of all the parties – that is the full file of letters from and to the client, from and to the government, from and to the accountant. This would be the full interaction, the full event, the set of social relations as it has been enacted. It embodies the full history of speech events as intertextual occurrences, but attending to the way that all the intertext is instantiated in generic form establishing the current act in relation to prior acts.

The notion of systems of genres is more comprehensive than the notion of genre sets, and is a very useful tool for investigating intertextually and interdiscursively related genres embedded within a specific professional activity. However, it is often necessary and more useful to go beyond a system of genres to consider a more general category of genres which are outside the boundaries of a particular professional activity, however broadly defined, and yet form a well-defined and closely linked group of genres in a particular professional or disciplinary domain, rather than just a particular professional activity on its own. In the case of law, for instance, we can identify a number of professional legal activities, such as lawyer–client consultation, drafting of wills, drawing contracts, conveyance of property, drafting affidavits, etc., each of which individually may require the legal professional to participate in the construction, interpretation and use of a particular system of genres (see Candlin and Bhatia 1998). However, all of these professional activities taken together may constitute the disciplinary domain of law, which may require the construction, interpretation, use and exploitation of a larger set of professional legal genres, such as legislation (statutes and ordinances), law reports and cases of various kind (Bhatia 1993: 119), agreements and contracts, legal briefs, title deeds, pleadings and other court documents, reference and textbooks, client files, and a host of other generic constructs, all of which together constitute a set of domain-specific *disciplinary genres*. Every disciplinary community has its own typical set of genres, which are used by most of its members in the achievement of the professional objectives. Domain-specific disciplinary genres can also be subcategorized in terms of academic or professional settings, in that one subset of disciplinary genres is more likely to be used in academic settings, whereas another is most often used in professional or workplace settings, though there may often be considerable overlap in the two subsets.

One may notice two interesting things here. Firstly, the typical genres associated with each discipline are rather distinct with absolutely no overlap whatsoever. Law centrally depends on two of the most conventionally standardized disciplinary genres, i.e. legislation and judgments to achieve its disciplinary goals, and this centrality is also signalled in the intertextual and interdiscursive patterning that these mutually dependent generic constructs display in all forms of legal discourse, including textbooks. Business studies, on the other hand, crucially depends on case studies, business reports, letters and memos to construct and communicate its typical disciplinary knowledge. Public administration, similarly, makes use of its own typical genres, such as government documents, political communiqués, policy statements, international treaties, joint statements or memoranda of understanding. To this extent, these disciplines are very much distinct.

There is, however, another factor, which makes things complex for those who have an interest in the analysis of discourse and genre, which is that some genres, especially those associated with academic settings, such as textbooks, journal articles, projects, examination questions, essays etc., have interesting generic overlaps across most of these academic disciplines. Therefore, although genres, by definition, cut across disciplinary boundaries, they do display subtle disciplinary differences, in addition to the use of specialist lexical realizations.

To sum up, domain-specific genres thus can be viewed as constituting three rather different categories, each incorporating a limited set of genres representing an increasing range and level of discursive practices. 'Genre set' incorporates a class of typical professional genres that a particular professional engages in as part of his or her routine professional activity (Devitt 1991). 'Genre system' represents a complete set of discursive forms that are invoked by all the participants involved in a professional activity. 'Disciplinary genres' extend such a system to include all those discursive forms that are invoked in all professional practices associated with a particular disciplinary or professional domain. This can be represented visually as in Diagram 2.3.

Although genres by their very nature cut across disciplinary boundaries, they also seem to share features across domains. Just as any set of discursive practices in a specific professional domain requires the use of a number of disciplinary genres, similarly a number of genres from a range of disciplines often display strikingly similar

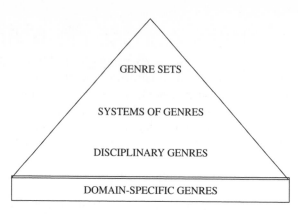

Diagram 2.3 *Domain-specific genres*

characteristics, which somehow put all these seemingly different genres in the same vicinity. Having looked at similarities and contrasts across a range of genres within a disciplinary or professional domain, we shall turn to similar genres across disciplinary and professional domains in the next chapter.

3 Genres across domains: Genre colonies

In the previous chapter, we looked at a number of genres within specific disciplinary domains, which gave us a number of interesting concepts for looking at genres, some of which include genre sets, systems of genres, and more generally disciplinary genres. We also found that most of them operated within disciplinary domains; some were configured broadly, others more narrowly. In addition to such disciplinary genres, we often find instances of super genres, incorporating a constellation of individually recognized genres that display strong similarities across disciplinary and professional boundaries. Such super genres are a natural consequence of the versatility of genres, in that they are identifiable at various levels of generalization. Just as genres can be identified at a very specific individual level, such as research article introductions (Swales 1990), advertisements, sales promotion letters, news reports (Bhatia 1993), business reports, book reviews (Hyland 2000), book blurbs (Kathpalia 1992), textbooks (Swales 1990; Myers 1992) and a number of others, at the same time they can also be identified at levels above these in the form of super genres, or below these as sub-genres. Most of these super genres can be more appropriately regarded as 'colonies' of related genres, with members not necessarily respecting disciplinary or domain boundaries. It must be pointed out that the concept of 'genre colony' serves a number of important functions in genre theory. Firstly, it brings a degree of versatility to genre identification and description, in that it allows genres to be viewed at different levels of generalization, making it possible to posit principled relationships between super or macro-genres, genres, and sub-genres. It also makes it possible to relate these subcategories to features of context. The concept itself incorporates two related meanings. Firstly, it represents a grouping of closely related genres, which to a large extent share their individual communicative purposes, although most of them will be different in a number of other respects, such as their disciplinary and professional affiliations, contexts of use and exploitations, participant relationships, audience constraints and so on. In this sense the concept of 'genre colony' is somewhat similar to the concept of 'discourse colony' suggested by Hoey (1986). However, at the same time, genre colony also incorporates the process of colonization, which Fairclough terms 'commodification' and defines as

> ... the process whereby social domains and institutions, whose concern is not producing commodities in the narrower economic sense of goods for sale, come nevertheless to be organized and conceptualized in terms of commodity production, distribution and consumption. ... In terms of orders of discourse, we can conceive of commodification as the colonization of institutional orders of discourse, and more broadly of the societal order of discourse, by discourse types associated with commodity production.
>
> (Fairclough 1992: 207)

Colonization as a process thus involves invasion of the integrity of one genre by another genre or genre convention, often leading to the creation of a hybrid form, which eventually shares some of its genre characteristics with the one that influenced it in the first place. So the concept of genre colony is therefore crucial to the present theoretical framework for genre theory, as it represents both a grouping of a number of genres within and across disciplinary domains which largely share the communicative purposes that each one of them tends to serve, and hence they are to be seen as primary members of the colony, and at the same time it represents a process whereby generic resources are exploited and appropriated to create hybrid (both mixed and embedded) forms, which may be considered secondary members of the colony.

In this chapter, I would like to take up the discussion of genre colony in the first sense, i.e. the grouping of related genres within and across disciplinary domains, and will take up the process of colonization in the next chapter when I discuss invasion of territorial integrity of genres and appropriation of generic resources. Before going into any elaborate discussion of these genre colonies, it must be pointed out that generic boundaries between and across domains are not easy to draw. In whatever manner one may define genre, the boundaries between different levels of genres will always be fluid to some extent. It has little to do with the framework one uses, but more to do with the complex and dynamic variation and constant development of generic forms used within and across disciplinary and professional cultures. Conventionally we have been using a number of terms to identify genres, such as *advertising* or *promotional genres, introductions, reports*, etc. which can be posited at various levels of generalization. As super or macro-genres, these can also be identified as colonies of 'promotional genres', 'academic introductions' and 'reporting genres'. Let me begin with a detailed discussion of promotional genres.

3.1 Promotional genres

As pointed out in the earlier section, genre colonies represent groupings of closely related genres serving broadly similar communicative purposes, but not necessarily all the communicative purposes in cases where they serve more than one. In addition they may not share a number of other features of context. It was also pointed out that a genre colony is a function of the versatility of the genre. Let me give some substance to this claim by representing the versatility of promotional genres in Diagram 3.1.

Although genres are essentially identified in terms of communicative purposes they tend to serve, these communicative purposes can be characterized at various levels of generalization, and at the same time realized in terms of a combination of rhetorical acts, which I

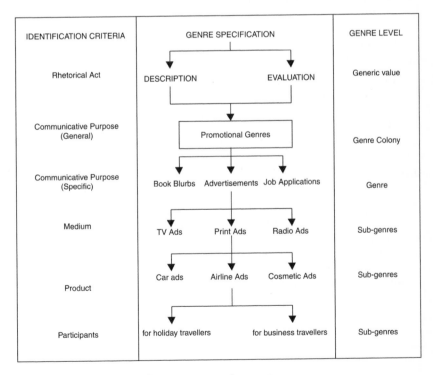

Diagram 3.1 *Versatility in generic description*

would like to call 'generic values' (Bhatia 2002). These generic values such as *arguments, narratives, descriptions, explanations* and *instructions* have been variously referred to as 'basic forms' (Werlich 1982) or 'primary speech genres' (Bakhtin 1986). I prefer the term 'generic value' because they can be and often are used in various combinations to give shape to different professional genres, as in promotional genres (descriptions and evaluations), reporting genres (narrations, arguments and descriptions) or introductions (descriptions, narrations, etc.). Since they do not seem to have any specific textual sequencing or cognitive structuring in terms of 'moves', it is more appropriate to treat them as 'generic values'. In professional genres, it is often possible to posit several levels of generalization. To take the case of promotional genres, one may find at the highest level of generalization 'promotional discourse' in the form of a constellation of several closely related genres with an overlapping communicative purpose of promoting a product or service to a potential customer. Some of the common examples of promotional genres may include advertisements, promotional letters, and book blurbs, which can be placed close to these, although they are different in terms of the specificity of the product they promote, i.e. books, the selection and size of the market or audience they target, and also the nature of the strategies and hence lexico-grammatical resources they employ, depending of course upon the subject discipline of the book. Very closely related to these will be job application letters, which have traditionally been regarded as very different from sales promotion letters, but as indicated in Bhatia (1993), they are very similar in terms of their communicative purpose and the use of lexico-grammatical and discoursal resources. Somewhat similar to these two types of letters, one may find the use of a reference letter or a testimonial, which, in principle, may essentially be a review of the candidate's suitability for a particular job, but in practice most often turns out to be a letter of recommendation, i.e. a positive evaluation of the competence of the candidate in question.

All these and a number of other instances of this kind have a large degree of overlap in the communicative purposes they tend to serve and that is the main reason why they are seen as forming a closely-related discourse colony, serving more or less a common promotional purpose, in spite of the fact that some of them, more than others, may also display subtle differences in their realizations. It is further possible for us to view any one of these genres – advertisements, for example – at a lower level of generalization and make distinctions between more specific realizations of this genre. Obvious examples will include print advertisements, TV commercials, radio advertisements and others. The differences between these are less discernible in terms of communicative purposes but more in terms of the medium of discourse, and therefore as genres they belong to the same broad category popularly known as advertisements. Taking a step further, this time considering only print advertisements, it is further possible to view these in terms of categories like straight-line advertisements, picture-caption reminder advertisements, image-building advertisements, testimonials, embedded genres etc. (Kathpalia 1992). Whatever the subcategory, all these advertisements serve the same set of communicative purposes, though most of them use different strategies to promote the product or service. Straight-line advertisements most often use 'product appraisal' as the main persuasive strategy, whereas image-building advertisements rely more heavily on establishing credentials as the main source of persuasion. Another variation one may find in the use of linguistic resources is that whereas some types rely on verbal strategies (straight-line advertisements using product appraisal), others, for example picture-caption advertisements, rely more on visual inputs. Once again, it is possible for us to take up straight-line advertisements and differentiate them further either in terms of their use of linguistic features for product evaluation, or maybe in terms of the kind of product they advertise, or even in terms of the audience they serve. In each case, we are sure to find subtle differences in the use of strategies for product description, evaluation and product differentiation, eventually giving rise to specific uses of linguistic resources. But the interesting thing is that all these variations become distinctive genres only at a level at which they start indicating a substantial difference in their communicative purposes.

Going beyond these primary members of this colony, we may find a number of other genres, which may not appear to be exactly advertisements but nevertheless have a strong promotional concern. Typical examples will include fundraising letters, travel brochures, grant proposals, public campaigns and several others, which tend to promote not necessarily a product or service, but possibly an idea, a research proposal, a public concern or an issue, a particular place of tourist attraction, or something similar. One may also find sufficient common promotional concerns in book reviews, film reviews, company reports, annual reports, company brochures, or what is often referred to as advertorials, many of which are hybrid genres, which may often be members of other colonies as well, as the case of annual reports. Diagram 3.2, though not exhaustive, can give a good indication of the primary and the secondary membership of such a genre colony.

As one can see, the colony has a variety of occupants, some of them having overlapping territorial claims, whereas others are somewhat more distinct from one another. This is in no way meant to be a

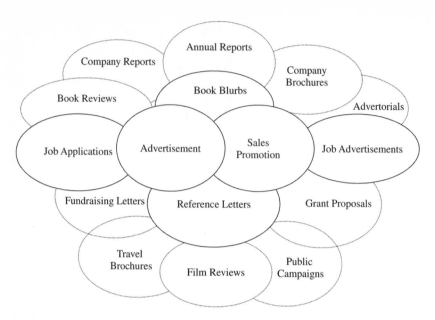

Diagram 3.2 *Colony of promotional genres*

complete picture. It is not only possible to add new members, it is also possible that over a period of time, the status of certain members can change, in that the genre may change, further develop or even become obsolete because of lack of use. The membership of the colony can also be displayed on various clines in terms of the degree and nature of appropriation of promotional elements. Advertisements, sales promotion letters, job advertisements and book blurbs are some of the primary members of the colony of promotional genres, whereas film reviews, travel brochures, public campaigns, grant proposals and several others of this kind are secondary members. If we take genres like book reviews, annual and company reports, company brochures, advertorials, etc. which are mixed genres, partly promotional, partly information-giving or opinion-giving, they can be considered only peripheral members of the colony. It is important to note that many of these secondary members of the colony may be primary members of some other genre colony, as in the case of annual company reports, which is a legitimate primary member of a colony of reporting genres. We will come back to this aspect in a later section of the chapter, but for the present let us look at the most central member of the colony in more detail.

Advertisements

Advertising, on the one hand, is the most traditional form of promotional activity, which is intended to inform and promote in order to sell ideas, goods or services to a selected group of people; on the other hand, it is also one of the most dynamic generic forms exhibiting some of the most innovative uses of lexico-grammatical and discoursal forms and rhetorical strategies. These innovations, however, are often used within, rather than outside, the typical generic boundaries of promotional discourse (for detailed accounts of this kind of variation, see Cook 1992; Kathpalia 1992, Bhatia 1995). Without going into any detailed generic specification of this genre, I would like to point out that most print advertisements of hard-sell type make use of a number of typical rhetorical moves to persuade potential customers to buy the product or service they promote, the most common of them being 'product appraisal'.

Although advertising has become a dynamic, innovative and versatile genre, which makes it difficult to give a comprehensive account of the strategies used to influence the targeted audience, one of the most favoured strategies in corporate advertising has been what is popularly known as *product differentiation*. The copywriters often analyse not only the detailed product information, but also the evidence to support their claim about what makes a particular product different from that of their competitors. An excellent illustration of this strategy one may find in an old story, which seems to capture the essential spirit of product differentiation in promotional advertising. It goes somewhat like this:

In the good old days, there were two shops selling sausages in the same street in London. Initially both were doing well, but as days went by, the competition became tough and the promotional activities intense. Suddenly, one fine morning the shop on the right side of the road put up a poster claiming, 'We sell the best sausages in London'. The next morning, the shop on the left side, in an attempt to outsmart its competitor came up with the claim 'We sell the best sausages in England'. The next day, the first one came up with the claim, 'Our sausages are the best in the world'. The second one responded by saying, 'We sell sausages to the Queen', to which the first one responded the following day by displaying a huge poster saying, 'God save the Queen!'

(Source unknown)

Today the traditional practice of direct comparison of products has become somewhat risky because of strict advertising laws, although subtle forms of comparison are still common, as in the case of a household product where *this special* brand is claimed to be superior to an *ordinary* one. However, the common denominator in most of the efforts for product differentiation is still the subtle use of **description** and **evaluation** as indicated in Diagram 3.1 above. Let us look at a typical example of advertising.

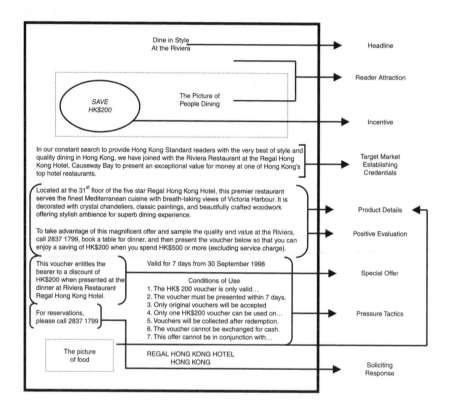

One of the most important moves in advertising discourse is 'offering a product description' that is good, positive and favourable. This is often realized through the generic values of 'description' and 'evaluation', which are most often called upon to serve the cause of millions of products and services across the corporate world. However, in order to give effect to the communicative purpose of product advertising, the copywriter makes use of a number of rhetorical moves, each of which contributes to the overall objectives of the advertisement. Following the move structure for sales promotion letters (Bhatia 1993; Kathpalia 1992), one may find the following rhetorical moves in a typical advertisement.

Move structure in advertisements

1. Headlines (for reader attraction)
2. Targeting the market
3. Justifying the product or service
   - *by indicating the importance or need of the product or service* and/or
   - *by establishing a niche*
4. Detailing the product or service
   - *by identifying the product or service*
   - *by describing the product or service*
   - *by indicating the value of the product or service*
5. Establishing credentials
6. Celebrity or typical user endorsement
7. Offering incentives
8. Using pressure tactics
9. Soliciting response

However there are a number of things worth pointing out. Firstly, advertisements have always been and in recent years are becoming increasingly creative in the use of multi-modality, sometimes for reader attraction, but often to highlight moves which have traditionally been realized in terms of typical lexico-grammatical resources. In the advertisement above, we have incentives highlighted as part of the picture of people dining. Similarly, at the bottom of the advertisement, we have displays of food to add to the move describing product and service. The highlighting by the picture of people dining is particularly attractive for the audience in Hong Kong, where the local people are extremely conscious of dining out in style at restaurants.

3.2 Academic introductions

Introduction, like a number of other terms of common currency, has also been overly used in academic discourse in a variety of ways. Although most of us have some idea of what an introduction is like, and we can identify many kinds of introductions when we see them in either written form or actual speech, it is rather difficult to have consensus in terms of its naming, function, distribution and discourse realizations. Like genre itself, introduction is also a very versatile concept, which can be posited at various levels of generalization.

Like promotional genres, *introductions* can be assigned a kind of super genre status, forming a colony of introductory genres, most of them closely related, but at the same time displaying subtle variations.

65

At a very general level, one could consider *introducing a friend, introducing a speaker in a symposium* or *a political meeting, introducing a business proposition, introducing a new product in the market, introducing a new book* or *a new research finding in a research article* or *a point of view in a student essay,* and several other introductions of this kind. All these are closely related genres and they all appear to form a colony, with members restricted not necessarily to the same domain or discipline. To take a more specific case, let us look at *academic introductions* more closely. Under this category of genre, we again find a number of variations, some easy to identify, others more difficult to distinguish.

The members at the level of academic introductions may include journal article introductions, book introductions, and essay introductions, all of which are used in academic contexts. They also share a broadly identified communicative purpose, a range of lexico-grammatical resources, and in a limited sense, especially when the instances are grounded in the same disciplinary context, academic knowledge. As argued in the previous chapter, they can be considered as part of the same disciplinary register, whether identified broadly as academic register, or more narrowly as the register of a specific discipline. However, the three genres are also distinct in terms of their more narrowly identified participant relations and their communicative objectives. In the case of research article introductions, the participants have an expectation of equal participation, which requires a tenor of discourse based on equal interaction, whereas in the case of book introductions, the situation can be more complex depending upon the subcategories we are dealing with. In the case of student essay introductions, the orientation is often based on unequal interaction, with the student making an attempt to communicate to the teacher his or her knowledge or understanding about the topic. It is possible to think of academic introductions as a colony of a number of related introductory genres often used within the academic world as indicated in Diagram 3.3.

These related genres could be identified in terms of a common communicative purpose of *introducing an academic work,* whether it is an academic discipline, a book, a research article, a student essay or a lecture. In its various manifestations, introduction has a general function of introducing a written or spoken academic action. If we move further down and look at its more specific realizations, more popularly known as *book introductions,* we find at least two major, though very different, types. We can distinguish an *introductory chapter* of a book, which is considered an important part of the book itself, from the *author's introduction* to the book, which is generally

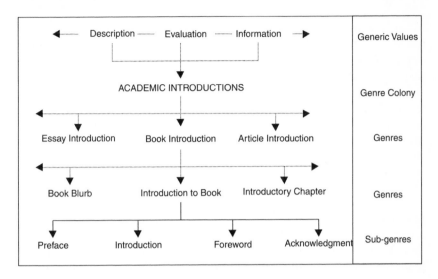

Diagram 3.3 *Versatility in academic introductions*

positioned outside the content of the book. At this level, we find a substantial difference in their communicative purposes. In the case of an introductory chapter of the book, its main communicative purpose is to introduce the content of the book, which eventually is meant to establish the context in which the rest of the book is understood. In this respect, the introductory chapter forms a preliminary part of the content of the book. This is often signalled by using the regular page numbers for this introductory chapter, which often begins with page 1 of the book, indicating that the chapter forms an integral part of the content of the book. In the case of a book introduction, however, its main communicative purpose is much more complex. Its main function is 'to introduce the book' by discussing the general purpose of the book and its intended scope, often giving a good description of the content of the book, combining it with positive aspects of the work. These book introductions typically occur outside the content of the book and are sometimes exploited by publishers to promote the book. It is these book introductions and their various manifestations that we would like to focus on in this section.

In the introductory pages of academic books one typically finds a number of introductory sections, some of which include *preface by the author, preface by the editor, foreword, introduction, acknowledge-ment* and occasionally *preamble* or *prologue*. Although, to a large extent, most of them share the same communicative purpose of introducing the book, some of them occasionally incorporate a number of other minor purposes too. Bhatia (1997a), in a small-scale survey based on information from university academics in Hong Kong, found considerable discrepancies in their understanding of the function, use and exploitation of these introductory genres. A majority of academics surveyed were unsure of the differences between the three main realizations of academic introductions, namely 'introduction', 'preface' and 'foreword', although a good number of them thought that these introductory sections represented significantly different genres. None of them considered them to be similar in their form or rhetorical function. When asked to indicate which of these were likely to have considerable overlap, most of them thought that there was a significant overlap between *introduction* and *preface*, and *introduction* and *foreword*, but less so between *preface* and *foreword*. An overwhelming majority of them thought that *preface* and *foreword* were mutually exclusive. On the question of authorship, a majority of them thought that introductions and prefaces are more likely to be written by the author of the book and foreword by someone other than the author. There were some who thought prefaces are sometimes written by the publishers, perhaps through the editors. Finally, on the question of the main communicative purpose(s) of these various discourse forms, almost all of them pointed out that an introduction had an academic purpose, whereas a preface served both academic and promotional purposes, and a foreword was more likely to have a rather distinctly promotional purpose. On the basis of this survey, which seems to represent elements of conventional wisdom, one could distinguish *preface, foreword, introduction* and *acknowledgment* along the following lines:

Preface: The main function is to outline the general purpose and scope of the book, often indicating steps leading to the preparation of the book.

Communicative purpose: Informational as well as promotional

Introduction: The main objective is to place the content of the book in the context of the field to which the book belongs, often outlining the work and advising readers how to go about the book.

Communicative purpose: Primarily informational

Foreword:	This is viewed as a comment on the book generally written by someone other than the author, often a well-known scholar.
Communicative purpose:	Mainly promotional
Acknowledgement:	The main purpose is to express gratitude to people who the author feels have helped in the preparation of the book.
Communicative purpose:	Mainly public relational and promotional

However, Bhatia (1997a) also found a considerable amount of overlap in their communicative purposes in actual academic practice, so much so that even the dictionaries find it difficult to distinguish them. This is what a well-known modern dictionary says about these genres:

Introduction:	An introduction is the first part of a book in which the author tells you what the rest of the book is about.
Preface:	A preface is an introduction at the beginning of a book which explains why the book was written or what it is about.
Foreword:	The foreword of a book is an introduction by the author or by someone else.
Preamble:	A preamble is an introduction that comes before something you say or write.
Prologue:	A prologue is a piece of text that is spoken or written at the beginning of a book in order to introduce it.

(Collins Cobuild English Language Dictionary 1987)

As one can see, there seems to be considerable overlap and circularity in the way these generic forms are explained by reference to lexical items such as *introduce, introduction*, etc. Other dictionaries are no more illuminating either. Moreover, these introductory sections are typically positioned outside the content of the book. There are conventions to page number them in Roman numerals rather than Arabic numbers. Most of them are short, although occasionally we find some which go beyond seven to eight pages, complete with a list of references (Poynton 1989). These introductory genres invariably introduce the content of the book, telling the reader why the book has been written and what it contains, although in some cases, especially in an editor's preface, it is possible to find a longish attempt to establish the field and position the new work within the established field, which often reminds one of a research article rather than a simple preface by the editor. This can be seen as a legitimate attempt on the part of the editor to 'bend' a conventional communicative purpose of the genre to make a more detailed academic statement (see Candlin's preface to Hyland 2000 and Luke's preface to Freedman and Medway 1994). They are generally written by the author or abstracted from his or her introduction. Sometimes it may be written by a well-known academic in the field or the editor of the series, if the book is published as part of a series, in which case it is generally called an editor's preface (exceptions are not very uncommon, though; see Cook 1989, where we find the author's introduction and the series editor's preface both put under the introduction). From the above description of these closely related genres I have called *academic introductions*, it is clear that all of them, whatever names they are given, have at least one main communicative purpose in common, and that is to introduce the book. This rather surprising overlap in the function and identification of academic introductions is not simply documented in modern dictionaries, it is evident in modern practice too. One may find instances of introductions, prefaces and forewords largely indistinguishable from each other. Let me take the following three instances of academic introductions, an *introduction*, a *preface* and a *foreword*.

(1)

Introduction **Discourse** Discourse analysis examines how stretches of language, considered in their full textual, social, and psychological context, become meaningful and unified for their users. ... (*It then continues with the discussion of the field, indicating its importance for language teaching.*)	Establishing Field
This book aims to explain the theory of discourse analysis and to demonstrate its practical relevance to language learning and teaching. Section one examines .... Section two explores ... (*It then gives the description of the content of the book.*)	Book Description
There are several people I want to thank for their friendship and help. ... (*The introduction ends with acknowledgements.*) <div align="right">(Cook 1989)</div>	Expressing Gratitude

(2)

PREFACE It is arguable that the most crucial problem at present facing foreign language teaching syllabus designers, and ultimately materials producers, in the field of language for specific purposes, is how to specify validly the target communicative competence. ... (*The introduction attempts to establish a niche for the book.*)	Establishing Niche Describing Book
In the preparation of this book I was influenced at the macro-level by the socio-linguistic writings of Dell Hymes and Michael Halliday, and at a more micro-level by the work of, in particular, Henry Widdowson, David Wilkins. ... (*The introduction ends with acknowledgements.*) <div align="right">(Munby 1978)</div>	Expressing Gratitude

(3)

Foreword	
This book, which is based on the teaching given in the Ordinary Course in Phonetics at Edinburgh University, is intended to provide an introduction to the subject as traditionally understood and practised in Britain: it deals ... with phonetics as part of general linguistics .... (*It begins by describing the book positively and establishing its orientation.*)	Establishing Niche Describing Book
My debt to the great phoneticians of the English speaking tradition – Alexander Melville Bell, Alexander J. Ellis, Henry Sweet, Daniel Jones, Kenneth Lee Pike – must be apparent on nearly every page. I owe especial thanks to ... (*The introduction ends with acknowledgements.*) <div align="right">(Abercrombie 1967)</div>	Expressing Gratitude

All three texts display a remarkable degree of overlap in terms of their use of lexico-grammatical resources and structural interpretation. In all of them we find a major concern with introducing the content of the books, which includes *establishing the field of study* and *establishing a niche in the relevant field of study*. The other major concern that is common to all three texts is the *expression of gratitude in terms of acknowledgements*, which forms an integral part of the texts, rather than an independent section of the book. In terms of their communicative purpose also, there seems to be a considerable overlap. However, all three of them have been given different generic names, which have been conventionally recognized and used with some degree of independent identification. This makes one question the conventional wisdom of giving the three texts different generic names. It is also possible that over a period of time these historically somewhat distinct genres have come so close to each other that they seem to have lost whatever traditional distinctions they may have had at one time. As things stand today, it is more than evident that these three academic introductions and perhaps many more of this kind, for instance *Overview* as in Johnson (1989), *Editorial* as in Brumfit (1984), *About this book* as in Kennedy and Bolitho (1984), *To the reader* as in Grellet (1981) and *Viewpoint* as in Gunderson (1991), to name a few, are instances of an overlapping form. Conventional analysis of genres in terms of move structures appears to be somewhat inadequate when one considers the realities of the world of discourse, underpinning the importance of taking into account interdiscursivity involved in similar or closely related genres.

There is another aspect of the development of academic introductions that prompts an even more interesting discussion. As briefly mentioned earlier, the dictionary definitions suggest introducing academic work as the main communicative purpose of academic introductions. There is no mention of any other concern in dictionaries or in any other published literature. However, as Swales (1990) points out in the case of 'Research Article Introductions' (RAIs), there is another subtle intention in writing RAIs, which can be identified as looking for readership, indirectly promoting research. In RAIs such promotional input is rather subtle, but in academic introductions, especially of the kind we have been discussing, the promotional input is becoming increasingly transparent and more direct and dominant in some cases. This obvious concern on the part of the writer of the academic introduction to promote the book often results in the use of specific linguistic resources and subtle rhetorical strategies, e.g. an extensive use of adjectives to describe aspects of the book, which reminds one of advertising. In the present-day practice, therefore, it is not uncommon to find a dual communicative purpose in academic introductions, that is to introduce the book and to promote it to the potential readers, who may be tempted to invest in the knowledge being offered. If we look at the current practice of writing academic introductions, we will find ample evidence of what might be the hidden agenda. There is a clear indication of the fact that publishers use a socially recognized communicative purpose (i.e. introducing the academic work) and genres which are considered appropriate for the fulfilment of this purpose to communicate 'private intentions' (i.e. to promote the book), which conventionally were not considered part of the book introduction.

This phenomenon of mixing 'private intentions' with 'socially recognized communicative purposes' is not characteristic of academic introductions alone; it is widely used in other professional genres too, resulting in a 'mixing' and often 'bending' of genres. We will take up the notion of genre bending in greater detail in the next chapter when we consider appropriation of genres and generic resources. At this stage, however, I would like to emphasize that these expressions of what I have called 'private intentions' to distinguish them from socially accepted and to some extent expected purposes are quite common in a number of professional genres as well. In newspapers, for instance, objective news reporting has long been regarded as a socially recognized communicative purpose of the genre of news reporting; however, we often find well-established news reporters giving what they think are legitimate slants to the events of the day, often mixing factual reporting with elements of opinions or interpretations in their writing. In the case of academic introductions, it is difficult to say to what extent they are contributed by the author of the book and what exactly is the role of the publisher, because these introductions are always attributed to the author, the series editor or some other established academic in the field. *Viewpoints* or *introductions* attributed to academics other than the author often have a very distinct and recognizable promotional flavour, which often reminds one of 'celebrity endorsements' in advertisements. In most cases, book blurbs, which are mostly attributed to publishers, though never explicitly, are almost always written by authors, and sometimes moderated by the publishers. There is so much of genre mixing in academic introductions that one is often surprised by what one least expects in academic introductions. It is generally true that the acknowledgement is written by the author and the foreword by somebody else, whereas in the case of the preface and the introduction one may find relatively less obvious claims in terms of authorship. We therefore expect a *foreword* to be written by an academic other than the author, and the *introduction* to be written by the author(s); however, in practice, we may be surprised to find an *introduction* written by somebody other than the author (Tay 1993) and a *foreword* written by the author (Gimson 1970, Poynton 1989). In one case I have found all three written by the author in the same book (Halliday 1994). Sometimes in the area of academic introductions, we find what Fairclough (1993) termed 'marketization' of academic discourse.

Similarly, in terms of promotional effort one is least likely to find authors directly promoting their own products and that is one reason why the *foreword*, which is more likely to promote the work, is often written by a well-known academic other than the author of the book. But in present-day practice it is not difficult to find forewords, prefaces, even introductions with a clearly dominant promotional input, so much so that even the main purpose of introduction becomes somewhat secondary to this promotional flavour. The following book introduction provides an interesting example.

(4)

Introduction	
The COBUILD approach to grammar is simple and direct. We study a large collection of English texts, and find out how people are actually using the language. We pick the most important points. ...	Positive Book Description
In this book we give explanations of the most important, frequent, and typical points of English grammar ... so that you can put the knowledge to use immediately. ...	Positive Book Description
... Our first grammar book has been well received, and we are continuing full-scale research on grammar in order to be more accurate and relevant to the needs of the teacher and student.	Establishing Credentials
I would be very glad to have your comments on this book. (Sinclair 1991)	Soliciting Response

In most promotional and advertising genres, adjectives are used to describe and positively evaluate products as the basis of selling power. The most characteristic feature of this text is the predominant use of adjectives, practically in every sentence of the text. Expressions such as the following

- The COBUILD approach to grammar is simple and direct.
- We pick the most important points ...
- You can be sure that ...
- You are presented with real English ...
- The most important, frequent, and typical points of English grammar ...
- This makes the book suitable both as a classroom text, and also for private study ...
- Very easy and direct to understand ...
- Necessary for clear understanding and accurate usage ...

are typical of product description in promotional letters. In addition to that, there are other indications of promotional input, especially the attempt *to establish credentials*:

- Our first grammar book has been well received, and we are continuing full-scale research on grammar in order to be more accurate and relevant to the needs of the teacher and student.

The final paragraph echoes a typical effort in promotional letters to solicit response, considering the fact that a vast majority of promotional discourse is largely unsolicited:

- I would be very glad to have your comments on this book, especially on how useful you find it.

This so-called introduction does not seem to be very different from a typical promotional letter. In fact, it contains all the crucial ingredients that are likely to make a typical promotional effort successful. One may be tempted to think that such a promotional input is very recent because of the intense competition in the publishing industry and the role of advertising in modern-day business. It is true that such promotional concerns have become increasingly more visible in recent times, but it would be inaccurate to say that they were completely

PREFACE	
The American Management Association has felt for some time the need for bringing together in convenient handbook form not only a digest of the best of its own publications ...	Establishing Customer Needs
That this tendency has gone too far is indicated by the opinion often expressed that it is extremely difficult to find men for promotion into positions of major managerial responsibility. ...	
The net result is an extremely difficult problem of coordinating different activities with a particular function ...	
This "Handbook of Business Administration" will, to a considerable extent, meet this educational need by providing in a form convenient for study the fundamentals and the procedures of managerial policy and technique which may be put to use by business	Positive Book Description to Meet Customer Needs

executives ...	
It is our hope, too, that this "Handbook of Business Administration" will find its way into the hands of many business executives ...	Targeting Market
Essentially the Handbook has been prepared to meet the needs of the following groups:	
1. Executives of general managerial ranks who ...	

2.   Those major functional executives who ...
   3.   Those business executives of ... specialized responsibilities who ...
   4. Those specialized executives who ...	

The contributors to the various sections of the Handbook have been carefully chosen as leaders in their respective fields ... (Donald, 1931)	Establishing Credentials

absent some 50 years ago. Bhatia (1997a) provides an interesting instance of such an introduction from the first half of the last century:

Very much like a typical promotional document, it begins by establishing the needs of a potential readership (a well-defined group of business executives) and then goes on to bring in a positive product description to suggest at least a partial fulfilment of such needs (Bhatia 1993: 46–52). The interesting point is that almost the whole of the preface is devoted to these two major moves. Also, like the example we had earlier of the introduction with similar promotional input, this one too relies on the use of positively evaluating expressions like 'a digest of the best of its own publications', 'a reasonably complete picture', 'a form convenient for study', 'contributors ... have been carefully chosen as leaders', 'contributions represent ... the best in modern managerial policies', etc., some of which are often associated with the field of advertising. So this mixing of promotional input to introductory purposes is not entirely new in academic introductions, although it has become a lot more visible in the last few decades than ever before.

This process of genre mixing, especially for the expression of private intentions within the socially-recognized communicative purposes, does not seem to be an exclusive property of academic introductions alone; it is found more commonly in many other forms of professional discourse. Bhatia (1995) documents several instances of genre mixing from advertising, news reporting and legal documents, as well as from bureaucratic communications. He explains:

> This dynamic complexity of professional communication is the result of several factors, including the ever-increasing use of multi-media, explosion of information technology, multi-disciplinary contexts of the world of work, increasingly competitive professional (academic as well as business) environment, and the overwhelmingly compulsive nature of promotional and advertising activities.
>
> (Bhatia 1995: 1)

He also points out that book introductions are becoming increasingly difficult to distinguish from publisher's blurbs, and that publishers seem to be appropriating from author introductions in constructing their blurbs. This raises a number of interesting questions about the conventional naming of genres. Although it is true that discourse communities give generic names to conventionalized communicative events, it may not necessarily be the case that such generic events continue to attract the same labels. It would be interesting to investigate to what extent genres, and therefore generic forms and conventions, can be exploited in order to introduce innovations and creativities to achieve more complex communicative purposes in order to respond to novel communicative situations. To what extent can one do it safely without opting out of the genre boundaries? To what extent are these boundaries crucial? And how can these boundaries be defined? We shall take up some of these issues in the next chapter, but in the meantime I would like to turn to genre embedding, where one often finds a particular generic form, maybe a poem, a story or an article, used as a template to give expression to another conventionally distinct generic form, as in the following advertisement for a job from the *South China Morning Post* (21 March 2003).

WANTED
DYNAMIC AND SPECIALIST SENIOR PRODUCT MANAGERS

1. SWEATERS
2. KNITS
3. DRESSES
If you have lots of *garment* experience,
this is the job for you
If you are *fashion* conscious,
this is the job for you
If you are not afraid of *hard work*,
this is the job for you
If you are a team player,
this is the job for you
If you use your *initiative*,
this is the job for you
If you enjoy *meeting* and *working* with overseas buyers,
this is the job for you
If you are looking for *financial* rewards
In *excess* of HK30,000 per month plus *bonus* and *generous* benefits,
This is the job for you

Now be *honest*
If you are *uncomfortable* with any of the above,
This is not the job for you
Only applicants who are ready for *tough* challenge and
Willing to go through a
rigorous interview need apply.

Your potential employer is Loyaltex Apparel Ltd.—a leading and progressive international trading group based in Hong Kong engaged in the export of garment products. The Group sources and sells a full range of apparel for men, women and children. If you are convinced this is the job for you, apply with your full particulars to:

The Personnel Manager
Loyaltex Apparel Ltd.
Tower B, Cheung Sha Wan Plaza
833 Cheung Sha Wan Road
Kowloon

Other generic forms, such as letters, dialogues, articles, scientific reports, reviews etc., are also very common in advertising genres. Look at the next one where we find two different genres embedded within the advertisement itself.

OVERHEARD AT FANLING GOLF COURSE:

1st PLAYER:	"How was your trip to Indonesia?"
2nd PLAYER:	"Great. Got all the business done … and got in a spot of golf."
1st PLAYER:	"Hear business is booming there?"
2nd PLAYER:	"Yes, We're very optimistic about the future, so we're opening an office in Jakarta next month."
1st PLAYER:	"So you're heavily invested there?"
2nd PLAYER:	"Well, the company is. My investments are more liquid. I prefer to buy shares in funds."
1st PLAYER:	"I thought you liked Indonesia?"
2nd PLAYER:	"I do. I've invested in the Barclays Indonesia Fund. It's up 66% over the past three years*."
1st PLAYER:	"Sounds good. Know anyone there?"
2nd PLAYER:	"Call my contact at Barclays, Sarah Robbins, on 826 1988, or your investment adviser can help."
1st PLAYER:	"Thanks. I'll follow it up. By the way, you just played my ball!"

*Source Micropal 01/010/94

Dear Sarah,
I recently heard about the great performance of the Barclays Indonesia Fund. Please send me information on how I too can benefit from Barclays' Asia expertise with as little as US$1,500. My business card is enclosed. Thanks.

BARCLAYS

Level 16, Two Pacific Place, 88 Queensway, Hong Kong

It must be remembered that the value of shares and income from them can decrease as well as increase and the past performance figures are not indicative of future performance.

In principle, the notion of pure genres is very attractive and extremely useful for a number of pedagogical applications; in practice, however, it is unlikely to capture the complex communicative realities of the present-day professional and academic world. In order to account for these complexities, do we need to abandon the notion of pure genres altogether, or should we extend it to cover a range of genres in a specific domain and then look for generic patterns? If we take it a little bit further, we might need to establish criteria to determine what kinds of communicative purposes can be legitimately mixed or embedded without opting out of the socially established generic boundaries. What kind of 'private intentions' are compatible with what kind of 'socially recognized communicative purposes'? To investigate some of these questions further we need to look closely at what we said in the beginning of this chapter, that is the process of colonization, which results in the appropriation of generic resources, sometimes leading to the bending of genres, and also to the creation of generic conflicts in professional contexts, all of which will be the focus of attention in the next section. But before we do that, I would like to introduce yet another important professional genre colony, that of reporting genres.

3.3 Reporting genres

Like the other two colonies we have just looked at, *reporting genres* form a similar colony. Reporting is perhaps one of the most popular and overly used 'generic values' in all contexts of professional discourse across disciplines and domains today. We are quite familiar with *news reports, business reports, law reports, accident reports, first information reports* (FIR), *inquiry reports*, etc., and one could add many more to the list from a range of disciplines. On the other hand, one could go further down the line and identify variations within *business reports*, for example *company report, financial report, feasibility report, investigation report, annual report*, etc. The emerging picture may be simplified by considering these reports within and across disciplines and domains, but in reality it will be much more dynamic, displaying distinctiveness as well as overlap in various ways. Let us look at the simplified classification first, and then variations within business reports.

Reports

- News reports
- Technical reports
- Business reports
- Accident reports
- Police reports
- First Information Reports
- Medical reports
- Scientist's reports

Although these reports from different domains and contexts of use share an overlapping communicative purpose, that of reporting on events, they are also likely to display lexico-grammatical as well as rhetorical variations. As an illustration, let us look at news reports, which are seen as the most common form of reporting events of the day. They are considered objective, detached and factual, though it is also true that oftentimes news reporters favour a particular interpretation, slant or perspective on specific events of the day. One may see news reports of various kinds as well, some of which include hard news, news on special topics such as science, business and economics, finance, agriculture, information technology, medicine, etc. As Bhatia (1993: 157–74) points out, although they share a common genre, they still display interesting differences, not only in terms of the use of specialist lexis, which is often the case, but also in terms of their rhetorical structuring. Similarly, it is possible to find a whole range of subtle variations in what is known as business reports, some of which may include the following:

Business reports

- Investigation report (suggesting solutions for existing problems)
- Performance report (evaluating an individual product, service or activity)
- Progress or Status report (reporting development as part of a project/activity)
- Process report (reporting on how-to aspects of projects or activities)
- Feasibility report (reporting on chances of failure or success of projects)
- Sales report (reporting on periodic sales figures; may include market analysis)
- Field trip report (recording business activities at various locations)
- Annual report (reporting on overall perspective on an organization)
- Audit report (indicating economic efficiency)

An interesting aspect of such a classification is that just as it is possible to view individual genres as part of a specific disciplinary domain, it is equally possible to view some other aspects of these very genres as displaying overlaps across a number of disciplinary domains.

Therefore the reality of the situation can only be captured by a much more complex and perhaps dynamic picture displaying similarities as well as overlaps within and across disciplinary frames and discursive practices. A more realistic picture of the colony of reporting genres will look like the one in Diagram 3.4.

The preceding discussion offers an increasingly complex and dynamically developing picture of genre colonies from a range of professional, academic and institutionalized contexts. It also highlights the versatility of genres in terms of their conceptualization, specification and hybridization, both in mixed and embedded forms. It also raises an interesting possibility of appropriation of generic resources across generic boundaries, which we referred to at the beginning of this chapter as the process of colonization. This appropriation of linguistic and discoursal resources is an unmistakable indication of the dynamic nature of genre (Swales 1990; Bhatia 1993, 1995; Berkenkotter and Huckin 1995). Although all genres undergo change and development over a period of time, colonization by promotional genres has a special significance in academic and professional contexts. This can be

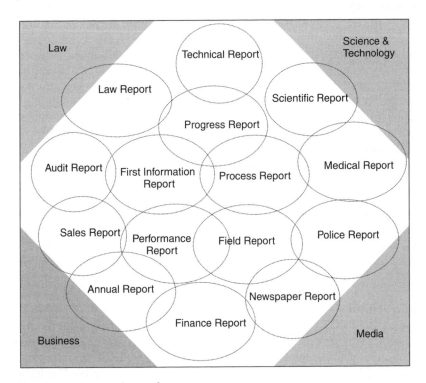

Diagram 3.4 *Colony of reporting genres*

attributed to a number of interesting and significant developments in recent years. An almost unprecedented exploitation of new technology to make public discourse accessible to large audiences across the globe has prompted millions of new 'makers' of discourse to give varied interpretations to conventional forms of discourse, often creating new forms. Appropriation of lexico-grammatical and rhetorical resources from the discourse of corporate advertising has offered a number of very attractive options because of its innovative character and creative use of language. Advertising has turned the process of writing into an art form, where writers constantly compete for attention not only by innovative use of language but also by the creative use of traditional expressions and clichés, which are often shunned by good writers in other forms of discourse. This process of colonization is given a further boost by the fact that the world we live in today provides an extremely competitive environment in which academics and professionals are required to perform. Universities, for example, until very recently have always maintained their special status and dignity in society because of their territorial demarcation and also because of their excellence in specialist areas of knowledge creation and consumption. However, in the present-day competitive environment, most of them are finding it extremely difficult to maintain their privileged status of excellence. As a result of an increasing number of students going for higher education, the universities are gradually coming closer to the concept of a marketplace, where every one has to compete with every one else for clients' attention. Similarly, in the corporate world, the events in the past few years have made it far more competitive than it was in the past. In the 1960s and 1970s, the corporate world was rather small and varied, with very few multinationals operating globally. The markets were also somewhat segmented and often protected by governments. With the competition in trade and commerce becoming more and more intense, multinationals started increasing in number and size in the 1980s and became almost the norm in the 1990s. From the point of view of discourse development, there were two important consequences: first, promotion and advertising activities became almost essential for survival, and second, cross-cultural variations became a significant factor in promotional and advertising discourse. The most important consequence of these developments on the discourse of advertising has been that in a very short period of time this has become one of the most dynamic and innovative forms of discourse today, which in turn has influenced the construction, interpretation, use and exploitation of most other forms of academic, professional and institutional genres, thus invading their territorial integrity to create appropriated, embedded, mixed or hybrid forms of discourse, which we shall discuss in the next chapter.

THE WORLD OF PRIVATE INTENTIONS

4 Appropriation of generic resources

So far we have considered genres as conventionalized discursive actions, in which participating individuals or institutions have shared perceptions of communicative purposes as well as those of constraints operating on their construction, interpretation and conditions of use. In this sense, genres are socially constructed, interpreted and used in specific academic, social, institutional and professional contexts, and have their own individual identity. We have also seen that expert members of professional discourse communities often mix socially accepted communicative purposes conventionally served by two different genres to create hybrid (both mixed and embedded) genres. Sometimes, we also find well-established genre writers exploiting generic conventions to communicate their 'private intentions' within the context of socially accepted communicative purposes that a particular genre is meant to serve (Bhatia 1995), often resulting not only in genre mixing and embedding, but also occasionally in genre bending, which can sometimes create genres in conflict. This is often done by appropriating generic resources from a specific genre for the construction of another. These resources may be lexico-grammatical, rhetorical, discoursal or other generic conventions, which are appropriated to give shape to more dynamic or innovative generic forms. This tendency to appropriate generic resources is becoming increasingly common in all areas of academic and professional discourse. These appropriations often lead to the colonization of one genre by the other by invading its integrity. In this chapter we shall consider two such exploitations of generic resources, but before we go to specific instances, some discussion of what I have called 'invasion of territorial integrity' is necessary.

4.1 Invasion of territorial integrity

As we have discussed earlier, genres often operate within their own territorial boundaries, displaying their individually recognizable integrity, which is accessible not only to established members of the professional community, but to discourse analysts too. However, in the context of the present-day interdisciplinary and dynamic world of work, it is often difficult to keep the individual generic boundaries intact, and it has become even more difficult because of the explosion of information technology, the use of new media and also the overpowering influence of promotional activities in today's competitive world. Of all the genres which have invaded the territorial integrity of many professional and academic genres, 'advertising' clearly stands out to be the most predominant instrument of colonization. It has successfully invaded a number of professional genres, including academic, corporate, political, journalistic and many of the reporting genres, displaying the use of a range of strategies from a relatively subtle appropriation of lexico-grammatical and discoursal resources to a much more conspicuous 'hybridization' (Fairclough 1993) or 'mixing' and 'embedding' of genres (Bhatia 1994, 1995, 1997a), which forms a very interesting aspect of the genre theory. We have already discussed in the last chapter one aspect of this while discussing the concept of genre colonies. In order to give some idea of the widespread nature of this kind of colonization of other genres from different domains, let us look at Diagram 4.1.

Bhatia (1995), in his discussion of professional discourse, gives examples from several settings where genre mixing and embedding has become increasingly common. He also mentions several instances where one may find an increasing use of promotional strategies in

---

Non-conventional use of generic resources for promotional purposes

ACADEMIC DISCOURSE
Academic course descriptions
Job descriptions
Academic Introductions: book introduction, preface, foreword
Book blurbs

CORPORATE DISCOURSE
Annual Reports
Company Brochures
Financial Statements
Investment Brochures

MEDIA DISCOURSE
News reports v. News stories
Editorials v. News analysis

POLITICAL DISCOURSE
Joint Declarations
Memorandum of understanding
Diplomatic Communiqués

Diagram 4.1   *Invasion of territorial integrity*

genres which are traditionally considered non-promotional in their communicative purposes. The examples include job advertisements and academic introductions, where he found rather explicit indications of promotional elements which traditionally have been regarded as purely informative or at best persuasive, but certainly not promotional in the marketing sense. A closer look at these instances will indicate that it often is the case that informative functions are more likely to be colonized by promotional functions than any other. As Bhatia (1993) points out, the most popular promotional strategy in advertising has been *to describe and evaluate a product or service in a positive manner*, which may be seen as the information-giving function of language. These two functions of language, i.e. informational and promotional, are therefore unlikely to create tension, even if they may not be entirely complementary to each other. A number of such instances of mixed genres are getting established and are being given innovative names, as in the case of *infomercial, infotainment* or *advertorial*. Although it may appear that this kind of genre mixing is more common in genres that are less likely to create functional tension, it will be wrong to assume that it will always be the case. It is possible to view this subtle colonization of genres in terms of appropriation and ultimate mixing of genres, depending upon the degree of invasion one may find in individual members of a colony. This can be diagrammatically represented as in Diagram 4.2.

The primary and most dominant form of promotional discourse is what is commonly known as advertising discourse, which of course has a number of exponents. A very closely related marketing genre that has remarkable similarities with advertising is what is popularly known as a book blurb or a publisher's blurb, to distinguish it from an author's introduction. Most traditional forms of advertisement have considerable overlap with book blurbs, especially in respect of the rhetorical moves that both of them use to persuade their readership to buy the advertised product or book. A sales promotional letter, though remarkably similar to a typical advertisement, is interdiscursively more complex, in that it is always embedded in a letter format.

This interdiscursivity is also partly responsible for bringing together yet another genre with advertising, i.e. the job application letter, which shares not only the embedded format with advertising, but also a striking range of lexico-grammatical resources, though sometimes different in form but remarkably similar in their functional value. In spite of their very different contextual configurations, as genres they display strong similarities in terms of their communicative purposes, the lexico-grammatical resources they use and also their move structure (Swales 1990). This probably is one of the most

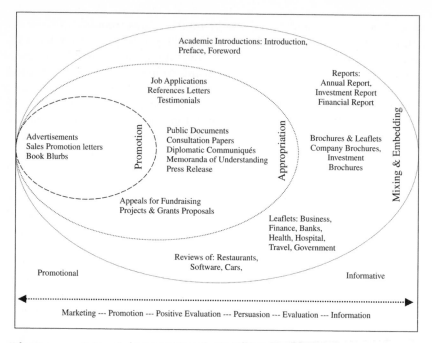

Diagram 4.2 *Colonization of academic, professional and other institutionalized genres*

interesting appropriations of generic resources across conventional socio-rhetorical boundaries. Somewhat similar but more radical appropriation of linguistic and discoursal resources we find in the case of philanthropic fundraising letters, which are different from sales promotional letters in terms of the rationale, the ideology and the nature of the appeal, but are remarkably similar in terms of their move structure (Bhatia 1998a). Closely related to job application letters, we have testimonials, reference letters and CVs, all of which tend to have promotional intentions. In addition to these appropriated forms, we do get a number of other public and professional genres, which tend to be persuasive though not in the sense of marketing. Some of the most notable candidates for inclusion in this category are genres related to socio-political and diplomatic contexts, such as consultation papers (Bhatia 1997b), diplomatic communiqués, press releases and what are popularly known as memoranda of understanding (Bhatia 2000). Although most of these are designed to serve informative purposes, they invariably focus on only positive aspects and incorporate persuasive and sometimes even promotional elements.

Somewhat more distant categories of discourse, which still have a number of genres, essentially informative and traditionally non-promotional in intent, are increasingly being influenced and even colonized by promotional concerns. The main communicative purpose they serve is still informative, but they can sometimes be mixed or hybrid in appearance. Fairclough (1993) discusses several interesting instances of academic course descriptions and job advertisements, which, he rightly claims, are becoming increasingly promotional. Similarly, we have seen in Chapter 3 the case of academic introductions, i.e. book introductions, prefaces and forewords (see also Bhatia 1995, 1997a), which brought into focus two issues. The one is that the traditional distinctions between these closely related genres are disappearing in practice, thus making it very difficult to distinguish them in terms of their individual generic identities. The second issue, and perhaps more interesting for this chapter, is that these forms of academic introductions are becoming increasingly promotional in practice, so that sometimes it becomes rather difficult not to take notice of such promotional elements in these essentially informative genres, particularly in the case of book introductions.

Coming to reviews as genre, one may continue to find book reviews as essentially balanced evaluations, where one may find reasonably balanced descriptions of books which may incorporate positive as well as negative aspects of the product in question. However, in the case of reviews of food and restaurants, software and other similar products, one may find a majority of them predominantly promotional in character, focusing mainly on positive description and evaluation, which is creating a new appropriated form of reviews, which are increasingly being used for 'recommending' products and services. In one of the most popular Hong Kong English language newspapers, the *South China Morning Post*, there is once a week a special write-up as part of their regular classified section which they call 'Classified Plus', a review of a particular product or service, which is almost entirely promotional, but is presented as if it is a kind of recommendation from the newspaper. If we compare this with any example of a mixed genre, such as an advertorial or a blurb, we can see the way it has been deceptively used as a recommendation or a review, whereas in fact it is no different from an advertisement. An example from this 'Classified Plus' section is produced below.

MIND-BODY WORKOUT FOR ALL AGES

Imagine an exercise programme that you look forward to, that engages you, and that leaves you refreshed and alert with a feeling of physical and metal well-being. The Pilates Method (pronounced puh-LAH-teez) of body-conditioning will do all this . . . and more.

The Pilates and Gyrotonic exercise methods, as a result of their user-friendliness, safety and effectiveness, have become the fastest-growing fitness methods in the United States over the past five years.

Developed in the 1920s by physical trainer Joseph Pilates, the programme is an exercise system for men and women of all fitness levels, focused on improving flexibility and strength for the total body without building bulk. Pilates is not just exercise, however, it is a series of controlled movements engaging your body and mind, performed on specifically designed exercise apparatus and on the mat supervised by trained teachers. The fundamentals of Gyrotonic Expansion System simultaneously stretches and strengthens the body with minimal effort, while increasing range of motion and developing co-ordination.

The system was specifically conceived incorporating key principles of gymnastics, swimming, ballet, and yoga through which major muscle groups are worked interdependently and in an integrated manner. It is served by a series of specially designed exercise equipment, which is built around the human body with all regards to total freedom in movement, no restriction to speed and versatility, and enhances co-ordination, stregth and flexibility.

All sporting activities demand strength, flexibility, co-ordination and range of motion. The Gyrotonic system also provides greater endurance, versatility and gracefulness to all performed competitive skills and movements.

When practiced correctly and consistently over time, the Pilates and Gyrotonic exercise will significantly enhance:

Aesthetic form, muscle tone and strength without increasing bulk;
- Posture and the structural alignment of the skeleton and musculature to promote efficiency of form and function for everyday activities;
- Movement flow and the corresponding breathing patterns;
- Flexibility and range of motion around the joints;
- Core strength; and
- Rehabilitation of injuries and certain physiological conditions.

Instruction in the Pilates and Gyrotonic methods at Iso Fit takes the form of studio instruction (private/semi-private coaching) and a full schedule and variety of group classes.

Isodynamic Fitness Centres
(South China Morning Post, 21 March 2003)

If we look at it closely, we find at least three of the most crucial rhetorical moves that are associated with promotional documents such as advertising, promotional letters or book blurbs. Let me illustrate this by analysing the move structure:

Imagine an exercise programme that you look forward to, that engages you, and that leaves you refreshed and alert with a feeling of physical and mental well-being.	**ESTABLISHING CREDENTIALS by referring to the needs of the customers**
The Pilates Method (pronounced puh-LAH-teez) of body-conditioning will do all this ... and more.	**INTRODUCING THE PRODUCT**
The Pilates and Gyrotonic exercise methods, as a result of their user-friendliness, safety and effectiveness, have become the fastest-growing fitness methods in the United States over the past five years.	**ESTABLISHING CREDENTIALS** ▲
Developed in the 1920s by physical trainer Joseph Pilates ... Pilates is not just exercise ... it is a series of controlled movements engaging your body and mind ... The fundamentals of Gyrotonic Expansion System simultaneously stretches and strengthens the body with minimal effort ...	**Detailing the product**
The system was specifically conceived incorporating key principles of gymnastics, swimming ... It is served by a series of specially designed exercise equipment ...	▼▲
All sporting activities demand strength, flexibility, co-ordination and range of motion. The Gyrotonic system also provides greater endurance, versatility and gracefulness to all performed competitive skills and movements.	
... the Pilates and Gyrotonic exercise will significantly enhance:	

• Aesthetic form, muscle tone and strength ...; • Posture and the structural alignment of the skeleton ...; • Movement flow and the corresponding breathing patterns; • Flexibility and range of motion around the joints; • Core strength; and • Rehabilitation of injuries ... Instruction in the Pilates and Gyrotonic methods at Iso Fit takes the form of studio instruction (private/semi-private coaching) and a full schedule and variety of group classes. Isodynamic Fitness Centres	**Indicating value of the product** ↓ **OFFERING INCENTIVES (?)** **SOLICITING RESPONSE (?)**

The text has two explicit realizations of 'ESTABLISHING CREDEN-TIALS' by referring to the needs of readers, i.e. the potential customers, and also by referring to established practice in the United States, as indicated by the use of the perfect tense with a time adverbial 'have become the fastest-growing fitness methods in the United States over the past five years'. It then goes on to describe the product positively as is often done in typical promotional documents, followed by a detailed section indicating the value of the product. One can notice the typical use of a string of adjectival and adverbial expressions within the syntactic structures of nominal as well as verbal components, such as 'specifically conceived incorporating key principles of gymnastics, swimming', 'greater endurance, versatility and gracefulness to all performed competitive skills and movements', 'aesthetic form, muscle tone and strength,' 'posture and the structural alignment of the skeleton ...', 'movement flow and the corresponding breathing patterns', ' flexibility and range of motion around the joints', etc. The text, however, does not contain any explicit indications of other typical rhetorical moves such as 'offering incentives' or 'soliciting response', though one may read a subtle hint of these in expressions in the last paragraph and in the name of the centres providing such services following it. The use of some of these features of lexico-grammar as well as some of the rhetorical moves as discussed above clearly indicates the hybrid nature of the text in question, which is partly informational and partly promotional. However, it differentiates itself clearly from review, as it is unlikely to incorporate any negative evaluation of the product. At least in several of these advertorials I have seen so far, I have not noticed any indication of a 'balanced' evaluation (containing negative as well as positive elements) of the product or service.

Leaflets on services from corporations, banking as well as financial, medical and health institutions, travel industries and government departments are primarily informative, but it is rare not to find any promotional or persuasive overtones in most of them. Similarly, brochures and reports, whether they report on the company services, financial matters, investment appreciation or travel opportunities, are essentially informative but are always exploited for promotional purposes.

Although appropriation of generic resources is often a natural socio-rhetorical option available to most genre writers, it will be inappropriate to assume that such appropriations are always legitimate. They often have a potential to create conflicts in genre construction and interpretation. Let me give more substance to this claim by taking up specific examples.

4.2 Philanthropic fundraising

Most forms of fundraising discourse are essentially promotional in nature, in the sense that they may promote a cause as in the case of direct mail fundraising, a public campaign for social events, an image or, as in brochures, the success of the institution concerned. We can place various forms of fundraising discourse on a continuum along with many others related to promotional discourse, including commercial advertisements of various kinds. At one end of the continuum we can have philanthropic purposes, while at the other end we can place commercial advertising (for corporate and individual profit), as shown in Diagram 4.3.

Philanthropic fundraising genres and commercial advertising genres can be grouped together in the same broad category of promotional discourse. The two sets of genres have a remarkable degree of overlap, though one could also notice subtle differences in the two categories. Let me explore the two sets of genres further to see how they compare.

Commercial advertising and philanthropic fundraising genres both primarily aim at capital raising. However, in the first one the main objective is to accumulate profit for corporate purposes, whereas in the second the objective is to raise money for social and welfare purposes, which is essentially a non-profit activity. In most cases of philanthropic fundraising the main driving force is the mission of the

Diagram 4.3 *Commercial advertising and philanthropic fundraising*

organization or the fundraising agency, which is primarily used as a strategy to mobilize fundraising successfully, as in the following example from Amnesty International:

> *Amnesty International's worldwide campaign to highlight the discrepancy between the human rights protection which those living in Russia have in international and national law, and the reality of widespread human rights abuses committed in a climate of impunity.*

In the case of corporate advertising, on the contrary, the primary mission is maximization of profits, either for individual or corporate purposes. Even in companies where explicit mission statements are publicized, the real intention invariably is capital growth, profit-enhancement and corporate success. In the case of philanthropic fundraising there is always a cause for which fundraising is under-taken and that cause very often is the mission. In either case, the cause is always taken to be more important than the mission. In the case of corporate advertising, however, profit maximization is the mission and the cause, if there is any.

The two sets of social actions (Miller 1984), however, differ significantly in terms of the motivating factors that make them successful. In the case of corporate advertising, it is the resources and expertise accessible in the form of a business proposition that will convince the audience about the potential strength and eventual success of the activity, whereas in the case of philanthropic fundraising, it is more a case of selfless motivation, social responsi-bility and an urge to take moral action that will ensure the eventual success of the enterprise. In spite of the similarities in terms of communicative purposes, and somewhat overlapping use of rhetorical strategies, the two social actions differ basically in that philanthropic

Community Purposes Philanthropic Fundraising	Corporate Purposes Commercial Advertising
Mission	Accumulation of capital
Non-profit	Individual or corporate profit
Cause: More important than the Mission	Profit as mission
Trustees: their public image and integrity	Success or track record of the company
Selfless motivation is crucial	Resources and expertise

Diagram 4.4 *Commercial advertising & philanthropic fundraising contrasts*

fundraising is essentially viewed as a form of moral action, whereas corporate advertising is seen as a business proposition. Diagram 4.4 summarizes some of these parallels.

In spite of some of these subtle variations, the two types of promotional discourse display remarkably similar surface-level rhetorical characteristics. Like most promotional letters in business contexts (see Bhatia 1993), fundraising letters also can have a seven-move cognitive structure, although in practice we do not see all of them in every instance.

1. Establishing credentials
2. Introducing the offer
3. Offering incentives
4. Enclosing documents
5. Soliciting response
6. Using pressure tactics
7. Ending politely

Let me give some evidence of this by analysing a direct mail fundraising letter produced below.

GIANT STEPS

Toward a New Black Cultural Center at Purdue University

March 1997

Dear Colleague:

Tony Harris, Purdue alumnus and Vice President for Business and Customer Service at Pacific Gas and Electric in San Francisco, wrote the following in an Exponent column: *"Purdue can be a lonely place for incoming freshman, particularly minority students. For me, the BCC represented a familiar setting, and made Purdue feel more like home. This story, I have heard repeated hundreds of times."*

1

Tony is only one of the many students, staff, and faculty of all races who have sought out the BCC over the years to make new friends, enjoy the fine arts performances and lectures the BCC sponsors, and broaden their understanding of African-American culture in an increasingly diverse and multicultural world. The BCC also helps Purdue departments recruit new faculty, staff, and students and supports academic excellence through its expanded library, computer lab, and outreach programs.

For nearly 27 years the <u>Black Culture Center has served the University and the community</u> from a small house built in 1905. If you've been there, you know the programs and services have outgrown the space. A new, much larger center is essential to carry on the mission of the BCC.

<u>Giant Steps --- a $3 million campaign to build a new center</u> at the Third and Russell Streets was started last fall. President Beering launched the campaign with a $1 million pledge from the University. As of March 1, another $270,000 had been pledged by corporations and individuals, including more than $135,000 raised recently by BCC students calling alumni and friends.

2

Now it's your turn to help. If you've already made a gift or pledge, we thank you. If not, please take this opportunity to demonstrate <u>your support</u> by returning the enclosed form with your gift. The CC is a cultural treasure that enriches our community. We believe strongly that the return to the campus will be well worth your investment and ours. Please join us in building a new Black Cultural Center. If you have any questions, call Renee Thomas of the BCC, at 494–3091.

3

4

5

Sincerely

John W Hicks
Senior Vice President Emeritus
Co-Chair, Campus Campaign

Judith M. Gappa
Vice President for Human Relations
Co-Chair, Campus Campaign

7

The Black Cultural Center Purdue University 315 University Street, West Lafayette, In 47906–2897
Fax 765–496–1915

1. **Establishing credentials**

Typical promotional letters begin by establishing the credentials of the company either by referring to the needs of the potential customers or by referring to the long-standing service of the company (Bhatia 1993). Fundraising letters, in a similar manner, attempt to establish the needs of the members of the community, in the fulfilment of which they have a shared interest. This is often done by using endorsement from a typical and credible beneficiary of the outcome of the desired action, as in the following case:

Tony is only one of the many students, staff, and faculty of all races who have sought out the BCC over the years to make new friends, enjoy the fine arts performances and lectures the BCC sponsors, and broaden their understanding of African-American culture in an increasingly diverse and multicultural world. The BCC also helps Purdue departments recruit new faculty, staff, and students and supports academic excellence through its expanded library, computer lab, and outreach programs.

Community cause is often established by mission statements, as in the following claim:

The BCC is a cultural treasure that enriches our community. We believe strongly that the return to the campus will be well worth your investment and ours. Please join us in building a new Black Cultural Center.

For establishing credentials in advertising discourse, we find the use of a positive and long-established track record of the corporation in providing the service or product, whereas in philanthropic fundraising we often find a record of past success in fulfilling community goals (Bhatia 1993):

For four years now, the Teddy Bear program has been supported by friends in the area who care ...

Or

For nearly 27 years the <u>Black Cultural Center has served the University and the community</u> from a small house built in 1905. If you've been there, you know the programs and services have outgrown the space. A new, much larger center is essential to carry on the mission of the BCC.

Celebrity endorsement is one of the most time-honoured advertising strategies for a whole range of promotional purposes, corporate or fundraising. Notice the following attempt from a fundraising brochure:

Tony Harris, Purdue alumnus and Vice President for Business and Customer Service at Pacific Gas and Electric in San Francisco, wrote the following in an Exponent column: 'Purdue can be a lonely place for incoming minority

*students. For me, the BCC represented a familiar setting, and made Purdue feel
more like home. This story, I have heard repeated hundreds of times.'*

In fundraising discourse, this strategy is also exploited when the
integrity and the public image of the trustees are used to emphasize the
honest intention of the fundraising activity. However, it must be
admitted that the exploitation of the image of the trustees is very subtle
and indirect, as compared with celebrity endorsement often used in
corporate advertising. The variety of strategies often used to realize this
move thus include

- incorporating celebrity endorsement
- referring to community needs
- referring to mission statements
- using images of the trustees
- invoking frameworks of consciousness
- invoking community involvement

2. **Introducing the product**

Although this move is common in both the sales promotion letters as
well as in fundraising letters, it is often expressed in terms of the cause
for which the funds are being raised:

*Giant Steps – a $3 million campaign to build a new center at the Third and
Russell Streets was started last fall. President Beering launched the campaign
with a $1 million pledge from the University. As of March 1, another $270,000
had been pledged by corporations and individuals, including more than
$135,000 raised recently by BCC students calling alumni and friends.*

In fundraising letters, this move often consists of the following stages:

- introducing the cause
- describing the cause
- indicating the value of the cause
- indicating the potential value of solicited support
- establishing the track record

3. **Offering incentives**

In fundraising letters incentives are not very common, except in the
form of a subtle mention of tax exemption possibilities.

4. **Enclosing documents**

Like typical promotional letters, philanthropic fundraising letters also
enclose supporting documents, especially the forms to be filled in to
pledge support, supporting brochures or leaflets.

Now it's your turn to help. If you've already made a gift or pledge, we thank you. If not, please take this opportunity to demonstrate your support by returning the enclosed form with your gift.

5. **Soliciting support**
Promotional efforts are never considered complete without soliciting support, which is the main communicative purpose of the activity. It is often realized in terms of a straightforward directive:

6. **Using pressure tactics**
Unlike many sales promotion letters, fundraising letters rarely if ever *use pressure tactics* to encourage donations.

7. **Ending politely**
Unlike typical advertisements or other forms of corporate promotional literature, one invariably finds the use of appeals encouraging personal involvement, and also with them some expression of gratitude for anticipated or completed gestures of support.

In addition, we also see the usual borrowings from the marketing world in the form of headlines, signature lines, and even slogans as in the following examples:

> The Center on Philanthropy – A Pillar of Community
> GIANTSTEPS – Toward a New Black Cultural Center at Purdue University

One can thus summarize the essential similarities and differences in advertising and philanthropic discourse in the terms indicated in Diagram 4.5.

One of the most fundamental features of philanthropic fundraising, which differentiates it from much of corporate advertising, is the assumption that the society has self-interest in the establishment and maintenance of community values. Corporations and other business organizations are also sometimes tempted to go beyond their profit motivation to sponsor or contribute to fundraising in the hope that it will bring them community recognition and hence give them an advantage over their competitors. However, this raises a number of interesting issues from the point of view of appropriation of generic resources and development in genres in the context of philanthropic fundraising discourse. Some of these include the relationship between the discourse of fundraising and corporate advertising, and the nature and extent of appropriation of rhetorical and linguistic devices to achieve fundraising objectives, which further raise a more general issue of the implications of this territorial invasion for the integrity of fundraising discourse. Although there are rhetorical similarities between corporate advertisements and philanthropic fundraising discourse, there are a few significant factors that give fundraising

ADVERTISING DISCOURSE		PHILANTHROPIC DISCOURSE
ESTABLISHING CREDENTIALS	1	ESTABLISHING CREDENTIALS
Individual needs Long established service Gratitude for past support Celebrity endorsement		Community needs Established cause Gratitude for past support Celebrity endorsement Mission statements Credentials of trustees Continued community support
INTRODUCING THE OFFER	2	INTRODUCING THE CAUSE
Offering product/service Detailing the offer Indicating value of offer		Introducing the cause Preparing for support Detailing cause/service Value of the support
OFFERING INCENTIVES Special offers discounts	3	OFFERING INCENTIVES Income tax rebates
ENCLOSING BROCHURES Details of offer Request/order forms	4	ENCLOSING BROCHURES Brochures, mission statements Pledge or donation form
SOLICITING RESPONSE	5	SOLICITING SUPPORT
USING PRESSURE TACTICS	6	(Rarely used)
ENDING POLITELY	7	EXPRESSING GRATITUDE

Diagram 4.5 *Advertising and fundraising discourses*

genres their very distinctive generic integrity, some of which are listed below.

Community participation: Unlike commercial advertising, which is targeted at individual customers, philanthropic fundraising highly values the concept of community participation. The success of the whole exercise is measured in terms of community participation. It is considered more valuable to collect a few hundred thousand dollars from many members of the community than to collect a similar amount from a handful of rich businessmen. As Payton *et al.* (1991: 4) rightly point out '... fund raising is ... inextricably tied to philanthropic values, purposes, and methods'. They identify fundraising as moral action, which is a major factor distinguishing philanthropic fundraising from much of corporate advertising. However, there seems to be a significant increase in the use of rhetorical strategies that are more commonly associated with the discourse of marketing, which are likely to undervalue the importance of philanthropic fundraising as a community activity.

Framework of social consciousness: Schervish (1997) identifies framework of social consciousness, with its own unique system of beliefs, goals, and ways of thinking and fulfilling social responsibility, as an important factor that often motivates charitable giving. Motivation for corporate success is essentially embedded within a more utilitarian framework (Scollon 1998). Any large-scale appropriation of rhetorical and linguistic resources associated with commercial advertising thus has the potential to undermine the value of even the most legitimate philanthropic fundraising cause. However, there is a need to distinguish motivations that encourage individuals and big corporations to donate for philanthropic activities. In much of corporate philanthropic donations there is a subtle underlying concern to attract corporate advantage, whereas individuals are often drawn by a relatively more selfless spirit.

Voluntary action: Although fundraising involves community participation, it is essentially a voluntary activity. It may need persuasion, which is often in the form of tax incentives, but there is hardly any scope for the use of pressure tactics, which are so very often used in commercial advertising. Even the incentives are nothing more than a simple and legitimate recognition of the act of donation. So far as the corporate donors are concerned, tax incentives are seen as the main driving force.

Non-competitiveness stance: Promotional concerns have been at the very heart of most business and professional activities and the discourse of fundraising is no exception. Although it appears to be very different from traditional commercial advertising, it shares an important characteristic with much of advertising in general, in that both the activities in recent years have become extremely competitive. Just as an increasing number of new products and services are competing for favourable attention from potential buyers, similarly the number of fundraising activities is on the increase and so is the competition to attract contributions from potential donors. In the context of these developments, it is hardly surprising that in fundraising discourse we notice an increasing appropriation of a wide range of rhetorical strategies and their linguistic realizations which have traditionally been associated with corporate advertising.

However, the two activities and hence their typical rhetorical forms are different in a number of ways. As discussed in Chapter 3 above, product differentiation, which is one of the main underlying considerations in typical commercial advertising, is rarely an issue in most forms of philanthropic discourse. Although many of these philanthropic organizations compete with one another for a limited pool of financial resources available in a particular society, any form of competitive stance is rarely reflected in the discourse of fundraising. On the other hand, we often find charitable collections being shared across a range of institutions.

Coming to the more general issue of appropriation of rhetorical strategies across closely related genres, I briefly mentioned in the earlier section that it is generally less problematic to appropriate generic features across areas of discourse which serve complementary communicative purposes to create mixed or hybrid genres, as in the case of *advertorial, infotainment, infomercial* and a number of others. However, it may become somewhat problematic to do so across genres which either serve conflicting communicative purposes or are associated with contexts that have conflicting or contradictory concerns or requirements, as we see in the case of philanthropic discourse. It is interesting to see that in a number of respects it appears to be very similar to much of commercial advertising discourse, especially when seen in the context of an increasingly liberal attitude towards appropriation of generic resources from a much more powerful and hence dominant promotional discourse. However, in spite of a number of very striking surface similarities, the two areas of discourse have somewhat different underlying concerns, which may demand the development of these two discourse-types in slightly different directions. The real danger in an indiscriminate and overwhelming appropriation of discoursal resources from the discourse of marketing is that it is likely to undermine the real value and strength of much of philanthropic discourse.

Another interesting example of such conflicts is that of the 'joint declaration' or what is more popularly known in bureaucratic contexts as the 'memorandum of understanding', which can be seen as a mixed or hybrid genre, incorporating two rather conflicting communicative purposes. Let me give more substance to this by considering an instance of partly legal and partly bureaucratic discourse, i.e. the 1984 Joint Declaration by the governments of Great Britain and the People's Republic of China on Hong Kong, which is an interesting example of misappropriation of generic resources.

4.3 Public discourse: Memorandum of understanding

Public legal discourse in Hong Kong, especially close to the period of handover of sovereignty from Britain to the People's Republic of China (PRC), provided an interesting opportunity to study how political decolonization gradually created conditions for an equally interesting colonization of some public discourse genres which have traditionally been regarded as conflicting, especially the promotional and legislative genres in the emerging political context. On the face of it, there seems to be hardly anything common between the two; legislation, which is meant to control public life, has primarily a regulative communicative purpose, whereas promotional discourse is essentially persuasive. Legislative writing is used to impose obligations and to confer rights. However, in order to control the capacity of humans to wriggle out of their obligations and to stretch their rights to unexpected limits, legislation is generally intended to be precise, clear, unambiguous, on the one hand, and all-inclusive, on the other, although the two sets of intentions may appear to be somewhat contradictory in certain ways.

Another aspect of public discourse which assumed increasing significance in the years leading to the handover of sovereignty was the concern on the part of both the British government and that of the PRC to assure the people of Hong Kong and also the rest of the world that transition of sovereignty was going to be smooth and free of any conflict. This was very important for both the governments in order to maintain confidence in the viability of Hong Kong as an important centre for international trade and finance. Although Hong Kong had been a British colony for almost 150 years, there was no doubt that Britain had made a very significant contribution to the making of what Hong Kong represents today, especially as a remarkable economic miracle in Asia. It was important for Britain to be seen as handing over Hong Kong gracefully and, at the same time, and perhaps more importantly, making sure that the confidence of the people of Hong Kong was in no way undermined. It could have become quite traumatic for many of the Hong Kong residents to adjust to communism after a consistent dosage of capitalism for such a long period of time. Besides, no government can afford to underestimate the diversificational interests of the financial industry in the age of rapidly expanding multinationalism.

The People's Republic of China, on the other hand, would not have liked to rock the boat at that critical juncture. It was certainly not in the interest of the PRC government to send wrong signals to the residents of Hong Kong, and, more importantly, to the people of Macau

105

and Taiwan as well. Macau was eventually handed over to the PRC in 1999, and the PRC government has always claimed Taiwan to be part of the People's Republic of China, and efforts for re-unification have always assumed the highest importance. The other factor that supports this hypothesis further is the economic freedom that the PRC has given to its southern regions, especially Shenzhen, Guandong and Shanghai. One country, two systems, which was the promise at the time, has become a reality now. Once again, it was not in the best interests of the PRC government to encourage conditions which were likely to be seen as detrimental to the survival of Hong Kong as an economic miracle, certainly not during and immediately after the handover of the territory.

In the circumstances it was absolutely crucial for both the parties to be seen to be working towards a smooth and conflict-free transfer of sovereignty. The most important indication of their good intention was in the public document that came to be known as the Sino-British Joint Declaration signed by the two governments in 1984. It is an interesting document which, on the one hand, was intended to signal to the people of Hong Kong and, of course, to the rest of the world, the importance the two countries attached to smoothness of transition of power, while on the other, it was also meant to be the basis in the light of which all future disputes were to be considered and perhaps settled. As one can see, the Joint Declaration was intended to have two somewhat conflicting intentions, one *legislative*, to provide solutions to all future disputes, and the other *diplomatic*, to promote and to give expression to mutual understanding, and perhaps to postpone, or even avoid, if necessary, painful and difficult decisions on contentious and unresolved issues of potential conflict so that they could be managed through further negotiations as and when necessary. The legislative function often requires clarity, precision, unambiguity and compre-hensiveness in the expression of such issues, whereas the most characteristic features of the diplomatic use of language are vagueness, indirectness, generality and flexibility of expression, which often help the user to avoid commitment to any specific interpretation. Con-sidered in this manner, the two communicative functions are conflicting and contradictory, to say the least. However, it is interesting to find both of them present in the same document.

Perhaps this duality of somewhat conflicting intentions is a typical feature of what in diplomatic contexts is also known as a *memorandum of understanding*. If one were to look at the diplomatic intentions in such documents, they are rightly called 'memorandum of understanding'. However, if one were to take seriously the other aspect of many of these documents, they can be just the opposite of what was intended in the first place and hence no better than *memorandum of (mis)understanding*. Let me give substance to this claim by looking at specific sections of the document in question.

The very first introductory section of the document sets the tone of the document when it expressly states:

> The Government of the United Kingdom of Great Britain and Northern Ireland and the Government of the People's Republic of China have ... agreed that a proper negotiated settlement of the question of Hong Kong ... is conducive to the maintenance of the prosperity and stability of Hong Kong and to the further strengthening and development of the relations between the two countries.
>
> (Joint Declaration 1984: 11)

In a nutshell, the Joint Declaration is a political or more appropriately a diplomatic statement with the effect of a legislative intention. It worked well as a political statement, but was pragmatically rather contentious as an instrument of legislative expression.

To illustrate the point, let me take up Section 3(3), which assigns all kinds of executive, legislative and judicial powers to the people of Hong Kong, with an assurance that the laws of Hong Kong will remain 'basically' unchanged for 50 years after the transfer of sovereignty. It is interesting to note the qualification 'basically' in an important statement that was to govern the life of six million people for the next 50 years. This deliberate vagueness was perhaps introduced in the statement to keep things flexible so far as the future legislative actions in and for Hong Kong were concerned.

> The Hong Kong Special Administrative Region will be vested with executive, legislative and independent judicial power, including that of final adjudication. The laws currently in force in Hong Kong will remain basically unchanged.
>
> (Section 3 (3) of the Joint Declaration 1984: 11)

To make things more complex, a subsection of section 3 (12) further provides that these basic policies will be stipulated in a Basic Law of the Hong Kong SAR, which will be drafted by the National People's Congress of the PRC:

> The above-stated basic policies of the People's Republic of China regarding Hong Kong and the elaboration of them in Annex I to this Joint Declaration will be stipulated, in a Basic Law of the Hong Kong Special Administrative Region of the People's Republic of China, by the National People's Congress of the People's Republic of China, and they will remain unchanged for 50 years.
>
> (Section 3(12) of the Joint Declaration 1984: 13)

These are very important overarching legislative provisions and were likely to play a crucial role in the governance of Hong Kong as part of 'one country, two systems', however they have been drafted in the form of simple and precise statements. More detailed information on some of these aspects is included in Annex I, which is a little more elaborate than the main document, but is still far from the traditional legislative rigour of British legislative writing.

> After the establishment of the Hong Kong Special Administrative Region, the laws previously in force in Hong Kong (i.e. the common law, rules of equity, ordinances, subordinate legislation and customary law) shall be maintained, save for any that contravene the Basic Law and subject to any amendment by the Hong Kong Special Administrative Region legislature.
>
> The legislative power of the Hong Kong Special Administrative Region shall be vested in the legislature of the Hong Kong Special Administrative Region. The legislature may on its own authority enact laws in accordance with the provisions of the Basic Law and legal procedures, and report them to the Standing Committee of the National People's Congress for the record. Laws enacted by the legislature, which are in accordance with the Basic Law and legal procedures, shall be regarded as valid.
>
> The laws of the Hong Kong Special Administrative region shall be the Basic Law, and the laws previously in force in Hong Kong and laws enacted by the Hong Kong Special Administrative Region legislature as above.
>
> (Annex I, Section II of the Joint Declaration 1984: 15)

From these sections, it is clear that the maintenance of the so-called status quo in Hong Kong for the next 50 years after the transfer of sovereignty crucially depends on the contents of the Basic Law, which was not written at the time of the Joint Declaration in 1984. Obviously, at the time when the Joint Declaration was signed, there was some understanding in terms of broad principles rather than on matters of detail. To illustrate the point, let us take up Article 12, which legislates on the relationship between the HKSAR and the Central Authorities of the PRC.

> Article 12
> The Hong Kong Special Administrative Region shall be a local administrative region of the People's Republic of China, which shall enjoy a high degree of autonomy and come directly under the Central People's Government.

As one can see, Article 12 on the one hand gives 'a high degree of autonomy' to the HKSAR region, while at the same time it categorically puts it directly under the Central People's Government, without any further specification of any kind. In the absence of any further specification, the expression 'a high degree of autonomy' can only be interpreted on a case-by-case basis and hence becomes a matter of fresh negotiation every time it is invoked in a particular context. In the first five years after establishment of the HKSAR, the number of contentious issues arising from this lack of adequate specification either in the Joint Declaration or the Basic Law bears testimony to the claim made above. Without going into such issues, some of which we shall take up in the next chapter, I would like to look at the provision for the amendment of the Basic Law under the Joint Declaration in order to substantiate the possibility of multiple interpretations of this section.

> **Provision under the Joint Declaration:**
> The National People's Congress of the People's Republic of China shall enact and promulgate a Basic Law of the Hong Kong Special Administrative Region of the People's Republic of China (hereinafter referred to as the Basic Law) in accordance with the Constitution of the People's Republic of China.
>
> (Para 1, Section 1, Annex 1)

Although the Joint Declaration clearly indicates that the National People's Congress will enact the Basic Law, it does not provide any indication for its amendment or interpretation, which, like many other contentious issues, was left open to be resolved by future negotiations. This lack of specification led to the setting up of a special group on the Basic Law in Hong Kong, which considered the issue of the amendment of the Basic Law in the context of the Joint Declaration and the Chinese Constitution, under which the Basic Law was to be enacted and promulgated, and suggested that there were several possible interpretations, most of them arising from the fact that this issue had failed to find adequate specification in any of the existing provisions, either in the Joint Declaration or anywhere else.

The Special Group thus raised the following pertinent points on the Relationship between the Central Government and the HKSAR.

It is generally held that since the Basic Law shall be enacted by the NPC, it and only it shall have the power to amend the Basic Law.

Who can propose amendments to the Basic Law?

Opinion A
Members note that under the Chinese Constitution, the NPC and the State Council have the right to propose amendments to basic statutes. The by-law of

the NPC provides that 30 members of the NPC together can initiate the proposal to amend the basic statutes. Therefore the NPC should have the power to initiate amendments to the Basic Law.

Opinion B
Nevertheless, it was proposed that the SAR Government or the SAR legislature should have the right to initiate proposals for amendments to the Basic Law.

Opinion C
An opposing view to this proposal is that if people of foreign nationality are permitted to sit on the SAR legislature, then they may change a very important law of China.

Opinion D
The Hong Kong delegates to the NPC shall have the sole right to propose amendments to the Basic Law.

Opinion E
Directly elected representatives from Hong Kong shall have the sole right to propose amendments to the Basic Law.

Opinion F
The Hong Kong Legislature shall have the sole right to propose amendments to the Basic Law with no restriction on the composition of the Legislature provided they are all local inhabitants as stated under the Joint Declaration.

It is interesting to note that such a multiplicity of interpretations arises from a general feeling that 'since the Basic Law shall be enacted by the NPC, it and only it shall have the power to amend the Basic Law'. Misconceptions such as these can be attributed to two factors: firstly, the conflicts inherent in the drafting of the Joint Declaration, some of which we have already discussed, and secondly, the conflicting legal systems in use in Hong Kong (HKSAR) and the PRC. Legislative style often associated with the mainland legal system is considered less detailed, and therefore less transparent, thus giving extensive interpretive power to the judiciary. In Hong Kong, on the other hand, legislative style is detailed and all-inclusive in the true Commonwealth tradition, giving supreme authority to the legislative body elected by the people rather than the government-appointed judiciary, which is consistent with the expectations in a typical democratic form of government. Much of the variation and potential conflict in the interpretation of the same constitutional document, therefore, is the result of a possible interaction of the two conflicting rhetorical contexts in which the documents are being construed, interpreted and eventually used, and the events of the past five years confirm this point of view.

110

In this chapter we have looked at the notion of appropriation of generic resources leading to the colonization and bending of genres, sometimes creating potential conflicts in specific areas of public discourse. Although mixing is common in genres that display a natural compatibility in their communicative intentions, and there are numerous instances of mixed genres that typically combine promotional concerns with some of those that are typically informative, mixing two very different communicative purposes within a single genre is somewhat less common. The phenomenon of genre mixing demonstrates the versatility of the generic framework, on the one hand, and the human capacity to exploit generic conventions to bend genres to create new forms of discourse to meet the challenges of novel and rapidly changing rhetorical situations, on the other. The universe of real life communicative behaviour is complex, dynamic and unpredictable, and the field of discourse and genre analysis, on the contrary, is relatively constrained, which always brings into focus the tension between integrity of genre, on the one hand, and its innovative exploitations, on the other. This is one of the most important issues in genre theory today, and will be the focus of the next chapter.

5 Generic integrity

The main focus in the last chapter was on the notion of appropriation of generic resources to manipulate and exploit genre conventions and lexico-grammatical and rhetorical resources to create new and hybrid forms. The assumption was that although every genre has its own individual integrity, which is often maintained in professional practice, it is still possible for experienced genre writers to take liberties with genre conventions, which gives the impression that generic integrity after all is not fixed or prescribed. This view seems to create a tension between generic integrity, on the one hand, and the possibility of appropriation of generic resources to create new forms, on the other, which warrants a more detailed discussion of the nature, function and importance of generic integrity in genre theory. This tension has become more problematic in applied linguistics because generic integrity is often viewed in terms of textual analysis and very rarely, if ever, from the point of view of other socio-cognitive and cultural factors that have a significant bearing on the way genres are constructed and interpreted in professional contexts. Let us look at this more closely.

In genre theory, there has often been an overwhelming emphasis on the analysis of linguistic resources, with very little attempt to integrate the socio-cognitive factors that so often contribute to the act of genre construction, interpretation, use and exploitation to achieve non-linguistic ends in real life professional contexts. One of the consequences of this lack of attention to the social and the cognitive aspects of genre has been that genre theory continues to be weak on the processes and procedures of genre participation, the receptivity of genres, and also the factors that make a particular instance of genre successful. For a comprehensible understanding of genres in action one is essentially required to integrate many of these perceptions into a comprehensive understanding of generic integrity and also of how this is related to professional competence or expertise in a particular profession. In order to achieve this, I will focus on three important aspects of generic integrity: firstly, to suggest a multi-perspective and multidimensional view of generic integrity in professional discourse; secondly, to illustrate the dynamic view of generic integrity by looking closely at some of the relevant examples of professional genres; and finally to establish a relationship between generic integrity, discursive competence, and the notion of expertise in a specific professional context. However, before going to the framework for identifying generic integrity, it is necessary to highlight a few important aspects of genre theory.

Although genres are highly conventionalized and standardized linguistic forms (Swales 1990), they often appear to be fuzzy. Investigating language use involves analysing human behaviour, which is not entirely predictable. Analysing genre, therefore, with any expectation of a high degree of predictability or certainty is like analysing the stock market in a highly complex and volatile economic environment, where it is almost impossible to take into account all the variables contributing to the movements of the stock market. Analysing genre within any framework is essentially an attempt to explain and account for most of the realities of the world, which are often complex, dynamic and unpredictable. There are, and will always be, a number of contributors to the construction, interpretation, exploitation and use of professional genres which it will not always be possible to take into account even in the most rigorous form of analysis. Even the status of communicative purpose, which is often used as a 'privileged criterion' (Swales 1990: 46), appears to be fuzzy and sometimes subjective. Swales (1990) finds considerable heuristic value in this difficulty because it 'may require the analyst to undertake a fair amount of independent and open-minded investigation'. Therefore, the difficulties in establishing a communicative purpose for a specific genre or a 'set of communicative purposes', as Swales (1990: 46) rightly points out, is very much part of the design, rather than a handicap, as some might see it. If one were looking for clear-cut, definite and objective criteria to define and identify communicative purposes for each genre, one would necessarily be frustrated by the complex realities of the world of discourse. But on the other hand this very unpredictability of the discursive realities of the world makes the analytical process challenging. It is precisely for this reason that the integrity of any generic form is also viewed as dynamic, flexible and sometimes 'contested' (Candlin and Plum 1999).

Another factor that makes the task of analysing genre rather difficult is that genre analysts are not practising members of the relevant disciplinary or professional cultures, and hence do not claim deep understanding of the discursive practices characteristic of these professional cultures. They often have expertise in text-internal aspects of language use, including an extensive understanding of the lexico-grammatical, rhetorical and discourse organizational features, all of which in various ways reflect the communicative purpose of the genre, and help them identify the nature of the genre in question;

113

however, these insights often need to be interpreted in the context of text-external aspects of the genre, i.e. the goals of the specialist community and the broader institutional and disciplinary contexts in which the genre is likely to be constructed, interpreted and used in real-life situations, to name only a few. In order for anyone to claim sufficient expertise in genre identification and analysis, one needs to have some understanding of both these aspects, text-internal as well as text-external, including socio-cognitive.

The most important issue emerging from this point of view is that in spite of such complex variations, expert genre writers do manage to identify, construct, interpret, use and exploit generic constructs in a socially acceptable manner to respond to a variety of familiar, and often not so familiar, rhetorical contexts. How do we explain this? How do we explain that a vast majority of good professionals from a specific disciplinary culture communicate through a set of genres which display a remarkable degree of overlap, not only in terms of their use of lexico-grammatical and discoursal resources, but also in terms of interpretive strategies and expectations? They do not always communicate within stringent or narrowly configured rhetorical circumstances. Often they exploit lexico-grammatical, discoursal and other generic resources to go beyond the narrowly configured generic objectives; however, all these variations are no more than subtle exploitations of social conventions within a narrow range of innovations. Expert members of professional or disciplinary communities rarely opt out of the professional, institutional or corporate games. They all tend to respect and maintain what I have been suggesting as 'generic integrity' of specific professional genres. How do we characterize generic integrity and what factors contribute to its understanding and use? In what way is it related to generic competence or professional expertise and how do expert professionals acquire such expertise? I will make an attempt to discuss some of these important issues in what follows.

5.1 Identifying generic integrity

The notion of *generic integrity* is important for most perspectives on genre, however diverse they may appear to be. It is important because it has the potential to enhance our understanding of the role and function of genres in everyday activities that we are all engaged in not only through language, but also through other semiotic means. Although I have discussed this notion in general terms elsewhere (see Bhatia 1993, 1994, 1997a, 1998b and 1999a), its detailed discussion and elaboration is necessary, especially in the light of our discussions in the preceding chapters. The explication of this notion will also, I hope, offer a much broader understanding of genre as a complex and increasingly dynamic, and at the same time, multifaceted construct, which in turn will need a much more multidimensional approach to its analysis than hitherto available.

The most important aspect of genre is that it is recognizable and is sufficiently standardized; it is based on a set of mutually accessible conventions which most members of a professional, academic or institutional organization share. In general terms, a typical instance of a specific genre looks like the one intended, in the sense that the members of the discourse or professional community with which it is often associated tend to recognize it as a typical or valid instance of the genre in question. Most successful constructions of professional genres have recognizable generic integrity (Bhatia 1993). It may be complex, in that it may reflect a specific form of mixing and/or embedding of two or more generic forms, or even dynamic, in the sense that it may reflect a gradual development over a period of time in response to subtle changes in the rhetorical contexts that it responds to; but it will certainly continue to have a recognizable generic character, which might undergo slow and subtle changes over a long period of time. This generic character is more easily accessible to the established members of the professional community than to those who have a peripheral involvement in the affairs of the professional community in question (Swales 1990). Let me take a few examples to illustrate this point. Consider the following text from which I have taken away all the obvious and surface indicators of its generic identity.

(1)

> When considering the establishment of a retirement scheme for your company one factor immediately springs to mind – security. Your staff are your company's future and they deserve the highest quality retirement package.
>
> That's where The Bank of Bermuda comes in. As an independent trustee and custodian we make it our responsibility to safekeep and protect the scheme assets on behalf of your employees. We provide full retirement scheme administration and reporting to substantially reduce your administrative workload. Our worldwide network of offices can provide you with the security of an offshore trust and the convenience of on-line access to employee information.
>
> For over 20 years we have been serving retirement schemes, mutual funds and unit trusts in Asia. Our quality approach to service and client

> satisfaction has earned us the respect and trust of the region's leading fund managers and corporations.
>
> For more information on our retirement scheme services in Hong Kong please call ... on ... or fax .... The Bank of Bermuda Limited, Hong Kong Branch, A Restricted Licence Bank, 39th Floor, Edinburgh Tower, The Landmark, 15 Queen's Road Central, Hong Kong.

The first thing about this text that strikes us is its use of the interpersonal 'I' and 'you' orientation, in which the party addressed as 'you' representing a company has been put in a position of well-identified need in respect of its employees, and the party 'I' is represented as the one in a position to fulfil that need. The expressions such as 'security' in the context of 'Your staff are your company's future and they deserve the highest quality retirement package' suggest a typical promotional situation, where the writer makes an attempt to establish customer needs, and then in the paragraph that follows makes an offer of a product in the form of a service, which is seen as beneficial to the other party. The 'I' and 'you' orientation continues, typically with the 'I' party as the provider, and the 'you' party as the beneficiary. In the next paragraph, we see a typical attempt on the part of the writer to establish his own credentials by referring to the long experience in providing the service of that kind. Expressions such as 'Our quality approach', 'client satisfaction' and 'the trust of the region's leading fund managers and corporations' are typical of advertising register. Even the four-part rhetorical move structure is also very typical of the advertising genre. See the following version of the same text.

(1A)

When considering the establishment of a retirement scheme for your company one factor immediately springs to mind – <u>security</u>. Your staff are your company's future and they <u>deserve the highest quality retirement package</u>.	Establishing Customer Needs
That's where The Bank of Bermuda comes in. As an independent trustee and custodian we make it <u>our responsibility</u> to safekeep and protect the scheme assets on behalf of your employees. We provide full retirement scheme administration and reporting to	Product Offering Product Description

substantially <u>reduce your administrative workload.</u> <u>Our worldwide network of offices can provide you</u> <u>with the security of an offshore trust and the</u> <u>convenience of on-line access</u> to employee information.	Product Evaluation
<u>For over 20 years we have been serving retirement</u> <u>schemes</u>, mutual funds and unit trusts in Asia. <u>Our</u> <u>quality approach to service and client satisfaction</u> has earned us the respect and trust of <u>the region's leading</u> <u>fund managers and corporations</u>.	Establishing Credentials
<u>For more information on our retirement scheme</u> <u>services in Hong Kong please call ... on ... or fax ...</u> . The Bank of Bermuda Limited, Hong Kong Branch, A Restricted Licence Bank, 39th Floor, Edinburgh Tower, The Landmark, 15 Queen's Road Central, Hong Kong.	Soliciting Response

Thus there seem to be a number of text-internal factors that identify the text as a promotional one. It is still not certain whether it is an advertisement or any other form of promotional genre.

In addition to lexico-grammatical, rhetorical and discoursal features, we also find a number of other factors which indicate that the text is more likely to be an advertisement rather than any other form of promotional genre. The picture at the top is more common in print advertisements than in any other form of promotional genre. The heading 'When the futures of others are balancing on your decisions, you owe them the best retirement scheme protection possible' also supports a similar conclusion. However, the listing of company sites at various international centres is rather problematic, as it can be part of a letterhead. Similarly, THE BANK OF BERMUDA at the bottom of the page can be equally ambiguous. In addition, we know from our understanding and prior knowledge of the world of work that business organizations are under pressure to provide attractive job security and retirement options in order to retain good employees, and that there are a number of competitors in the market offering a range of products and services to meet such requirements. Thus in order to make sense of a text such as this, we need to go beyond the text to factors very much external to the language of the text. Let me give you the original version of the text, which will add a number of other features to the generic artefact, and thus help one to identify its true generic character. Bhatia

When the futures of others are balancing on your decisions, you owe them the best retirement scheme protection possible.

Bermuda. British Virgin Islands. Cayman. Cook Islands. Dublin. Guernsey. Hong Kong. Isle of Man. Jersey. London. Luxembourg. Mauritius. New Zealand. Singapore. Western Samoa.

When considering the establishment of a retirement scheme for your company one factor immediately springs to mind – security. Your staff are your company's future and they deserve the highest quality retirement package.

That's where the Bank of Bermuda comes in. As an independent trustee and custodian we make it our responsibility to safekeep and protect the scheme assets on behalf of your employees. We provide full retirement scheme administration and reporting to substantially reduce your administrative workload. Our worldwide network of offices can provide you with the security of an offshore trust and the convenience of on-line access to employee information.

For over 20 years we have been servicing retirement schemes, mutual funds and unit trusts in Asia. Our quality approach to service and client satisfaction has earned us the respect and trust of the region's leading fund managers and corporations.

For more information on our retirement scheme services in Hong Kong please call ... on ... or fax ... The Bank of Bermuda Limited, Hong Kong Branch, A Restricted Licence Bank, 39th Floor, Edinburgh Tower, The Landmark, 15 Queen's Road Central, Hong Kong.

THE BANK OF BERMUDA

(1993: 22–3) points out some of the factors that are helpful in identifying genres, some of which include the following:

- placement of the text in a situational context by looking at prior experience and encyclopaedic knowledge of the conventions associated with the professional culture the text might be seen to belong to
- background knowledge of the disciplinary discourse community, which may include their shared objectives, ways of doing

business, concerns and constraints, and a number of other factors
- typical participants, their relationship and their goals
- knowledge of the historical, socio-cultural, philosophic and occupational background of the profession which typically uses the genre in question
- awareness of the network of surrounding texts and genres from the same domain and systems of genres that may have some impact on the construction and interpretation of the genre in question
- awareness of the topic, subject and extra-textual reality that the genre is representing, or changing, in particular the relationship between the genre and that reality
- the communicative purpose of the genre, and often some understanding of the 'private intentions' that are likely to be signalled, conveyed or communicated within such a genre
- the most likely recipients of the genre in question, whether individuals, groups, organizations or institutions.

All these factors are crucial to our understanding of the genre, and contribute significantly to the notion of generic integrity of the text in question. Although text-internal factors are important for the identification of communicative purposes, they can give misleading insights when used on their own. Textual factors typically depend on their form–function correlation and it is not always possible to have one-to-one correlation in this area. There are linguistic forms that can attract several discoursal values; on the other hand, a particular discourse value can be realized through several syntactic forms. However, it is not as chaotic a situation as it may seem. Linguistic forms do carry specific generic values, but the only way one can assign the right generic value to any linguistic feature of the genre is by reference to text-external factors. Similarly, any conclusion arrived at purely on the basis of text-external factors needs to be confirmed by reference to text-internal factors. In Chapter 1, I discussed the case of complex nominals in three different genres: advertising, academic scientific genres and legislation, on the basis of which we concluded that although one may find an above-average use of complex nominals in the three genres, their form, distribution and generic values are very different in the three cases (see also Bhatia 1992 and 1993).

Let me take up another example, this time from an academic context.

(2)

> Over the years, the concept of genre has changed from being a static and classificatory type to a more fluid and dynamic one where genres may be "manipulated according to the conditions of use" (Berkenkotter and Huckin, 1995). Using a case study approach, articles on the same topic of research that have been published in the local newspaper and several newsletters will be examined and compared with the original version of the article. The rhetorical shifts of these articles will be analysed in order to determine how the situational constraints of a discourse can shape the overall structure of the genre as well as its realization at different linguistic levels. It is hoped that this paper will illustrate how the same information is expressed in different genres depending upon factors such as purpose, audience and medium that govern the conventions of these genres.

I shall begin with some very general observations first. It is a brief, coherent and tightly textured complete text. One notices a number of lexico-grammatical expressions, such as *the concept of genre, static and classificatory, fluid and dynamic, case study approach, topic of research, examined and compared, original version, rhetorical shifts, articles, analysed, situational constraints, discourse, overall structure, realization, linguistic levels, information is expressed, purpose, audience and medium, conventions of genres,* which overwhelmingly indicate the formal academic nature of the text. The use of academic lexis without any explanation or glossing also indicates the background and academic expertise of the audience, and to some extent the nature of participant relationships. Then there is the quote from an academic book, with a conventional referencing device, once again confirming the academic and research nature of the text. Furthermore, the text has an average sentence length of 35 words, with a reasonably high incidence of what Halliday (1994) called 'grammatical metaphor', suggesting the text as an instance of 'language of thinking', which is rather typical of academic research genres, as against the 'language of doing' which is typical of news reports. Let us look at the following version of the same text.

(2A)

<u>Over the years</u>, the <u>concept of genre has changed</u> from being a static and classificatory type to a more fluid and dynamic one where genres may be "manipulated according to the conditions of use" (<u>Berkenkotter and Huckin 1995</u>).	Establishing the field, and identifying the topic
<u>Using a case study approach</u>, articles on the same topic of research that have been published in the local newspaper and several newsletters <u>will be examined and compared</u> with the original version of the article.	Research methods used
The rhetorical shifts of these articles will be analysed <u>in order to determine</u> how the situational constraints of a discourse can shape the overall structure of the genre as well as its realization at different linguistic levels.	Focus of investigation
<u>It is hoped that this paper will illustrate</u> how the same information is expressed in different genres depending upon factors such as purpose, audience and medium that govern the conventions of these genres.	Results and conclusions expected

Let me now highlight the cognitive structuring in the text. It begins by establishing the field and identifying the topic of discourse, followed by the research methodology used to investigate the topic, followed by the main purpose of research investigation, and ends with the kind of results and conclusion expected from such an investigation. These and several other features of the text make it possible for a genre analyst to identify the broad nature and function of the text as one commonly found in a research article abstract.

Beyond these text-internal features, one may need to go to a number of other text-external features to identify and establish this text as representing an academic abstract of a research article, or conference paper. Much of the evidence to confirm such identification will come from the understanding, awareness and background knowledge of the established conventions of the disciplinary and professional community, in this case the academic research community, most of which will be essentially external to the text being analysed. One may also need to consider intertextuality and interdiscursivity with respect to other surrounding texts in order to establish what I have called the generic integrity of the text. We get a much better and fuller account of the grounding and integrity of the text as a genre by looking at the original version, which I am reproducing here.

(2B)

International Conference on
"Research & Practice in Professional Discourse"
15–17 Nov 2000

City University of Hong Kong
Centre for English Language and Communication Research
Department of English
Faculty of Humanities & Social Sciences

Programme
KATHPALIA, Sujata S.
KRISHNAN Lakshmy A.
Nanyang Technological University, Singapore

Spreading the news: texts and contexts

Over the years, the concept of genre has changed from being a static and classificatory type to a more fluid and dynamic one where genres may be "manipulated according to the conditions of use" (Berkenkotter and Huckin, 1995). Using a case study approach, articles on the same topic of research that have been published in the local newspaper and several newsletters will be examined and compared with the original version of the article. The rhetorical shifts of these articles will be analysed in order to determine how the situational constraints of a discourse can shape the overall structure of the genre as well as its realisation at different linguistic levels. It is hoped that this paper will illustrate how the same information is expressed in different genres depending upon factors such as purpose, audience and medium that govern the conventions of these genres.

This original version positions the text in the context of a section of a conference brochure, setting off a number of institutional and disciplinary expectations, including those on the nature and function of these conference presentations, on participants and their relationships, and on shared expertise in areas of academic interest, as well as on more narrowly defined situational contexts in which the conference may be taking place. One can even go further and consider the status and background of expected participation, including the audience, and a number of other factors. A thoroughly grounded analysis of discourse genres thus requires analysis not only of text-internal lexico-grammatical, rhetorical and cognitive features of the genre in question, and a complete analysis of intertextual as well as interdiscursive aspects of the text, but also a thick analysis of the text-external, which includes situational as well as a number of socio-cognitive factors related to text construction, interpretation, use and exploitation by expert members of the disciplinary cultures in question. For instance, the text above will make a limited sense on its own, unless it is analysed in the context of other surrounding texts such as the information that points out that it was an abstract submitted for a conference on a particular topic. One may even need to go beyond the text-internal factors to consider the theme of the conference and also the other relevant materials, including instructions available to the authors imposing constraints on their construction of the abstract as well as the interpretations of the theme of the conference. Based on the discussion so far, let me summarize the notion of generic integrity in professional and institutional written discourse.

Generic integrity may be understood in terms of a socially constructed typical constellation of form–function correlations representing a specific professional, academic or institutional communicative construct realizing a specific communicative purpose of the genre in question. It is essentially constructed in the context of the goals of the professional or disciplinary culture that it is often associated with. It is possible to characterize it in terms of text-internal and/or text-external or a combination of such features. It is not static, fixed or prescribed, but is often flexible, negotiable or sometimes contested. There are a number of diverse indications of generic integrity, some of which I have already alluded to in the analyses of the two examples discussed above. Let me give here a much broader and more comprehensive picture of some of the important indicators of generic integrity.

Indicators of generic integrity can be viewed in terms of two broad categories, those that are text-internal and others that are text-external. I am using these terms to conveniently reflect analytical practices in the last few years, rather than to clearly identify and comprehensively distinguish all the factors that may have implications for genre construction. In this sense, the term text-internal refers to factors generally related to the construction and interpretation of the text in question, whereas text-external factors are those that are more appropriately related to the wider context of the disciplinary community and culture in which the text is used and interpreted. I realize that these distinctions may seem somewhat artificial and occasionally blurred, but they are useful in the discussion of generic integrity. Let me identify and explain some of the factors I find particularly helpful in the discussion of generic integrity.

Discourse and genre analysts have long been focusing predominantly on text-internal factors, which may incorporate some aspects of immediate context, and most of the textual and intertextual information. Textual indicators include not only lexico-grammatical but also rhetorical as well as discoursal features. It is necessary to point out that these text-internal indicators of generic integrity are relatively easily accessible to discourse and genre analysts rather than to the members of professional cultures, who often use these genres but pay little attention to a conscious understanding of the linguistic resources that realize these genres. However, in addition to the text-internal indicators of generic integrity, there are a number of text-external indicators of generic integrity, which are more easily accessible to experienced professionals and expert practitioners of specific genres. They often use these text-external features to identify, construct, interpret, use and exploit these genres to achieve their professional objectives. Some of these include the professional or institutional context in which the genre is used, typical 'sites of engagement' (Scollon 1998) that invoke the use of the genre in question, the disciplinary practices to achieve disciplinary or institutional goals, and typical processes and procedures employed to represent institutional, organizational or professional identities.

To account for such text-external perspectives of genre I would like to propose at least three categories of indicators of generic integrity, 'discursive practices', 'discursive procedures' and 'disciplinary culture'. Discursive practices, in turn, include factors such as the choice of genre and mode of communication to suit a particular professional action; discursive procedures are essentially processes of genre construction, and include factors such as 'who contributes what', 'at what stage and by what mechanisms' one can contribute to the construction of a genre, and the role of other contributing genres; and disciplinary culture provides information about goals and objectives of the professional community, about norms and conventions of the genres in use, and also about the nature of professional and organizational identity one is allowed to construct as part of a particular professional activity. These two major types of indicators of generic integrity therefore are text-internal and text-external.

Text-internal indicators are primarily of three major kinds. These can be represented as in Diagram 5.1.

Since discourse and genre analysts are familiar with most of these indicators and have been using them for a long time to analyse genres

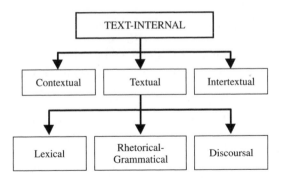

Diagram 5.1 *Text-internal indicators of generic integrity*

of various kinds, I would not like to dwell too much on these. They can be interpreted to represent the following.

Text-internal aspects of generic integrity

CONTEXTUAL

Context includes both the most immediate context and the more general context in which the text is placed. In a more general sense, contextual indicators incorporate the communicative purpose and the communicative context. In the narrow sense, context provides information on those aspects of the text that are part of the immediate surroundings of the text. Both are crucial to its placement in a particular communicative environment, and include some of the following:

- the speaker/writer of the text and the audience, their relationship, attitude, social distance or proximity and their goals;
- the network of surrounding texts and linguistic traditions that form the background to this particular genre-text;
- the complexities of the medium in use.

In the broader sense, context provides information on:

- the historical, socio-cultural, philosophic and/or occupational nature of the discipline the genre is embedded in;
- the social structure, interactions, history, beliefs, goals etc. of the relevant professional, academic or workplace discourse community;
- the extra-textual reality which the text is trying to represent, change or use and its relationship with the text.

One may notice that context in a broader sense may seem to be problematic, as it can be seen in different ways. In one sense, it may have direct implications for the construction of a particular genre, in which sense it will be considered text-internal. However, interpretation of broader context may also validly contribute to the nature and function of the disciplinary community or culture in question and hence only indirectly to the construction or interpretation of a particular text, in which case it can be considered text-external. In text example (2) above, for instance, the general context of 'abstract for a conference' will be considered a text-external factor, whereas the interpretation of a specific conference on the theme, 'Research and Practice in Professional Discourse', though an aspect of broader context, will be seen as text-internal helping the authors more directly to position their abstract more appropriately in the desired context.

TEXTUAL

Textual features include primarily three kinds of linguistic resources, *lexical, rhetorical-grammatical* and *discoursal*. The kinds of information that are often found useful in determining the generic integrity of a specific genre include:

- statistically significant aspects of lexico-grammar
- text patterning or textualizations of generic purposes and concerns
- cognitive patterning or discourse structuring of the genre.

Analyses of genres in terms of these textual features have dominated much of text, discourse and genre studies in the past literature (Bhatia 1993). We have discussed some of these textual features extensively in Chapter 1 also. Discoursal indicators have been variedly considered as organizational elements, often in terms of information structures, rhetorical structures, schematic structures, discourse structures, move structures or cognitive structures, to name just a few.

INTERTEXTUAL

Intertextuality refers to a number of relationships that the text in question may have with those which in some way have been used, referred to or exploited either directly or indirectly in the construction of the text in question, and may include some of the following:

- texts providing a context (a letter to which the one in question is a reply)

- texts within and around the text (a chapter in the context of a book)
- texts explicitly referred to in the text (references in academic journals)
- texts referred to implicitly in the text (*The Sun never sets over Lufthansa territory* used in an advertisement, with an implicit reference to *The sun never sets over the British Empire*)
- texts embedded within the text (conversation within a story)
- texts mixed with the text (quotations etc.).

All these text-internal indicators of generic integrity are powerful instruments for discourse and genre analysts to account for the way texts and genres are constructed and interpreted.

The other major category of indicators of generic integrity is what I referred to earlier as text-external, which incorporates the subcategories shown in Diagram 5.2.

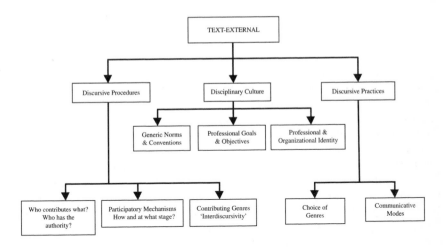

Diagram 5.2 *Text-external indicators of generic integrity*

Let me take up these text-external indicators of generic integrity one at a time.

Text-external aspects of generic integrity

The three main types of text-external factors indicating generic integrity are *discursive practices, discursive procedures* and *disciplinary or professional culture.*

DISCURSIVE PRACTICES

Discursive practices include information about the choice of appropriate genres to achieve professional objectives in specific professional contexts; in other words, the knowledge of genre appropriacy allows one to choose relevant genres to suit specific professional activities. Discursive practices also include knowledge about what modes of communication are appropriate to what kind of professional action. At which stage of a professional activity one may use telephone, fax or e-mail mode, and where one may like to use a formal written communication, are all part of established discursive practices of individual professions. Some of the typical questions that can be raised in the context of discursive practices are:

- What kinds of genres are typically used for what kind of disciplinary goals?
- What modes of communications are conventionally employed to achieve these goals?
- What organizational constraints operate on these practices?

DISCURSIVE PROCEDURES

Discursive procedures, the second set of text-external indicators of generic integrity, include three types of factors, which essentially constrain the procedural aspects of genre construction, such as *'who'* contributes *'what'* to the construction and interpretation of specific generic actions; 'participatory mechanisms' which indicate *'at what stage'* and *'by which means'* does one participate in the genre construction and interpretation activities; and 'contributing genres' which allow one to choose the appropriate and relevant generic knowledge and information to make the genre in question possible. Some of these contributing genres are also responsible for the introduction of 'interdiscursivity' in genre construction, which may include some or all of the following:

- genre mixing (promotion in academic introductions)
- genre embedding (letter format in job advertisements)
- one set of generic conventions used to exploit another (parodies)
- system of genres (legislation, cases, textbook and legal problem)
- change and development in genres (academic introduction → book blurbs)

- appropriation of genres (fundraising letters → sales promotional letters).

Genres in most of the professional contexts are often the result of collaborative activities on the part of a number of professionals, who have specific roles to play in the genre construction activities. Discursive processes provide relevant and necessary answers to the following kinds of questions:

- How do professionals construct, interpret, use and exploit professional genres?
- Who are the participants in the genre construction activity?
- Who have the authority to contribute what to the construction of specific genres?
- How does the participatory mechanism work in specific contexts?
- Who takes control at which stage of the process?

The next most typical characteristic of professional genres is that they are often products of a set of established procedures that form an important part of the disciplinary culture within a profession. A generic artefact often acquires its typical identity as a result of a set of conventionalized discursive practices, both written and spoken, that professionals routinely engage in as part of their daily work. Many of these discursive practices have distinct stages, with identifiable inputs and outputs. These discursive practices are often characterized by the involvement of more than one participant, which, to a large extent, assigns multiple authorship to the resulting artefact. This also gives the resultant document a distinctly rich intertextual and interdiscursive patterning.

A business client's request for a loan to fund a specific business proposition, for example, is part of a larger business activity, which can be characterized by several discursive processes and stages. A typical request for a business loan made at the front-desk banking counter initiates a series of discursive activities, some of which may include detailed client consultation with a banking official, either in person or in writing, followed by a report by the banking official to the appropriate department for further consideration. The department may, if it decides to take the request further, involve the risk evaluation department in the further evaluation of the request. On the basis of the report from the risk evaluation team, the loan department may decide to proceed further, which might involve further consultation within the bank or negotiation with the client, before any final decision is taken either to accept or reject the loan request. Whichever way it may finally go, it is the result of a series of discursive procedures which are routinely undertaken by the professionals in the conduct of their business. Although neither the final textual artefact(s), nor the intervening textual outputs (e.g. reports by the front-desk banking official to his superior, or those by the risk management department, etc.), may directly reflect the involvement or contribution made by these discursive processes and procedures, these are very much part of the whole business activity. The emerging textual products, whichever generic form(s) they may finally take, are the outcomes of a range of diverse discursive processes and consultations engaged in by several professionals, rather than just the person who ultimately has the privilege or authority to claim the sole authorship. That may be one of the reasons why so many of these professional genres have a somewhat predominant impersonal quality. Two important points emerge from this; firstly, most of these genres, through which various professionals or departments participate in this banking activity, are mutually shared by the professional community, and secondly, these genres make more sense as part of the business activity rather than on their own.

DISCIPLINARY CULTURE

Disciplinary culture, the third subset of text-external indicators, specifically includes 'professional goals and objectives', 'generic norms and conventions', and 'professional and organizational identity'.

'Professional goals and objectives' provide relevant information on what objectives and goals are considered valid and desirable for the members of a particular professional group. They may be identified at the level of a specific profession, or at the level of a specific organization or corporation within a profession. Both can be useful in the analysis of professional genres. Generic intentions and norms and conventions are unstated behavioural principles that most professionals observe when they participate in their everyday activities related to their professional lives. These norms and conventions also constrain the discursive practices of members of professional communities when they exploit these professional genres to express additional private intentions within the socially accepted and shared communicative purposes. These norms and conventions also indicate the ways in which they often preserve and express their professional and/or corporate identity when they respond to recurring and novel rhetorical contexts as part of their professional activities.

Such information about the use of specific genres is invariably provided in the context of the historical, socio-cultural, philosophic and/or occupational nature of the discipline the genre is embedded in, and the social structure, interactions, history, beliefs, goals etc. of the relevant professional, academic or workplace discourse community. One may notice some overlap here with the discussion of context earlier in this chapter; however, discussion here is much more specifically focused on institutional concerns, rather than on the texts as was the case in the earlier discussion. Some of the typical questions that may require information based on the background knowledge about the disciplinary or professional culture are:

- How do they exploit generic conventions to respond to recurring and novel rhetorical contexts as part of their professional activities?
- How do members of a disciplinary culture express private intentions within the context of disciplinary practices?
- What are the critical sites of engagement in which specific genres are used to achieve specific disciplinary goals and objectives?
- What physical circumstances influence the nature and construction of such professional activities?
- What are the critical moments of engagement or interaction?
- What modes of genre construction or communication are available at the critical moments or sites?

Although communicative purpose has been assigned a privileged status in the identification of genre (Swales 1990), its detailed specification also includes the 'private intentions' that the genre writer can validly communicate, on the one hand, and much broader disciplinary or professional goals of the specialist community, on the other. These goals are more widely recognized than those of the genres in question. Communicative purposes, though most often in harmony with professional goals, can sometimes be more easily exploited to achieve private intentions, so long as they do not conflict with disciplinary or professional objectives. And finally, most genres reflect a kind of 'professional identity' that makes outsiders wonder why most professionals write specific genres more or less the same way, though with subtle variations within a small range!

To sum up, I have presented the concept of generic integrity as a key element in our understanding of genre, which includes its construction, interpretation, use and exploitation to respond to familiar and not so familiar rhetorical contexts. I have also pointed out some of the important indicators of generic integrity, without claiming to have given a comprehensive list; however these indicators offer a number of perspectives on generic integrity, which can be represented as in Diagram 5.3.

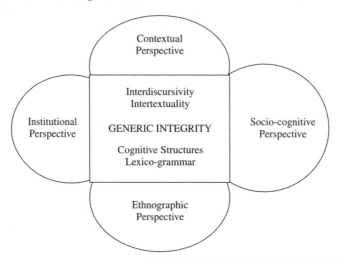

Diagram 5.3 *Perspectives on generic integrity*

In the discussion of generic integrity one may get the impression that the integrity of a genre is rather static or fixed, which to some extent may be true also; however, it would be wrong to assume that it is always so, and in all forms of discourse. There are numerous contextual factors operating on or constraining genres, and some of these factors introduce flexibility in the construction, interpretation and use of genres. Configurations of situational and contextual factors do not always repeat in exactly the same form, and genre users often need to adjust their responses accordingly, which introduces an element of flexibility into the conception of generic integrity. Sometimes participant perspectives are different, which may be due to changing contextual factors, or some other considerations of power and control over rhetorical action, and as a result, the integrity of a particular genre may be contested. As extensively discussed in Chapter 1, textual perspective may include textualization of lexico-grammar, organization of discourse and aspects of intertextuality and interdiscursivity. Ethnographic perspective covers a range of features which constrain the construction of genre from the point of view of factors such as the impressions, beliefs and perceptions of experts associated with a particular genre, the processes of its construction, choice of modes available, etc. Institutional perspective offers insights into the demands and concerns imposed by the membership requirements of a particular institution, and the use and exploitation of rhetorical strategies to maintain institutional harmony and integrity. Socio-critical perspective, on the other hand, provides information on patterns of language, ideology and power associated with a particular use of genre. This also provides useful information on the interaction between genre and social practices, including intercultural constraints. Let us take some of these aspects of generic integrity in the next section.

5.2 Dynamics of generic integrity

Although genres are stable textual artefacts with conventions shared by most participants in the professional event, generic integrity is not something given, but tentatively understood and shared by members of discourse communities. It is versatile, often blurred at the edges, sometimes contested, giving rise to differing perceptions. This may be the result of the dynamic changes in the nature of a particular genre over a period of time, or the complexity of contextual factors constraining the genre in question. As illustration of the first kind, I shall take up an instance of a mixed genre from travel and tourism, and of the second kind, an instance from a legal context.

(A) Advertorial as a mixed genre

As discussed in Chapter 3, advertisements have their own integrity as a persuasive genre, which is characterized by a number of factors, internal as well as external to the genre. They may have different contextual configurations depending upon a number of factors: they show variation in participants or participant relations, as in advertisements for holidaymakers v. business travellers, variation in medium, as in advertisements on television v. those in the print media, variation in terms of the products, services or ideas, as advertisements for cars and those for household products, and maybe others, as discussed in earlier chapters. However, all of them display an overlapping generic integrity, though using a wide variety of linguistic resources and rhetorical strategies. They are essentially persuasive and are meant to promote a particular product, service or idea to an intended audience. They often incorporate a positive description and evaluation of the product, service or idea being promoted. Most essentially, they almost always solicit response from the intended audience. However, at the same time it is not uncommon to see advertisements mixed with other genres, which raises an important question about the generic integrity of such mixed genres. How do professionals in disciplinary contexts recognize and reflect the status of such a mixing, and what constraints operate on such constructions. As illustration, let me take up an example of what has become very popular in the context of the present-day culture of advertising and media exploitation, where advertisers are always on the lookout for novel strategies to promote their products and services. They are well aware of a general feeling of disbelief on the part of the masses to take much of advertising seriously, and are constantly in search of new forms of influencing potential buyers. One such strategy that has become popular in recent times is to promote products and services through reviews, opinions and editorials, by bending these genres to promote products or services or mixing them with advertising. One such popular mixed genre is known as the advertorial, or a hybrid of editorial and advertisement. Let us look at a typical illustration of this mixed genre from a travel magazine.

The text of the advertorial represents two somewhat different kinds of realities. There are undoubtedly a number of text-internal indicators of advertising genres, some of which include the two colourful and attractive pictures, typical of advertising genres, a logo, an explicitly promotional sub-heading exploiting an established clich. 'The Jewel in the Crown' and a very positive and attractive description of the product 'Fairways & Bluewater Resort and Country Club'. The description is typically enticing, almost poetic in character: *Straddling a hundred hectares of gently rolling terrain and spanning the entire width of Boracay* ... If one were to look at the whole description, it would seem to be overwhelmingly nominal in structure, and since nominal phrases are the carriers of adjectives, the whole description seems to be full of positive attributes. ... *luxury and comforts of an international-caliber resort community; Boracay's stunning sights: sparkling white beaches, glassy acquamarine waters and miles and miles of tree-lined slopes*: they all seem to add to the positive description of the product, which is very typical of advertising genres. In fact, more than 75 per cent of the total number of words in the whole text accounts for positive description of the product (see the text below, with all the noun phrases italicized.

However, crucially missing from this positive description of the product is any direct attempt to 'establish credentials of the company' which owns the product, except through the logo of the company or a very low-key reference to 'For Fairways & Bluewater, Marsh maximizes ...' Also missing from this text is any direct or indirect attempt 'to solicit response' from readers, which again is a very typical characteristic of advertising genres. Therefore in certain respects the example is

---

Fairways and Bluewater
The Jewel of the Pacific

Straddling a hundred hectares of gently rolling terrain and spanning the entire width of Boracay at its very center, Fairways and Bluewater Resort Golf & Country Club, a private, high-end membership club, puts together the luxury and comforts of an international-caliber resort community and Boracay's stunning sights: sparkling white beaches, glassy aquamarine waters and miles and miles of tree-lined slopes.

At the core of this landmark project – owned and developed by Fil-Estate Properties Inc. – is an 18-hole, par 72 golf course designed by master designer and golfer Graham V. Marsh, whose world-class designs are highly rated in Australia, Japan and Southeast Asia. For Fairways & Bluewater, Marsh maximizes Boracay's aesthetic opportunities and combines them with ingenious landscaping that disturbs as little as possible the natural curve of the land. Says Marsh "[Boracay] is such a naturally beautiful sight that what we really want to achieve is a golf course that nature created ... There is absolutely no doubt in my mind that when people come out and play this golf course, they will be able to walk away with the feeling that they had just had a golfing experience which they may not experience anywhere else in the world."

---

similar to that of a typical advertisement, whereas in some other sense it does not fulfil the typical expectations one may have from an advertisement. On the other hand, it seems to incorporate a number of typical features of editorials, one of which is the way the writer argues for positive aspects of the place that he seems to favour as a destination for golf enthusiasts. It definitely highlights the opinion of the author, arguing favourably, but the interesting aspect of this argument is that unlike typical editorials, it does not incorporate any of the negative elements in the description. The main reason for this is that any negative elements would have created conflicts for the advertising or promotional aspects of the genre. Therefore in terms of textual input, just as the writer stops short of 'soliciting response' from the reader to make it a typical advertisement, similarly on the other hand, to avoid a generic conflict, the writer avoids mentioning any negative aspects about the product. The mixing of the two generic elements is further reinforced by some of the text-external factors, like the discourse community (holidaymakers) it is addressed to, the situational context in which it is published (a vacation magazine sent to members only), the editorial page on which it appears, and the regularity with which the section appears under the heading 'advertorial'.

This was a rather simple illustration of generic integrity in a mixed genre, highlighting the role of text-internal factors. I shall next take up a more complex issue that highlights contested perceptions of integrity as perceived by a wide and varied range of participants, focusing this time on text-external factors in legislative discourse.

(B) Contested generic integrity: legislative provisions

Every discipline or profession has its own language. It is true of academics, whether economists, physicists, political scientists, marketing specialists, legal academics or linguists; it is equally true of professionals, whether they are doctors, lawyers, scientists, computer specialists, recipe writers or even politicians. It is difficult to imagine a profession without their use of specialist discourse. Hudson (1979: 1) rightly points out: 'If one wished to kill a profession, to remove its cohesion and its strength, the most effective way would be to forbid the use of its characteristic language'. However, perceptions about the exact nature and form of legal discourse and hence of the generic integrity of legal discourse are rather varied and often contested. In the case of legislative genres, there are a variety of perspectives held by participants, members of the professional legal community, and people in general. One frequently comes across a variety of comments about the use of legal language, generally negative, often contradictory. The reformist movement in the use of plain language in legislative contexts is firmly established in most of the western democracies, and is fast becoming almost a global phenomenon, often generating deep divisions between those who support the use of conventional legislative language and those who oppose it. Although the contesting perceptions, arguments and beliefs are generally drawn along the 'insiders v. outsiders' lines, it is not always so. This is what Jonathan Swift, as outsider to legal professions, said in *Gulliver's Travels*.

> It is likewise to be observed, that this Society hath a peculiar Cant and Jargon of their own, that no other Mortal can understand, and wherein all their Laws are written, which they take special Care to multiply; whereby they have wholly confounded the very Essence of Truth and Falsehood, of Right and Wrong; so that it will take Thirty

> Years to decide whether the Field, left by my Ancestors for six
> Generations, belong to me, or to a Stranger three Hundred Miles off.
> (Jonathan Swift, *Gulliver's Travels*)

On the other hand, even members of the legal profession themselves
have started reacting against conventional legal expression. This is
what a newly initiated member of the profession says:

> I've dropped out of plain legal writing. I used to avoid, but now I
> embrace, convoluted sentences and legal gobbledygook. ... In law
> school, one of my favourite professors taught me that when I write,
> I should communicate effectively, not sound like a lawyer. But
> when I became an associate in a law firm, my writing style – clean,
> brisk, straightforward – exasperated the other lawyers. I just didn't
> sound like one of them. ... One partner summoned all his
> patience, pulled me aside, and gently asked, 'Didn't they teach you
> how to write in law school?' The real answer was, 'Yes, and that's
> what seems to be the problem.' Instead I said, 'I guess not.'
> (Bresler 1998–2000: 29)

The Scribes Journal of Legal Writing, devoted to reform movement in
legal writing, often goes to extremes to identify and make fun of
conventional legal language by setting up a number of awards such as
The Splitting Headache award, *The Serpentine Sentence Award* and a
number of others targeting inappropriate instances of specialist
discourses. Let us look at the following award-winning example.

[*The Scribes Journal of Legal Writing*, Vol.4, (1993), p.121]
The "Splitting Headache" Award
For the Legal Drafting Most Likely to Induce Migraines

(B) FAMILY.---In the case of an individual enrolled under a health
plan under a family class enrolment (as defined in section 1011(c)
(2) (A)), the family out-of-pocket limit on cost sharing schedule
offered by the plan represents the amount of expenses that
members of the individual's family, in the aggregate, may be
required to incur under the plan in a year because of a general
deductible, separate deductibles, copayments, and coinsurance
before the plan may no longer impose any cost sharing with respect
to items or services covered by the comprehensive benefit package
that are provided to any member of the individual's family, except
as provided in subsections (d)(2)(D) and (e)(2)(D) of section 1115.

[Health Security Act of 1993, s. 1131(c)(4)(B) from the Clinton
Administration's 1,300-page proposed health-care legislation]

The important question we ask here is, 'why do we have such extreme reactions against legal writing, when all other forms of specialist writing escape such reactions?' The answer perhaps lies in the fact that these rather complex forms of legislative writing are invariably meant to control the lives of millions of people in civilized societies. This is not necessarily so in the case of any other form of professional writing; at least one's life is not directly controlled by specialist discourses. In the case of law, whether one understands it or not, one is supposed to have read and understood any new piece of legislation the moment it comes into effect. In that sense ordinary citizens are the real audience for most forms of legislative rules and regulations, whereas in reality this form of writing makes little sense to anyone without legal expertise. Even for legal experts, it is not readily accessible all the time. In the good old days life was rather simple as there was very little awareness about one's rights and obligations in society; however in today's world when the general level of education and awareness of rights and obligations is on the increase, one often feels that it is one's right to demand easy accessibility to legal rules and regulations. The other factor that makes this task of accessibility even more difficult is the rapid increase in the size of the statute book in democratic societies, especially in the common law countries. On the one hand, this makes it impossible for the drafting community to introduce any drastic changes to their drafting practices and style, and on the other, it continues to reinforce the inaccessibility of such genres. In spite of such extreme perceptions about the generic integrity of the legislative genre, the reality is not as simple and clear-cut as it may appear to be. In fact, there has rarely been a significant effort to understand why this legislative is written the way it is. Neither the members of the legal profession, nor the ordinary users of this genre, and not even the linguists and discourse analysts, have really come to terms with the notion of the generic integrity of this public genre. Most approaches to text and genre analysis have yet to come to grips with this notion of contestation in generic integrity. Perhaps one needs to be aware of varying degrees of generic integrity in such genres. An equally important issue will be to investigate how one understands and expresses such varying perceptions of generic integrity. In order to make sense of such intricacies of legislative drafting, it is essential to consider some of the text-external factors, especially the participants and their institutional roles, and their shared background knowledge that make this genre possible.

PARTICIPANTS: STAKEHOLDERS, CONSUMERS OR VICTIMS

In any other form of writing it is often easy to identify the reader and the writer of a text. In this case, it is almost impossible to do so. There are so many participants and institutions with varying degrees of stakes involved in the construction and consumption of this legal genre that the exact nature of the dynamics is almost impossible to realize. There are specific aspects of correlations between various participating institutions in the making of legislative discourse, which are interesting, and there are equally important and interesting participant relationships which give rise to a complexity of dynamics of language and power, which require answers to a number of questions, some of which I would like to consider first.

Who are the real writers?

- Are they draftsmen, who actually are responsible for constructing legislative genres? But then, one must remember that they do not provide the substance, which is generally provided through the deliberations of members of the legislature, in which the draftsman is not a participant, and where he is not even present.
- Are they legislators who deliberate on the substance of these genres as part of their legislative responsibilities? Although legislators collectively provide substance to legislative process, and often go through several drafts of legislation, they do not write the documents.
- Are they government departments, who often initiate some of these rules and regulations and often are responsible for input to these legislative processes, and are ultimately responsible for implementing them? Although government departments often initiate the process in the form of bills to be tabled in the legislature, they have no role in the actual writing of legislation. They have vested interest in the nature and function of the actual output, they rarely have any direct control over it.

The interesting issue is that these three sets of participants do not share the same level of legal and background knowledge in the discipline.

Let us see the other side of the coin as well.

Who are the real readers?

- Are they the ordinary citizens, who are invariably controlled by these legislative acts? Maybe that is the case, at least in principle. Most plain English pressure groups maintain that these are the real recipients, but the drafting community has its loyalty elsewhere.

- Are they the lawyers, who have to read and (mis?)interpret these rules and regulations in the court of law in the course of their negotiation of justice, which, in fact, means that it must suit the requirements of their clients? In practice, this seems to be the case. Since members of the legal profession have the privilege to argue for convenient (mis?)interpretations, they are often controlled by making legislative sentences not simply clear, precise and unambiguous, but all-inclusive as well.
- Are they the judges, who are responsible for providing the final interpretation of these legislative acts? Although the judiciary, especially in common law countries, is privileged to have the last say in the matter of interpretation of legislation, the real power to legislate rests with the legislature; hence in the drafting of legislation every attempt is made to 'box the judge firmly into a corner from which he cannot escape' (Caldwell 1982).
- Are they the members of the executive arms of the governments, who often have their own government interests in mind and as such are important parties to the process? Although executives (government) are primarily responsible for implementing legislative propositions, and most often are given extensive powers to execute legislative decisions and intentions, they seem to be only marginally regarded as the real readers of legislative discourse, certainly not to the extent members of the legal profession are.

Once again, the degree of overlap in legal knowledge in these varied groups is rather diverse. Moreover, all these parties do not enjoy the same level of authority to interpret these legislative genres. Although lawyers have the privilege to offer their own interpretations, the final responsibility and privilege rests with judges. Members of the executive arms of the government or the bureaucracy also have some role but only in a limited sense, and in some cases.

INSTITUTIONAL ROLES

This raises another issue: the participation and involvement of the institutions, especially the judiciary, the administration or bureaucracy, the legislature, the drafting community, the public and of course the government. Who gets power, and who is impoverished? And how does any advantage on the part of one institution become a disadvantage for the other?

The answers to many of these questions are not straightforward, and not easy to find either. Unlike many other forms of language use, legal contexts give rise to generic artefacts that are multifaceted and multidimensional, in that they are constructed as a result of the efforts of a number of adversaries who are supposed to be collaborating in the process to create a truly impersonal document. On the surface, the real writer is a parliamentary draftsman, but he rarely contributes to the content of the document, and is never present in the deliberations of the parliamentary debates that give rise to the content of legislation. Legislators, who actually contribute to the content of the document, are never involved in the writing of the document. The real consumers are lawyers and judges who need to interpret or perhaps misinterpret legislative language but are never directly recipients of any cost or benefit arising from such adventures. The two adversaries in the legal battle are supposed to be experts through intensive training and experience in legislative interpretation but are not supposed to agree with each other on any aspect of legislative interpretation.

The whole issue of generic integrity is much more complex than might appear on the surface. In fact, it has a number of different yet overlapping dimensions, with varying perspectives, interests and power dynamics, giving rise to a number of tensions, some of which can be represented as in Diagram 5.4.

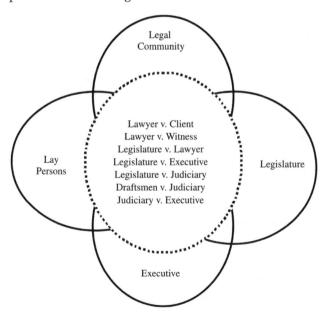

Diagram 5.4 *Participant and institutional conflicts in legislative discourse*

As one can see there are four major institutional involvements in the construction, interpretation and use of legislative discourse, giving rise to multiple perspectives and potential conflicts of interest. One can identify at least seven such possibilities, distinct like the colours of a rainbow, though overlapping in some respects.

Lawyer v. Client	Unequal distribution of power, shared background knowledge
Lawyer v. Witness	Setting: unequal distribution of institutional power, specialist knowledge, specific professional role assignment
Legislature v. Executive	Political power v. bureaucratic privilege
Legislator v. Lawyer	Political power and control v. institutional privilege
Legislature v. Judiciary	Who has the ultimate power?
Draftsman v. Judiciary	Clarity, precision, unambiguity and all-inclusiveness, to box the judge firmly into a corner
Judiciary v. Executive	Freedom to interpret v. socio-political control

With so many different participants, institutions and conflicting interests and stakes operating on the processes and procedures of discourse construction and consumption, it is only natural to expect contestations about the generic integrity of legislative genres. In recent years, the awareness of these conflicting perspectives about legal discourse have assumed critical importance, raising a number of interesting issues about the empowerment of legal professionals at the cost of disempowerment of society at large. We will revisit such realities of power and the politics of legislative genres in the final chapter, when we consider the world of applications. But before we do that, let me briefly discuss the notion of acquisition of generic expertise, which throws further light on the dynamics of the lay – professional relationship, and has not been raised anywhere in available literature in the field.

5.3 Generic competence and professional expertise

Closely related to generic integrity is the concept of generic competence, which not only makes it possible for members of a professional community to construct, interpret and use genres appropriately, but is also an important measure of professional expertise (Candlin 1999). Although the exact relationship between generic competence and professional expertise is still not very clear, we have some idea of how one contributes to the other. How specialists acquire professional expertise is even more difficult to investigate, and it is hardly surprising that acquisition of generic competence and professional expertise continues to be a major problem for current theories of genre. This may be partly because it has two seemingly divergent affiliations. If, on the one hand, it has strong connections with the notions of linguistic and communicative competence (perhaps because of historical development), then on the other hand it also has inseparable links with the notion of academic and professional practice (certainly a matter of relevant and effective application). Consequently, it needs to negotiate textual space, on the one hand, and socio-cognitive space, on the other. Since there is very little research work in second language acquisition which focuses on discourse and genre acquisition, and hence provides little under-standing of this complex and often dynamic process of the acquisition of professional genres, I will make an attempt to identify and discuss some of the major issues involved in the definition, function, use, exploitation and acquisition of generic expertise, which seems to be the key to pragmatic success in the use of language in wide-ranging professional contexts.

Traditional terms such as *competence* and *performance* (Chomsky 1965) or *communicative competence* (Hymes 1972) are unfortunately not very helpful when we attempt to understand more precisely what makes it possible for expert professionals to be able to 'own' and use specific systems of genres or more broadly a range of disciplinary genres in their everyday professional activities. Hymes (1972) proposed *communicative competence* to contrast it with *linguistic competence* in the sense in which Chomsky (1965) used it. Canale and Swain (1980) further specified this concept in terms of the underlying systems of knowledge and skill required for communica-tion, which may include knowledge of lexico-grammar and skill in using socio-linguistic conventions for a given language. However valid *communicative competence* may be for general ability to use language in social contexts, it undermines the specific concerns of individual professions and institutions. It seems too general to be of any value in the context of specific professional cultures. Moreover, the notion of *communicative competence* tends to blur the finer distinctions recent work on discourse studies needs to make. More recent work in discourse and genre analysis and its application to educational practice (especially in ESP, both EAP and EOP, professional and corporate communication) demands a more precise specification of such a competence. Moreover, whichever way one may specify it, it

143

must be consistent with the model of discourse that we have outlined in Chapter 1 (Diagram 1.3).

I would like to propose *discursive competence* as a general concept to cover various levels of competence we all need in order to expertly operate within well-defined professional as well as general socio-cultural contexts. Consistent with our four-space model of discourse proposed in Chapter 1, we can more narrowly differentiate *discursive competence* at various levels depending upon the kind of focus we may have on the nature of inquiry, and the framework within which we decide to operate. I would like to differentiate discursive competence at three levels consisting of the following:

- textual competence
- generic competence
- social competence

Textual competence represents not only an ability to master the linguistic code, but also an ability to use textual, contextual and pragmatic knowledge to construct and interpret contextually appropriate texts. Confined primarily to what we referred to as textual space, *textual competence* is much more powerful than what has been traditionally referred to as *linguistic competence* in (applied) linguistic literature, in that it includes an ability to construct grammatically correct and textually appropriate (cohesive as well as coherent) stretches of language, but does not include parameters which make communication socio-culturally effective, politically correct and socially acceptable within specific communities of disciplinary cultures or in a more general sense, within broadly defined socio-culturally appropriate contexts. In this sense, it incorporates both the *linguistic competence* and some aspects of what in applied linguistic literature is popularly known as the *communicative competence*. Then we may like to distinguish *generic competence*, which is the ability to respond to recurrent and novel rhetorical situations by constructing, interpreting, using and often exploiting generic conventions embedded in specific disciplinary cultures and practices to achieve professional ends. The third level at which *discursive competence* can operate is the *social competence*, which incorporates an ability to use language more widely to participate effectively in a variety of social and institutional contexts to give expression to one's social identity, in the context of constraining social structures and social processes.

Discursive competence, of which generic competence is an important part, thus incorporates three different kinds of competence, only one of which is predominantly text-internal or language-related.

The other two are much more complex, dynamic and constrained or conditioned by non-linguistic text-external factors, such as professional or social contexts, disciplinary or social knowledge, level of expertise or sophistication required and awareness of socio-cultural conventions, in addition to a number of other factors. In the case of generic competence, in particular, it is not only difficult but undesirable too to understand and investigate it without any reference to either professional practice, of which it is an integral part, or disciplinary knowledge, in the construction and communication of which it plays a central role.

Generic competence means the ability to identify, construct, interpret and successfully exploit a specific repertoire of professional, disciplinary or workplace genres to participate in the daily activities and to achieve the goals of a specific professional community or what Lave and Wenger (1991) call 'community of practice'; more specifically:

- to select the appropriate set of genres (or system of genres) to suit a rhetorical purpose in a specific professional, disciplinary or workplace context,
- to construct, interpret and use generic resources to achieve the goals of the professional community,
- to exploit generic knowledge to create new forms to express 'private intentions' within the socially recognized goals, and
- to participate effectively not only in the discursive procedures that give shape to such generic constructs, but also in the professional practices of which these form an important component.

(Bhatia 1999a)

Genres, in this sense, are reflections of disciplinary practices and the *acquisition of generic competence* is a matter of acquiring *specialist competence* or *expertise* in the knowledge-producing and knowledge-consuming activities of disciplinary, professional and workplace cultures.

Generic competence is an important contributor to *professional expertise*, and is often embedded in specific disciplinary cultures and invariably reflected in the typical disciplinary practices of professional communities. Any investigation of the acquisition of such professional expertise must seek to answer some or all of the following key questions not only on what it means, but also on how we specify, acquire, teach and measure it.

- What constitutes expert behaviour in a specific professional field? In other words, how do we characterize an expert accountant or lawyer?
- What role does discursive competence play in professional practice?
- Is it possible to specify professional expertise in terms of key competencies?
- How does one acquire and use these professional competencies?
- Are these competencies teachable/learnable?
- How does one appraise/measure expertise in a specialist area?

Viewed in this way, *professional expertise* tends to integrate the following three key elements:

- discursive competence (which includes generic competence)
- disciplinary knowledge
- professional practice.

This can be represented as in Diagram 5.5. Much of the literature on both first and second language acquisition has so far focused only on certain aspects of discursive competence, especially on textual or in some cases social competence, with very little attention to the acquisition of generic competence or specialist expertise (Candlin 2000; Bhatia and Candlin 2001).

In order to attempt to understand in some detail how expert members of disciplinary cultures acquire professional expertise and exploit it in their day-to-day professional work, it is necessary to integrate the three elements, that is, the knowledge of the system of genres they own, the knowledge of the specific discipline they use in order to conduct their everyday affairs, and the nature of the professional practice they are required to be part of. In the context of

Diagram 5.5 *Specification of professional expertise*

these aspects of professional expertise, we then need to find answers to the following three crucial questions:

1. What constitutes expert behaviour in a specialist disciplinary culture?
2. How does one acquire this expertise?
3. How can one measure it?

It seems that there is no single way of acquiring this kind of expertise. Professionals seem to acquire different aspects of this expertise in different ways and at different stages of their career development. Some of the key contributors to this process of acquisition may be the following:

- education
- professional training
- apprenticeship
- on the job learning (legitimate peripheral participation)
- ESP (English for Specific Purposes)
- communication skills training

These influences can be reflected as in Diagram 5.6.

As is obvious from Diagram 5.6, the process of becoming a competent professional requires the development of professional competence, which is measured in terms of a combination of *discursive knowledge* and *disciplinary knowledge*, in the context of *professional practices*. One may point out that although a sound understanding of *generic knowledge* is adequate in most professional contexts, I have chosen to focus on a more general *discursive competence* here. This is to highlight that fact that although understanding of genres gives a desired focus to discourse, *discursive knowledge* provides a necessary broad social vision within which genres are placed. Integrating these three in a realistic professional context is one of the greatest challenges that genre theory faces today. Of these influences and opportunities for development, especially in academic contexts, including applied linguistics, we seem to be paying considerable attention to disciplinary as well discursive knowledge independently of each other, but unfortunately there has been somewhat limited attention paid to the integration of these two, and perhaps no attention at all to the integration of these two with discursive practices in professional contexts. This is invariably left for the profession itself to take on independently, which makes the life of new entrants to various professions difficult and sometimes quite traumatic. The argument that I have tried to develop so far is that although disciplinary and

147

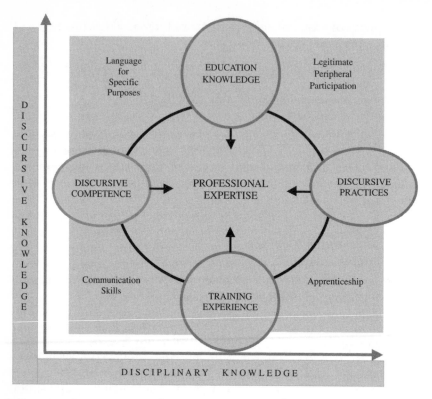

Diagram 5.6 *Key contributors to acquisition of professional expertise*

discursive knowledge is essential to the development of professional expertise, it can only be acquired and appraised in the context of professional practices, the third key contributor to any understanding of such expertise. It is for this reason alone that new entrants to any profession are trained as apprentices. However apprenticeship often carries with it long periods of training followed by uncertainties about eventual admittance to the professional community.

Lave and Wenger (1991: 33) propose an alternative in the form of *Legitimate Peripheral Participation*, as part of their theory of *Situated Learning* and *Communities of Practice*. Using situated activity as the basis of claims about the relational character of knowledge and learning, the negotiated character of meaning, and the concerned (engaged, dilemma-driven) nature of learning activity for the people involved in professional development, they characterize learning as 'Legitimate Peripheral Participation in Communities of Practice ... as a descriptor of engagement in social practice that entails learning as an integral constituent ... ' (Lave and Wenger 1991:31). Unlike apprentices, these peripheral members are treated as legitimate participants in a community, and being a legitimate member involves 'learning how to talk (and be silent) in the manner of full participants' (Lave and Wenger 1991: 105). This concept of *Legitimate Peripheral Participation* has implications for the conventional notions of *apprenticeship, situated learning* and *educational training*, adding significantly to our understanding and experience of participation in professional activities, especially with respect to professional knowledge, its location and the learning activity itself, effectively combining the cumulative advantages of training and apprenticeship without any of the disadvantages they tend to bring in.

Lave and Wenger (1991: 98) view a *community of practice* as a set of relations among persons, activities and the world over time and in relation with other tangential and overlapping communities of practice. A community of practice is an intrinsic condition for the existence of knowledge, not least because it provides the interpretive support necessary for making sense of its heritage. In *discourse communities*, the focus is on lexico-grammar, texts and genres that enable members throughout the world to maintain their goals, regulate their membership and communicate efficiently with one another. In *communities of practice*, on the other hand, the emphasis is on *practices* and *values* that hold the communities together, or separate them from one another. Ideally, one needs to integrate the two without sacrificing any of the strengths of either of these concepts. In order to do this, we must look at these three aspects of professional expertise from the point of view of multiple perspectives, such as the institutional as well as the professional perspective, where 'workplaces are seen as social institutions, which are held together by communicative practices, and where resources are produced and regulated, problems are solved, identities are played out and professional knowledge is constituted' (Sarangi and Roberts 1999).

To integrate these concepts, Sarangi and Roberts (1999) suggest two key concepts of *interaction order*, which includes talk, texts, media, spaces, categories, rules, codes, etc., and *institutional order*, which means shared practices, values and beliefs, rules of conduct, events, routines, etc. Referring to the context of medicine and health, they distinguish *professional discourse* from *institutional discourse* as follows:

> A medical setting would include the clinician's narratives which work up patients as cases, the diagnosis of the medical problem in doctor–patient interaction, or the display of medical authority as

> evidence. The institutional discourses would include the gate-keeping functions of selection, training and assessment, the discourses around the management of hospitals, General Practitioners' surgery and so on, and the voices used by the institution to represent itself to the outside world.
>
> (Sarangi and Roberts 1999: 16)

They further suggest that there could be changes in interactional activity occasioned by changes in public policy and public expectations (Sarangi and Roberts 1999: 18). As in the educational scenario, health and social care professionals, they claim, are also subject to changed practices and discourses as a result of changes within the social institution of health and family welfare. Increasingly, one may find that caring professions like social work are adopting the role of service providers in conjunction with a market economy model, which may have implications for community care and consumer ethics. Similarly, in professional legal contexts, members of the legal profession are adopting the role of service providers within a market economy model, and their practices, standards of services, attitudes towards their professional expertise and professional identities have also undergone changes. It is hardly surprising that, in the United States, one often finds lawyers arriving at the site of a road accident long before the police. All these developments have significant implications for a good understanding of professional expertise and the discursive practices and discourses associated with them.

Another perspective that may contribute significantly to our understanding of professional practice is the socio-cognitive perspective. In this context, Goffman (1959) introduces two interesting concepts of frontstage and backstage. Frontstage, as we know, is 'where the performance is given' and backstage is 'a place, relative to a given performance, where the impression fostered by the performance is knowingly contradicted as a matter of course'. For Goffman, these stages are differentiated by activities and behaviours and by language and interactions. In the context of professional expertise, we may need to know 'how expert one needs to be on both *stages*, and how do these *stages* interact?' Backstages are where knowledge is produced and often negotiated, and may involve different actors than frontstages. In order to have a good understanding of how professional discourses are collaboratively produced we certainly need to understand typical *backstage* interactions. We may also need to know 'who are legitimately allowed to participate in a particular discursive activity, at what stage, and with what kind of contribution?' 'What kinds of discourses might occur in any of those backstage interactions and

150

negotiations?' It is possible that frontstage participants may have different roles backstage, and may even use different kinds of language. As Sarangi and Roberts (1999) point out, it is also possible that *frontstages* and *backstages* get blurred, and the distinction may not always be easily made. Changes in work practices and work relationships encourage such blurring. These and many other socio-cognitive aspects of professional practices are crucial for a good understanding of professional expertise.

Similarly, Watson (1996) discusses expertise as a combination of professional and communicative abilities, underpinning the importance of both being an expert and being able to communicate like an expert. If this is true, then the actual discourses of such encounters will provide valuable information and evidence about what constitutes professional expertise. Just as *talk at work* can be drawn on as evidence of variable work expertise, *talk about work* may also provide significant evidence to support our understanding of professional expertise. This provides another important perspective through *personal narratives* or *accounts* in the investigation of professional expertise. As Watson (1996) reiterates,

> Whenever we wish to understand 'what actually happened' in the lives of the people we are studying, we have little to go on other than the words that are spoken to us by these people themselves or by people who know them. To reach our 'own interpretation' of 'what happened' it is therefore vital to recognize the importance of the interpretative work which the individuals have themselves engaged in when constructing their accounts.
>
> (Watson 1996: 261)

From the discussion above, it is clear that professional expertise, to which generic competence is a significant contributor, is a complex multidimensional concept, and hence may require an equally complex and multidimensional approach to the understanding of its nature, specification and acquisition by members of various professional cultures.

In this chapter, I have made an attempt to outline the notion of generic integrity as a key characteristic feature of every established genre. However, it is not to be seen as something static or given, but more flexible and dynamic. I also identified a number of perspectives (text-internal as well as text-external) which can help us identify and analyse the generic integrity of a specific genre. I also discussed a few examples to illustrate the use and function of generic integrity in specific professional contexts. To sum up, I have been suggesting a multidimensional and multi-perspective view of professional discourse, often highlighting its complexities, chaotic realities and dynamic development. Obviously, a multidimensional analysis of language use such as this would require an integration of a variety of tools of analysis available for genre analysis today, rather than any narrowly defined framework highlighting only some aspects of genre. These are important questions in genre theory today, and we shall take them up in detail in the next chapter.

THE WORLD OF
ANALYTICAL
PERSPECTIVES

6 Integrating research methods

Having looked at the complexities of the world of discourse from the point of view of genre analysis, it is time to turn to methods one can employ to achieve comprehensive, insightful and useful analyses of written discourse from academic, professional and other institutional contexts. Like any other area of multidisciplinary activity, analysis of written discourse has also been sliced off as rather independent territories by individual disciplines, with somewhat differential spotlights, specific perspectives, varied applications, and more importantly, distinct methodological procedures. As a consequence, we see a diverse range of multidisciplinary engagements with the discursive practices of disciplinary and professional cultures. Although there is an acknowledged diversity of interests for under-taking analyses of professional discourses, there has been, at the same time, a growing realization that we can understand the 'critical moments of engagement' (Scollon 1998) better if we are in a position to see the whole of the elephant, as it were, rather than only a part of it. As a result, there is increasing, though often selective, interest in appropriation of research methodologies across disciplinary bound-aries. Secondly, since interest in the analyses of written discourses has been motivated by a variety of applications within and across disciplinary boundaries, many of which tend to benefit from a multidimensional view of analysis, there has been a growing interest in the integration of research methodologies and frameworks for analysing professional discourses and practices.

The focus of analysis has also shifted to more complex and dynamic aspects of discourse construction and interpretation, and the demands on the analysts have become more challenging, as one is required to account for not only the use of textual genres, but also the way they influence and are in turn influenced by the recipients of discourse, including their attitudes, opinions, decisions and identities. As we have seen in the last few chapters, it is a complex multi-dimensional, multidisciplinary and multi-perspective task, and hence will require an equally complex research methodology to accomplish it. Using just the textual analytical methods, no doubt, will give us useful insights about the way the text is constructed, but this method, on its own, will provide information only on certain aspects of the textual construct. Linguistic perspective alone will only allow one to see part of the elephant. The question is 'how do we see the whole of the elephant?' The answer to this very important question, I think, will require the use of a range of methodological procedures which have rarely been used for the analysis of written discourse, such as the ethnographic, socio-cognitive and socio-critical. The important thing is not that one needs to use several procedures; the most important thing is how to integrate these different methodological procedures into a coherent genre analytical tool, which is the focus of this chapter.

In order to construct a model of analytical procedures for a comprehensive investigation of genres in the real world of discourse, we need to go back to our model of discourse analysis presented in the opening chapter in terms of three overlapping concepts of space. We need to investigate the textual space to take into account the use of text-internal features of language use, which include lexico-grammatical features, especially the values they carry in the context of rhetorical moves, discourse strategies, regularities of organization, intertextuality and some aspects of interdiscursivity. Then we need to investigate the broad socio-cognitive space to take into account the tactical aspects of language use, in particular the correlation between text-internal and text-external factors, especially the questions of interdiscursivity. In addition, it is necessary to explore professional space, which accounts for participant relationships, and their contributions to the process of genre construction, interpretation, use and exploitation in the context of disciplinary, professional and other institutional practices and constraints. This aspect of investigation will also take into account the way expert users of language exploit and manipulate generic resources to create hybrid genres, which may include mixing, embedding, bending and appropriating of generic resources. We also need to pay some attention to the way experts use their specialist knowledge to maintain and often assert their control over the genres they often use to achieve their professional objectives. Beyond this, we are often called upon to investigate the social space in an attempt to account for the influence of broad social actions in creating and sustaining social identities, social structures and the functioning of social institutions through discursive practices. Such a critical look at language use is crucial to our understanding of social and institutional practices in a broader framework of language as social action. Considering the proposed model as the basis of a comprehensive analysis of discourse as genre-based professional practice, we find that our primary objective in this book has been to investigate the performance of professional activities through language and to place it in the context of professional and institutional constraints, concerns and cultures.

6.1 Investigation goals

Based on the discussion so far, the main goals of genre analysis of written discourse could be manifold, some of which include the following.

(1) To understand and account for the realities of the world of discourse

Much of the earlier work on professional discourse analysis has focused on standardized and conventionalized generic forms, which has served the cause of language teaching and learning extremely well, particularly in the context of ESP and professional communication. However, there has been a negative impact of this practice as well, in the sense that it has encouraged analysts to focus on idealized and somewhat pure generic forms, and in the process, to overlook the realities of the professional world. There is a need to understand and account for the realities of the world as we see them, complex, dynamic and constantly changing. In other words, there is a strong need to look at the world as we find it, not necessarily as we would like to see it. However, this should not be seen as undermining the value of such analytical studies. On the contrary, it should be viewed as a development of genre theory in its quest for increased validation and relevance to the world of professions.

(2) To understand 'private intentions' within professional genres

With the invasion of new media and modes of communication in public life, and the more recent increase in the interdisciplinary nature of academic and professional discourse, appropriation of lexico-grammatical resources and discoursal strategies across discourse communities and genres is becoming increasingly common. We have discussed some of these issues in earlier sections, especially those focusing on discourse manipulation by expert members of professional communities. We have also focused on various forms of 'generic appropriation' giving rise to mixed and embedded forms, sometimes even creating conflicts through this process of hybridization. Although the freedom to exploit available resources for the expression of 'private intentions' seems to go against the concept of genre as social construction, it is only natural that experts and experienced writers always look for innovations of this kind in order to achieve their individual and corporate objectives at the same time. One of the main concerns of genre analysis should be to account for such appropriations within its methodological framework. It is important to realize that these appropriations are legitimate and creative extensions of available linguistic and generic resources and not necessarily breaches or flouting of conventions. This concern to account for such innovations will only add greater validity to genre theory.

(3) To understand individual, organizational, professional and social identities constructed through discursive practices within specific disciplinary cultures

Although it is important to study how professional and organizational discourses are constrained by professional practices and identities and organizational hierarchies, it is equally important to study how discursive practices in professional organizations determine and redefine professional and organizational identities and practices (Boswood 2000). Genre analysis has focused on how expert members of the community not only create and express their own identities but also question and undermine social identities of the outsiders (Candlin and Plum 1999). Although it is relatively easy to see the relationship between professional discourse and social structures, it is not easy to investigate the tensions between social and professional identities, on the one hand, and preferred professional or organizational practices, on the other. There are several identities that a professional may be required to negotiate and give expression to simultaneously in the same piece of discourse: his *professional identity* as member of a particular disciplinary community, his *organizational identity* as member of a specific organization or institution, his *social identity* as a valued member of one or more social groups, and of course his *individual identity* as indication of his self-expression. It should be of interest to any genre analyst to investigate how established professionals negotiate these different and often-conflicting identities in their discourses.

(4) To understand how professional boundaries are negotiated through discourse practices

Recontextualization of discourse in professional and institutional contexts is yet another interesting area of language use in genre-based investigations, because it raises very significant issues about variation in disciplinary and institutional practices and their use of contrasting methodologies. As Sarangi and Candlin (2001: 383) rightly point out:

In the context of communication in public and professional life, discourse analysts are bound to remain outsiders while seeking to make sense of the practices of the professional group, in a very similar way to the workings of Lave and Wenger's (1991) concept of 'legitimate peripheral participation'. Considerable time and effort, and considerable negotiation, is needed in order to immerse oneself in the research site so as to enable access to necessary tacit knowledge. Equally, a lack of methodological fit, as for example entering a site of professional and public communication without any *motivational relevancies*, as is the case with so-called open-ended discourse analytic studies, has to be viewed with considerable suspicion (Clarke 2000). Against this backdrop, reflexivity and collaborative interdisciplinary research become a necessity. Nor is this merely a matter of 'professional' sites. The issue of shared perspectives of analyst and participant is, quite clearly and routinely, an issue of access to mutuality.

In addition, it also underpins the issues of *power* and *dominance, authority* and *relevance* in institutionalized discourses (Candlin, Bhatia and Jensen 2002; Sarangi 2002; Wodak 2002).

(5) To investigate language as action in socio-critical environments

Professional genres are invariably used to do things; to give voice to social actions (Miller 1984; Martin 1985, 1993; Martin *et al.* 1987). It is often claimed that since language is only an instrument to achieve social ends, we do not need to pay so much attention to the analysis of language, and will do well to focus more or rather exclusively on 'action' (Gee 1999). This emphasis on social action in recent literature is on the increase, especially in investigation by scholars from a predominantly socio-cognitive background. Although we have not been able to pay any significant attention to this aspect of public discourse, it nevertheless remains one of the primary concerns of the genre-based theory of discourse. It is always good to see a balance between analysis of text, on the one hand, and social action, on the other. The tendency to focus exclusively on what was identified as 'social' or 'textual' space is more likely to discourage analysts from making informed judgements about the use of professional discourse.

(6) To offer effective pedagogical solutions

Although genre theory so far has been able to offer significant linguistic insights for the teaching and learning of languages under English for Specific Purposes, more popularly known as ESP (Swales 1990; Bhatia

1993), the learners have been constrained in two important ways: firstly, they remain exposed to classroom models of genre analyses and have often been shocked by the complex requirements of the workplace; and secondly, there has been a significant gap between the perceptions of the discourse and genre analysts and those of the practising professionals. There has been very little understanding or collaboration between the two communities, either in the form of jointly undertaken research projects or team taught ESP courses. There is little shared interest in each other's practices. There is still very little understanding of what counts as specialist expertise in a particular professional community. For instance, it is important for ESP practitioners to understand the nature and acquisition of professional expertise in specialist disciplines in order to design and teach ESP programmes, but our understanding of the nature, function and acquisition of specialist knowledge is still very rudimentary.

(7) To negotiate interactions between discourse practices and professional practices

The tension between discursive practices and professional or organizational practices is probably one of the most difficult areas to handle. There seems to be little understanding of the two processes across disciplinary boundaries. Often it has been found that two disciplinary cultures do not even share the same language. The *identity* and *membership* of different professional communities are more likely to create tensions rather than bridge the gap between their varying epistemological orientations, even in a context in which it is advantageous for both to cooperate and collaborate (Sarangi 2000). One of the main concerns of any framework for studying discourse is to create a better understanding of the shared concerns of the two professional communities.

In the next section, we shall make an attempt to move towards such a challenge.

6.2   Towards a multi-perspective model

The seven main goals of genre-based analysis of written discourse identified here can be realized in terms of the three concepts of space (*textual, socio-cognitive*, which incorporates *tactical* and *professional*, and *social*) I have proposed in this study. Investigation of textual space invariably focuses on the surface of the text, which may include analyses of statistical significance of lexico-grammar based on a corpus of texts, textualization of lexico-grammatical resources used in the corpus, patterns of discoursal, rhetorical or cognitive structuring, and intertextuality as well as interdiscursivity, all analysed within the context of generic conventions and practices.

Although investigations within textual space have been very popular in applied linguistics, especially for their usefulness in the design of language teaching and learning courses for specific purposes, they have been found rather constraining for learners when they leave the academy and join the world of work. Nevertheless, such a textual perspective continues to be attractive and useful, though not sufficient on its own, from the point of view of applications to other contexts as well. One may find textual analyses of specific instances of texts too simple, and inadequate, often undermining the complex realities of language use in the world of professions. However, rigorous analyses of lexico-grammatical and discoursal aspects of data are a valuable resource, which can be useful in the identification of and accounting for the subtle variations within and across disciplinary and discourse domains. The analyses of large corpora, made possible in recent years, have been useful in the analysis of surface realities of large corpora of textual genres, which were unthinkable only a few years ago. Textual space also overlaps with socio-cognitive space to facilitate analyses of genres, especially in the area of cognitive or rhetorical move structures embedded in genre conventions.

Investigations of socio-cognitive dimensions of space primarily facilitate two major perspectives on genre construction and interpretation, ethnographic and socio-cognitive. Ethnographic investigations focus on typical sites of engagement or interaction (Scollon 1998), highlighting analysis and understanding of practitioner advice and guidance, social structure, interactions, history, beliefs, goals of the professional community, physical circumstances influencing genre construction and modes available for genre construction and communication, all in the context of the historical development of the genre in question.

Socio-cognitive perspective, on the other hand, leads to the identification and analysis of various aspects of the integrity of systems of genres employed as part of the typical discursive practices of specific disciplinary cultures. These involve not only the analysis of genre construction procedures, but also of audience reception procedures and insights. They may also include analysis of rhetorical strategies, as well as appropriation of generic resources to respond to familiar and novel rhetorical situations. In addition, socio-cognitive investigations typically encourage a community perspective on discourse practices as against a purely individual perspective. This is often done by grounding the regularities of textual patterns within the context of specific professional practices and disciplinary cultures, which often leads to a more realistic and comprehensive under-standing of professional or disciplinary goals and objectives.

Investigation of socio-cognitive or tactical space thus makes it possible for the discourse analyst to observe genres in action, and ground textual analysis in the interpretive ethnographic contexts of genre use, on the one hand, and in socio-cognitive analyses of the conditions under which specific professional practices take shape, on the other. Grounded and interpretive ethnographic investigations of professional practice are essential to any analysis and understanding of the discursive practices of a professional community. Pare and Smart (1994) convincingly demonstrate the usefulness of observing genres in action and grounding analyses beyond the regularities of textual organization to incorporate patterns of three other kinds, i.e. the patterns of the composing process involved in genre construction, the patterns in the reading practices used to interpret them, and the patterns of the social roles performed by the participants. Taking the genre of *the predisposition report*, which is 'written by a social worker as an advisory report to a judge on the sentencing of an adolescent found guilty of a criminal offence', they point out that the report can make better sense if one considers a number of interrelated patterns. The genre shows not only the typicality of structural organization, rhetorical moves and styles of writing, but also the typical roles assigned to individual participants in the production and use of the generic text, the typical patterns of composing processes involved (which may include an initiating event, an information gathering phase, some analysis of information, followed by individual writing and rewriting, followed by a number of collaborative tasks, culminat-ing in the technological production of the document), and the typical ways the reader approaches the text, negotiates his or her way to construct knowledge and finally uses the resulting knowledge.

Investigations of socio-cognitive or tactical space also lead one to go beyond the confines of typical professional or disciplinary practices, and consider their analyses within a wider network of socio-critical practices, which may include concepts such as ideology and power, wider social structures, social changes, more general social practices, identities and motives and cross-cultural and intercultural environment, within which most of these discursive and disciplinary practices and genres are more generally embedded. When Fairclough (1992) proposed a three-dimensional framework for critical discourse analysis, his primary concern was that the analysis of texts should not be artificially isolated from analysis of institutional and discoursal practices within which texts are embedded. Institutional and

162

discoursal practices in Fairclough (1992) include analyses of broader social and political structures, which we have identified separately within social space. Nevertheless, the necessity to explore 'the imbrications between language and social-institutional practices and between these, taken together, with broader social and political structures' (Candlin 1995: vii) can hardly be overemphasized. Hence the need to investigate not only the social space to analyse the issues related to language, ideology and power, but language and social structures, social changes, social identities and motives, too.

The investigations based on the model here provide a four-part multidimensional analytical perspective, which can be represented as in Diagram 6.1.

In order to analyse genre within the multidimensional perspective framework being proposed here, genre analysts need to employ a number of tools or instruments, in addition to those traditionally employed in linguistic and discourse analytical practice, often from disciplines other than linguistics and discourse analysis. Some of

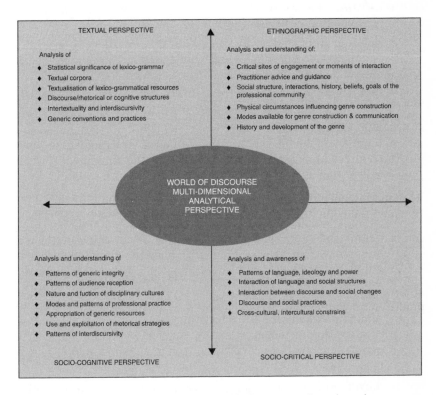

Diagram 6.1 *World of discourse multidimensional analytical perspective*

these I have discussed in Bhatia (1993: 22), but I would like to develop them further here.

(1) Placing the given genre-text in a situational context

(2) Surveying existing literature on:

- linguistic analyses of the genre in question or other related or similar genres;
- tools, methods or theories of linguistic/discourse/genre analysis which might be relevant to this situation;
- practitioner advice, guide books, manuals etc. relevant to the speech community in question;
- discussions of the social structure, interactions, history, beliefs, goals, etc. of the professional or academic community that uses the genre in question.

(3) Refining situational/contextual analysis

- defining the speaker/writer of the text, the audience, their relationship and their goals;
- defining the historical, socio-cultural, philosophic and/or occupational placement of the community in which the discourse takes place;
- identifying the network of surrounding texts and linguistic traditions that form the background to this particular genre-text; and
- identifying the topic/subject/extra-textual reality that the text is trying to represent, change or use and the relationship of the text to that reality.

(4) Selecting corpus
To select the right kind and size of the corpus, one may need to:

- define the genre/sub-genre that one is working with well enough so that it may be distinguishable from other genres either similar or closely related in some ways. The definition may be based on the communicative purposes and the situational context(s) in which it is generally used, and some distinctive textual characteristics of the genre-text or some combination of these;
- make sure that one's criteria for deciding whether a text belongs to a specific genre are clearly stated;
- decide on one's criteria for an adequate selection of the corpus for one's specific purpose(s). A long single typical text for

detailed analysis, a few randomly chosen texts for exploratory investigation, a large statistical sample to investigate a few specified features through easily identified indicators, etc.

(5) Textual, intertextual and interdiscursive perspective

- statistical significance of lexico-grammar
- text patterning or textualization
- cognitive or discourse structuring
- analysis of the role of intertextuality and interdiscursivity.

(6) Ethnographic analysis

This may focus on some of the following issues in the context of the typical sites of engagement:

- What physical circumstances influence the nature and construction of genre?
- What are the critical moments of engagement or interaction?
- What modes of genre construction or communication are available at the critical moments or sites?

Information on most of these aspects may be achieved through a set of ethnographical procedures, which may include the following:

- accounts of tools, methods or theories of linguistic, discourse and genre analysis conventionally used in discourse studies;
- accounts of practitioner advice, guide books, manuals written for members of the relevant professional discourse community in question, often describing and explaining what one may need to do in order to become initiated into a specific professional community;
- discussions of the social structure, interactions, history, beliefs, goals, etc. of the professional community that uses the genre or system of genres in question;
- detached observational accounts of expert behaviour. Since generic integrity is dynamic and often contested, rather than fixed, it is important that grounded ethnographic procedures, including detached participant observation of professional practice, be a crucial methodological procedure to serve this end. Long-term association with any context of professional site can often lead to personal involvement, which can lead to bias one way or the other, hence detachment is absolutely necessary;

- lived experiences of expert members of the community of practice. Genres are conventionalized discursive events, based on shared communicative purposes, but can be exploited for expressing private intentions, hence emphasis on institutional membership, historical accounts of discursive practices, and accumulated views on gate-keeping practices and power relationships at work can be very interesting and useful;

- convergent narrative accounts of first-hand experiences of active professionals. Genres are representations of social, institutional and professional practices, and hence there is a strong emphasis on the analysis of social, institutional and professional structures, roles, ideologies and distribution of power in specific professional contexts. Convergence on such perceptions is essential for this purpose and at this stage;

- textography of discursive practices (Swales 1998). Genres are social actions situated in disciplinary practices, and are products of the environment in which each takes shape. Investigating 'the discursive lives of individuals made within complexes of organized communications and social relations, mediated through writing' (Bazerman 1998), Swales adds a significant new dimension to our understanding of what we mean by a text being 'situated' in a particular context. He explains, 'On the one hand, I examine how writing is located within and along the evolution of a particular career; on the other, I try to place these various bodies of text both within a particular set of disciplinary norms and expectations, and within the local, institutional context of their production' (Swales 1998: 1).

(7) Studying institutional context

The study of institutional context may include the system and methodology in which the genre is used and the disciplinary conventions that govern the use of language in such institutional settings. These conventions are most often implicitly understood and unconsciously followed by the participants taking part in the communicative situation in which the genre in question is used, or even explicitly enforced in some institutional settings (e.g. cross-examination in the law court). Considerable information on these aspects of institutional contexts is available from guidebooks, manuals, practitioner advice and discussions of the social structure, interactions, history, beliefs and goals of the community etc. in published or otherwise available literature. This may also include the study of the organizational context, if that is seen to have influenced the genre construction in any way. This becomes particularly important if the data is collected from a specific organization; it is often found that they impose their own organizational constraints and prerequisites for genre construction. More specifically, studies, accounts or discussions of social structure and interactions, goals of disciplinary cultures, audience reception and relevant disciplinary cultures, etc. provide useful background knowledge against which analyses of genres can be adequately grounded. Besides, analyses of other texts that intertextually and interdiscursively contribute to the construction and interpretation of the genre in question can also be crucial. Studies of reading and interpretive behaviour can also contribute to an insightful analysis of the genre in question. These various research procedures can be visually represented as in Diagram 6.2.

Candlin, Bhatia and Jensen (2002) also emphasize the importance of grounding textual analysis of discourse as genre:

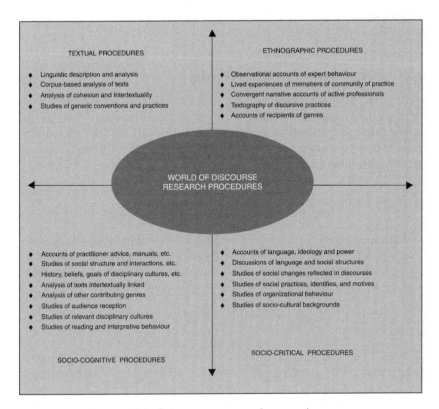

Diagram 6.2 *World of discourse research procedures*

> ... There will be a need to incorporate in such research into academic literacies explorations of social and social-psychological issues surrounding persons' identity and membership of particular academic disciplinary communities as these impinge on literacy practices, together with evaluations of the sources and exercises of authority over such persons and the determined relevance of their practices.

Multidimensional and multi-perspective approach to genre-based analysis of written discourse thus draws on several types of analytical data. It draws on textual data by treating genre as a reflection of discursive practices of disciplinary communities. It draws on ethno-graphic data, in that it seeks to observe genres in action, grounded in narrated insightful experiences of expert members of the community of practice. It also draws on socio-cognitive and institutional data, as it draws on historically and structurally grounded accounts of the conditions under which systems of genre are constructed, interpreted, used and exploited by expert members of disciplinary cultures to achieve their typical goals within the construct of their everyday professional activities.

6.3 Integrating perspectives

In order to illustrate some of the concerns of the multi-perspective and multi-dimensional analyses of genres in professional contexts, I would like to take up the following example of a publisher's blurb from the book jacket of *Genre Analysis: English in Academic and Research Settings*, by John M. Swales.

GENRE ANALYSIS
English in academic and research settings

Genre Analysis is the study of how language is used within a particular setting. It focuses on such issues as rhetorical styles and discourse types and relates research in socio-linguistics, text linguistics and discourse analysis to the study of specialist areas of language.

In Genre Analysis John Swales offers an approach to the understanding of academic discourse, and provides a theoretical framework which can be applied to a variety of practical situations such as the teaching of advanced writing and English for Academic Purposes. He demonstrates the value of genre analysis as a means of studying spoken and written discourse and shows how a genre-based approach can be used to shape language learning and development activities.

The book examines and develops the three key concepts of discourse community, genre and language learning task, each of which is extensively discussed and then defined. It goes on to explore a number of research genres with particular emphasis on the research article. Finally, it presents case studies of non-native student writing and examples of genre-based teaching materials designed to develop students' communicative competence in academic settings.

Genre Analysis will be important reading for all those directly involved in EAP and the analysis of academic discourse. It will also be of key interest to those working in post-secondary writing and composition.

John M. Swales is the Director of the English Language Institute and Professor of Linguistics at the University of Michigan.

For a multidimensional and multi-perspective analysis of this text as genre, one does not have to start in any specific way or at any specific point. Assuming that we have very little information about the genre in question, it is always advantageous to begin with some background information about the genre that this particular text seems to represent. Conventionally known as a publisher's blurb, it is often found on the book jacket. The genre has been in existence for quite some time now, and if one were to find the historical development of this genre, one could trace it back to the early twentieth century. The term is said to have been originated in 1907 by Gellett Burgess in a comic book jacket, which was decorated with a drawing of an extremely beautiful young lady whom he referred to as Miss Blurb. In 1914 in *Burgess Unabridged* he explained blurb as 'a flamboyant advertisement', 'an inspired testimonial' and 'fulsome praise', abounding in agile adjectives and adverbs, attesting that this book is the 'sensation of the year'. Similarly, Burchfield *et al.* (1972) defined blurb as 'a brief descriptive paragraph or note of the contents or characters of a book, printed as a commendatory advertisement, on the jacket or wrapper of a newly published book'. Coming to 1982, the *Longman Dictionary of Mass Media and Communication* reminds us that blurb is a 'commendatory publicity release or advertisement, one which is often inordinate in its praise or boosting of a new subject; also called PUFF PIECE, often appearing on a book jacket'. On the basis of information of this kind it is possible to find out a number of significant things about the background and origin of the genre. Let us now try to construct a general configuration of contextual features of this genre.

Communicative purpose:	Description and evaluation of the book in order to influence the future actions, attitudes and judgements of the readers.
Situation-type:	The message has to be brief, effective and adequate to fit the constraints of the book jacket.
Content:	To a large extent influenced by the subject matter of the book. However, there will be elements of description, which can be predictable. It will be interesting to see whether the content of blurbs of non-fictional and fictional books will be different. If so, in what respects will they differ?
Participants:	It is a bit difficult to decide who actually writes the blurb. Is it the author of the book or the publisher? Or may both of them have a role to play?
Medium/Channel:	Mainly written medium. It allows the writer to develop topics, issues and arguments as fully as necessary. A necessary consequence of this, from the readers' point of view, is that the written medium reflects avoidance of textual patterns of repetition and predominance of grammatical metaphor (Halliday 1994: 342) thus requiring frequent unpacking of content.

The blurb taken as illustration here represents an attractive, favourable and positive 'academic description' of the book. It is interesting to note the nature and range of adjectives, complex-nominals and verbs, all typical of academic writing used throughout the text. We will come back to a fuller discussion of the nature of these adjectives later, but at this stage I would like to see how an attractive, favourable and positive and yet *academic description* of the book is realized through the use of a range of adjectives, complex-nominals and verbs, all typical of academic writing.

- *study* of how language is used within a *particular setting*

- issues as *rhetorical styles* ... *discourse types* ... relates research ... *socio-linguistics* ... *text-linguistics* ... *discourse analysis*
- *offers* an approach to *the understanding of academic discourse*
- *provides* a *theoretical framework*
- *demonstrates* the *value of genre analysis* as a means of studying spoken and written discourse
- *shows* how *a genre-based approach* can ... *shape language learning and development* ...
- *develops* ... *key concepts* of *discourse community, genre and language learning task*
- *extensively discussed and defined*
- *explore a number of research genres*
- *presents case studies*
- *designed to develop* students' *communicative competence* in *academic settings*
- *important reading* for those directly involved in *EAP* and the *analysis of academic discourse* ... *of key interest* to those working *in post-secondary writing and composition.*

It is interesting to note the range of verbs such as *offers, provides, demonstrates, develops, discussed and defined, explore,* etc. used in conjunction with nominals like *setting, rhetorical styles, discourse types, theoretical framework, genre analysis, language learning and development, key concepts of discourse community, case studies, communicative competence in academic settings, analysis of academic discourse, post-secondary writing and composition,* etc. to develop academic discourse. It is also interesting to see that as the discourse develops, the nominals also become increasingly complex, from a *setting* to *communicative competence in academic settings, key concepts of discourse community, language learning and development,* etc. an unmistakable sign of academic research writing (Bhatia 1992, 1993). These nominals signal a number of interesting things about the text: firstly, from lexical choice one can safely predict that the text belongs to an academic research genre; and secondly, on the basis of an overwhelming use of positive adjectives it can be further concluded that it is predominantly promotional in its communicative objectives. One could go beyond these indications to analyse the exact nature of potential audiences being targeted, especially the nature of the sub-discipline, the level of the audience, the nature of the writer–audience relationship, etc. One could then go beyond it as well to see how the text has been structured or organized, to analyse the nature of what we have referred to in this book as its typical move structure.

GENRE ANALYSIS **English in academic and research settings**	Headline
Genre Analysis is the study of how language is used within a particular setting. It focuses on such issues as rhetorical styles and discourse types and relates research in socio-linguistics, text-linguistics and discourse analysis to the study of specialist areas of language.	**Establishing field**
In Genre Analysis John Swales offers an approach to the understanding of academic discourse, and provides a theoretical framework which can be applied to a variety of practical situations such as the teaching of advanced writing and English for Academic Purposes. He demonstrates the value of genre analysis as a means of studying spoken and written discourse and shows how a genre-based approach can be used to shape language learning and development activities.	**Appraising the book** *Previewing the book* *Indicating value of the book*
The book examines and develops the three key concepts of discourse community, genre and language learning task, each of which is extensively discussed and then defined. It goes on to explore a number of research genres with particular emphasis on the research article. Finally, it presents case studies of non-native student writing and examples of genre-based teaching materials designed to develop students' communicative competence in academic settings.	*Describing the book*
Genre Analysis will be important reading for all those directly involved in EAP and the analysis of academic discourse. It will also be of key interest to those working in post-secondary writing and composition.	**Targeting the market**
John M. Swales is the Director of the English Language Institute and Professor of Linguistics at the University of Michigan.	**Establishing credentials**

172

In order to see how closely blurbs resemble each other in terms of their disciplinary characteristics, particularly in terms of their lexical choice, I would like to consider another blurb from an area of study that is very much similar to the one we have just looked at. This time it is James Paul Gee's *An Introduction to Discourse Analysis*, published more recently. Here's the text of the blurb.

An Introduction to Discourse Analysis

"If you only read one book on discourse analysis, this is the one to read. Gee shows us that discourse analysis is about a lot more than linguistic study; it's about how to keep from, as he says, 'getting physically, socially, culturally, or morally "bitten" by the world'."
Ron Scollon, Georgetown University

James Paul Gee presents here his unique integrated approach to discourse analysis: the analysis of spoken and written language as it is used to enact social and cultural perspectives and identities.

Assuming no prior knowledge of linguistics, James Paul Gee presents both a theory of language-in-use, as well as a method of research. This method is made up of a set of "tools of inquiry" and strategies for using them.

Clearly structured and written in highly accessible style, the book presents these tools of inquiry alongside the theory of language-in-use. They are then placed in the framework of an overall approach to discourse analysis. Finally an extended example of discourse analysis is presented using some of the tools and strategies developed earlier in the book.

Perspectives from a variety of approaches and disciplines, including applied linguistics, education, psychology, anthropology, and communication, are incorporated to help students and scholars from a range of backgrounds formulate their own views on discourse and engage in their own discourse analyses.

James Paul Gee is the Tashia Morgridge Professor of Reading at the University of Wisconsin at Madison. His previous publications include *Social Linguistics and Literacies, The Social Mind*, and *The New Work Order* (with Glynda Hull and Colin Lankshear).

Since both the blurbs are written for books in the same field, they resemble each other very much in terms of their lexico-grammatical realizations as well as in their rhetorical structuring, except that in the second one we have an additional move that can be viewed as an *endorsement* from an established authority in the field, very much like *celebrity endorsements* in commercial advertisements. So if one were to assign a move structure to this blurb, it will be somewhat like the following:

An Introduction to Discourse Analysis	**Headline**
"If you only read one book on discourse analysis, this is the one to read. Gee shows us that discourse analysis is about a lot more than linguistic study; it's about how to keep from, as he says, 'getting physically, socially, culturally, or morally "bitten" by the worlds'." Ron Scollon, Georgetown University	**Endorse-ment**
James Paul Gee presents here his unique integrated approach to discourse analysis: the analysis of spoken and written language as it is used to enact social and cultural perspectives and identities.	**Appraising the book** *Previewing the book*
Assuming no prior knowledge of linguistics, James Paul Gee presents both a theory of language-in-use, as well as a method of research. This method is made up of a set of "tools of inquiry" and strategies for using them.	*Describing the book*
Clearly structured and written in highly accessible style, the book presents these tools of inquiry along-side the theory of language-in-use. They are then placed in the framework of an overall approach to discourse analysis. Finally an extended example of discourse analysis is presented using some of the tools and strategies developed earlier in the book.	*Indicating value of the book*
Perspectives from a variety of approaches and dis-ciplines, including applied linguistics, education, psychology, anthropology, and communication, are incorporated to help students and scholars from a range of backgrounds formulate their own views on discourse and engage in their own discourse analyses.	**Targeting the market**
James Paul Gee is the Tashia Morgridge Professor of Reading at the University of Wisconsin at Madison. His previous publications include *Social Linguistics and Literacies*, *The Social Mind*, and *The New Work Order* (with Glynda Hull and Colin Lankshear).	**Establishing credentials**

Following Kathpalia (1992) and Bhatia (1993), it is possible to assign the following six-move structure to typical instances of blurbs:

- headlines: *reader attraction*
- justifying the book *by establishing field, establishing a niche*
- appraising the book *by presenting a preview, describing the book, and indicating value of the book*
- establishing credentials
- endorsements
- targeting the market

One may also notice that the moves do not necessarily occur in the same order in all cases, and may not occur all at the same time. There may be variations depending upon the nature of the book, the target audience, the publishing house responsible for it and above all the kind of discipline it belongs to. Headlines, for example, are more common in bestsellers than in academic research books. Endorsements are also common in second editions, rather than the very first ones, as these are generally appropriated from reviews of the first edition. Sometimes, when forewords are written by established academics other than the author, extracts from such forewords are used as endorsements. Similarly, moves can be discontinuous or embedded one with the other, especially in the case of book justification and appraisal.

Let us look at some of the predominant lexico-grammatical features of the text, in particular the nature of nominals and adjectives:

- unique integrated approach to discourse analysis
- analysis of spoken and written language
- enact social and cultural perspectives and identities
- prior knowledge of linguistics
- a theory of language-in-use, as well as a method of research
- method is ... a set of "tools of inquiry" and strategies for using them
- tools of inquiry alongside the theory of language-in-use
- the framework of an overall approach to discourse analysis
- an extended example of discourse analysis
- the tools and strategies developed ... in the book
- perspectives from a variety of approaches and disciplines
- applied linguistics, education, psychology, anthropology, and communication

175

The broad outline of analysis suggested so far is in line with much of the established work on genre analysis. However, one does not need to stop there, and perhaps would like to extend the investigation more centrally to the socio-cognitive and socio-critical space, focusing on areas of intertextuality and interdiscursivity that may not be obvious on the surface. An interesting line of research would be to investigate the relationship between book reviews and the blurb, on the one hand, and book reviews and book introductions of various kinds (forewords, prefaces, introductions, etc.) on the other. Some of these investigations may lead one into areas of interdiscursivity highlighting appropriation of generic resources from the genre of marketing and advertising and the mixing of informative and purely promotional genres, such as advertising. One could also investigate disciplinary variations within book blurbs. To take just one simple instance of disciplinary variation, I will take up another blurb, this time of a fiction bestseller by Jeffrey Archer.

A MATTER OF HONOR

As Adam Scott opens the yellowed envelope bequeathed to him in his father's will, incredible drama begins. The terrible secret that shadowed his father's military career unfolds a time bomb of intrigue, passion, and greed, reaching back to the Nazi plunder of Europe ... into the mysterious heart of Tsarist Russia. In the deepest vault of a Swiss bank, Scott discovers a priceless icon, the key to an amazing document that could forever change the balance of power between America and the Soviet Union. Few men know of its existence. All will kill for it.

When his lover is brutally murdered, Scott is forced to flee across Europe, fighting desperately for his life against the KGB, the CIA, and even his own countrymen.

A MATTER OF HONOR is a novel of spine-tingling danger and unrelenting suspense, shocking climax ... Jeffrey Archer once again at the top of his form.

Without going into any detailed structural description or extensive lexico-grammatical analysis of the two blurbs, where I am sure one will find interesting analytical comparative insights, I would like to compare just the nominals in the two descriptions. Although both the blurbs are rich in terms of their use of nominals incorporating adjectives indicating positive book descriptions, the nature of nominals, especially the adjectives, are very different. Let me compare some of them here.

A Matter of Honor	An Introduction of Discourse Analysis
• the yellowed envelope • his father's will • incredible drama • The terrible secret • a time bomb of intrigue, passion, and greed, • the Nazi plunder of Europe • the mysterious heart of Tsarist Russia • the deepest vault of a Swiss bank • a priceless icon • the key to an amazing document • the KGB, the CIA, • a novel of spine-tingling danger and unrelenting suspense, shocking climax	• unique integrated approach • social and cultural perspectives and identities • prior knowledge of linguistics • theory of language-in-use • tools of inquiry alongside the theory of language-in-use • framework of an overall approach to discourse analysis • extended example of discourse analysis • the tools and strategies • perspectives from a variety of approaches and disciplines • applied linguistics, education, psychology, anthropology, and communication

Looking at the list above, *A Matter of Honor* contains nominals such as 'yellowed envelope', 'father's will', 'priceless icon', mostly related to mundane everyday life, on the one hand, but at the same time, there is an extensive use of nominals such as 'incredible drama', 'the terrible secret', 'time bomb of intrigue, passion, and greed', 'the Nazi plunder of Europe', 'mysterious heart of Tsarist Russia', and the one that gives it away is 'a novel of spine-tingling danger and unrelenting suspense, shocking climax'. Although the book is concerned with the realities of everyday life, these realities are made mysterious, suspenseful and spine-tingling, all of which indicate a fictional world of mystery, suspense and intrigue, a perfect combination for a bestseller. Compared to this *An Introduction of Discourse Analysis* is a 'unique world of research in applied linguistics, education, psychology, anthropology, and communication'. It offers 'socio-cultural perspectives and identities', 'the tools and strategies', etc. all within and as part of 'a framework for discourse analysis'. It offers 'a theory of language use', but 'requires no prior knowledge of linguistics'.

Although both the blurbs realize the same communicative purpose and represent the same genre, and even share similar grammatical resources, the choice of lexis makes them very different in terms of their disciplinary affiliation and use of persuasive appeals, indicating differences in the choice of audience. Like the use of nominals in blurbs from academic books and thrillers, one might like to investigate the use of nominals in promoting books and cosmetics, the use of language in books blurbs and book reviews from the same discipline, strategies in promoting classics and books by new authors, or classical fiction and detective fiction. Many of these are quite legitimate areas of investigation, and have been studied as part of genre analytical framework. However, it is also possible, and often necessary, to look at critical or socio-cognitive aspects of the construction and interpretation of blurbs, relating them to professional constraints, highlighting in particular the processes of discourse construction and reception. In order to investigate some of these perspectives, one will have to address questions such as the following:

- Are these blurbs seen embedded more in marketing practices or academic practices?
- Who are responsible for writing the blurbs?
- Is it often the publisher, as it may seem, or the author?
- Or is it written collaboratively? If so, who contributes what at what stage, and who has the final say?
- What kind of social and/or professional relationship develops between the writer and the publisher as a result of this collaboration? Do different publishers have different policies?
- As compared with new writers, especially the first-timers, how are established writers treated? Are there any areas of conflict?
- How are the audiences selected?
- Is there any possibility of conflict in the selection of audience?
- How do audiences receive such blurbs? Are these like advertisements? How many people actually read these blurbs before they buy the book?
- Is there any indication of appropriation of linguistic or other resources from the world of marketing?

The list is not intended to be exhaustive but just indicative of the kinds of questions one may be tempted to investigate in an attempt to provide explanatory answers to some of the questions that might legitimately be raised on the basis of a detailed textual analysis of blurbs as genre. In order to investigate these and many other questions

178

of this kind, one may need to resort to what I have suggested as a multi-perspective and multidimensional analytical framework incorporating a number of research procedures discussed above, in particular the use of socio-cognitive and ethnographic procedures to relate discursive practices of professionals with their professional practices.

In short, the integration of analytical tools suggested here should not be seen at the expense of the textual analysis that we have always been relying on for so long. Textual analysis gives us information about the use of lexico-grammatical and rhetorical resources, however it tells us very little about the use and success of the text when actually exploited in real life contexts and what could be called the 'rhetorical performance' of the text, which can be studied only by going beyond the text to genre and professional practice. How do we then study text as part of professional practice? As indicated above, genre is a rhetorical strategy used within a professional culture to organize knowledge in the form of professional action to achieve the objectives of professional communities. Genres in this way tell us how professional communities develop, use and exploit genres to construct professional knowledge to conduct their specific business. Genres, in other words, are constructions of professional community discourse whose meaning is created by and for the consumption of the members of the professional community. This implies that any comprehensive and useful understanding of discourses of this kind must necessarily be informed by the perceptions, experiences and practices of the professional community. Smart (1998) proposes the use of 'interpretive ethnography' to investigate the network of shared meanings that constitute reality within a professional community. This also allows us to study how members of a specific professional community participate in knowledge-producing and knowledge-consuming activities within their professional culture, which he rightly claims will help us understand more fully the community's meaning-making activity. Interpretive ethnography makes use of the following to make sense of it all:

- convergent data, which may include both oral and written genres, including the first-hand experiences of the community members and their specialist terminology and stories about the historical development of the community;
- convergent perspectives, which offer commonalities across informants' first-order constructs, which point to significant areas of intersubjectivity;
- observed areas of intersubjectivity, which help the researcher to map out the community's ideology, which is a form of 'social construction of reality'.

179

Interpretive ethnography is thus intended to map out the ideology of the discourse community through extended social engagement with informants. However, Smart (1998) is quick to caution that this must be done in such a way that one preserves an adequate 'distance' from the ideology of the community so as to gain sufficient 'analytic space' to work in as one develops an account or representation of the culture. This requires achieving a balance between engagement and detachment in exploring the ideology of the community, because in the community one may always find large areas of convergence but also signs of divergence, because key aspects of ideology are invariably both supported and contested within the profession.

To sum up, it is necessary to maintain a balance of engagement with and detachment from the local reality of the community, to portray the community in a way that encompasses both the intersubjectivity which enables intellectual collaboration and the differences which animate it.

In another interesting study of the significance of ethnographic procedures under the name of 'textography', Swales (1998) traces 'the journey into the textual lives of artifacts produced by members of three different discourse communities' (Bazerman 1998). Through analysis of texts, textual forms and systems of texts he studies the lives, life commitments and life projects of members of these communities, which share the same building. He points out that although people share the same building, their textual lives are maintained in different times and spaces, measured by the dimensions of their knowledge production and consumption, through texts they produce and circulate. He also finds interesting evidence to support the claim that the domains of text, time and space are differentiated and constrained by their different disciplinary cultures.

Similarly, drawing on Layder's (1993) 'resource map' for research on lawyer–client discourse, Candlin (2002) also suggests a multi-perspective approach seen from the point of view of the analyst, who attempts to explain 'motivational relevances' and 'practical relevance' in relation to participants' perspectives. In doing so, the analyst attempts to integrate the conventional *textual perspective* with three other perspectives, namely a *social action perspective*, which according to him 'interprets action as socially-situated practice', a *social/ institutional perspective*, which 'explains the contextual conditions in which discursive practices arise', and a *participants' perspective*, which 'recounts participants' interpretations' of discursive practices. All these multiple perspectives on the *discursive practices* of institutional cultures put together create the world of the analyst. Interactions between these different perspectives motivate several kinds of interdiscursive relations, through which the analyst seeks to explain his or her analytical insights into the discursive practices associated with specific institutions.

Using a combination of some or all of the procedures discussed here, it is possible to arrive at different methodological frameworks, depending upon the nature of the task and the applications intended. However, I must end the chapter with a word of caution that as we move from a textually oriented analysis of specific instances of genres towards a more multidimensional and multi-perspective analysis of complex realities of professional discourses, we are more likely to find increasing flexibility, fluidity and tentativeness in our understanding of generic integrity. This may be a consequence of blurred boundaries between genres, increasing tendencies toward mixing and embedding of genres, and a natural inclination on the part of expert users of language for innovation and creativity in their construction as well as consumption of genres in real-life contexts.

THE WORLD OF
APPLICATIONS

7 Applications of genre theory

Genre knowledge plays an important role in the packing and unpacking of texts used in wide-ranging institutional and professional contexts. If on the one hand it imposes constraints on an uninitiated genre writer to conform to the conventions and rhetorical expectations of the relevant professional community, on the other hand it also allows an experienced and established writer of the genre to exploit conventions to create new forms to suit specific contexts. However, this privilege of exploiting generic conventions to create new forms becomes available only to those few who enjoy a certain degree of visibility in the relevant professional community; for a wide majority of others, it is more a matter of apprenticeship in accommodating the expectations of disciplinary cultures. This section reviews current research to investigate the way the power and the politics of genre are often exploited by the so-called established membership of disciplinary communities to keep outsiders at a safe distance.

All discourse forms, especially those used in institutionalized contexts, are socially constructed and negotiated. At the very heart of most frameworks for the analysis of discourse, especially as genre, is the belief that there is nothing like a universal form of discourse for structuring knowledge. There can only be a 'consensus or an agreement' (Bruffee 1986: 777) among the members of specific disciplinary communities to express their concerns in specific discursive forms. Goodrich (1987) explains this institutionalization of discoursal practices in terms of 'social authorship' as against the more familiar subjective authorship.

> The right to a discourse is organized and restricted by a wide variety of means, to particular roles, statuses, professions and so on. Similarly the institutionalisation of discourse is limited in terms of its legitimate appropriation, and the restrictive situations of its reception – church, court, school, hustings and so on.

Foucault (1981) also sees social authorship of discourse in terms of two interrelated aspects. The first one, according to him, is:

> Who is speaking? Who, among the totality of speaking individuals, is accorded the right to use this sort of language? Who is qualified to do so? Who derives from it his own special quality, his prestige, and from whom, in return, does he receive if not the assurance, at least the presumption that what he says is true? What is the status of the individual who – alone – has the right, sanctioned by law or tradition, juridically defined or spontaneously accepted, to proffer such a discourse?

The second he explains in terms of institutional sites from which the authorized speaker makes his discourse and from which the discourse derives its 'legitimate source and point of application'.

Like other forms of discourse, genres are also socially constructed and even more intimately controlled by social practices. Genres are the media through which members of professional or academic communities communicate with each other. They are, as Berkenkotter and Huckin (1995) point out, 'intimately linked to a discipline's methodology, and they package information in ways that conform to a discipline's norms, values and ideology'.

Myers also points out:

> Disciplines are like cultures in that their members have shared, taken for granted beliefs; these beliefs can be mutually incomprehensible between cultures; these beliefs are encoded in a language; they are embodied in practices; new members are brought into culture through rituals.
>
> (Myers 1995: 5)

The consensus is arrived at and negotiated through professional conversations and practices amongst the informed and practising members of a professional community. Interactions and conversations enable consensus, on the one hand, and have a regulatory or limiting effect on the other as to what should or should not be admitted into a community's body of knowledge.

Genres, in other words, are socially authorized through conventions, which, in turn, are embedded in the discursive practices of members of specific disciplinary cultures. These discursive practices reflect not only conventions used by disciplinary communities, but also social conventions, including social changes, social institutions and social knowledge, all of which, in a way, could be seen as significantly contributing to what in genre theory is regarded as 'genre knowledge'. Genres are products of an understanding or a prior knowledge of disciplinary or institutional conventions, which are responsible for regulating generic constructs, giving them an identity and internal ordering.

Although generic forms are products of conventional knowledge embedded in disciplinary cultures, they are dynamic constructs. As discussed in earlier chapters, typical realizations of these institutionalized forms are often characterized by their generic integrity, on the one hand, and their propensity for innovation, on the other. As Dubrow (1982: 39) points out, 'a concern for generic traditions, far from precluding originality, often helps to produce it'. Similarly, Fowler says:

> Far from inhibiting the author, genres are a positive support. They offer room, as one might say, for him to write in – a habitation of mediated definiteness; a proportioned mental space; a literary matrix by which to order his experience during composition. ...
> The writer is invited to match experience and form in a specific yet undetermined way. Accepting the invitation does not solve his problems of expression. ... But it gives him access to formal ideas as to how a variety of constituents might suitably be combined. Genre also offers a challenge by provoking a free spirit to transcend the limitations of previous examples.
>
> (Fowler 1982: 31)

In fact, a subtle exploitation of a certain aspect of generic construct is always seen as tactically superior and effective. It is almost like the advertiser's exploitation of the cliché *The shape of things to come* in the following opening headline of an advertisement for a car, which goes like this: *The shape of things to come: Mitsubishi Cordia*. Or the use of the famous statement about the British colonial empire in the Lufthansa advertisement, *The sun never sets on Lufthansa territory*, or in the following slogan for energy conservation, which says *Don't be fuelish*, where the idea of waste of energy is lost unless it is associated with 'Don't be foolish'. Another example from an advertisement for a hotel makes use of the association of Easter with eggs to promote accommodation during Easter holidays:

Give yourself and your family
an eggscuse to *eggsplore* an *eggstraordinary*
holiday this *Easter.*

At the Gold Coast Hotel, Hong Kong's first resort hotel,
our *EASTER EGGSCAPE* package offers an *eggscellent* combination of
a Superior Room, daily breakfast, free ferry rides/carparking, and use of
recreational facilities.
All at the *eggsceptional* price of....

To reinforce the association between Easter and eggs, the new coinages are all highlighted in italics. Obviously, anyone who is not familiar with this association would find this advertisement rather strange. The important point about such associations is that they communicate best in the context of what is already familiar. In such contexts, words, on their own, carry no meanings; it is the experience that gives them the desired effect. Therefore, if one is not familiar with the original, the value of the novel expression is undermined. Just as the advertiser makes use of the well-known and the familiar in existing knowledge, a clever genre writer makes use of what is conventionally available to a discourse community to further his or her own subtle ends. The innovation, the creativity or the exploitation becomes effective only in the context of the already available and familiar. Therefore the constraints on generic construction, or the pre-knowledge of it, gives power to insiders of specific discourse communities, and the understanding of such processes of exploitation of this power to achieve familiar or not-so-familiar novel objectives is one of the main concerns of genre theory.

The other interesting area of generic power and control, although within a restricted range, we find in organizational preferences. In the case of academic publications, we often come across preferred house styles. Although every single journal claims to have its own style sheet, most of them can be characterized more by their overlap rather than their distinct variations.

Similarly, in the case of newspaper genres, such as news reports and editorials, we find that newspapers have their own preferences in style, stance and substance. Some may be more objective, while others more interpretive, some more socially responsible, while others more sensational. In spite of all these differences, most of them display common characteristics in terms of their use of generic resources, in terms of their structure, interpretation and communication of intentions. Their somewhat different orientations to the events of the day do not mark their stories as very different in terms of their generic form.

Even in the case of business communities, we often find different organizations displaying their unique identities through their organizational preferences in the matters of their choice of generic forms, but the broad range of genres they tend to exploit to further their organizational objectives shows remarkable similarities because it encompasses instances of similar genres. All these areas of generic use indicate that although their preferred generic forms show subtle degrees of variation for what could be seen as 'tactical advantage', they never disregard some of the basic features of individual generic constructs, which give these genres their essential identities.

7.1 The power and politics of genre

Language is power, and the power of language is the 'power of genre'. Power of genre is not only to construct, use, interpret and exploit genres, but also to innovate novel generic forms. This is the function of the knowledge of genre, which is accessible only to the expert members of disciplinary communities. How do these disciplinary communities maintain what we have called generic integrity in their discursive practices and, by employing these discursive practices, maintain their professional and personal identities and at the same time achieve their disciplinary goals? Let me consider the academic community first.

(A) Academic culture

EDITORIAL INTERVENTION

In some forms of academic discourse, especially the research articles, one can generally see two kinds of mechanisms in place to ensure generic integrity: the peer review process and the editorial intervention. Both these mechanisms, though operating at different levels, are actively invoked to ensure that all accounts of new knowledge conform to the standards of institutionalized behaviour that is expected by a community of established peers in a specific discipline. Although individual judgements can vary within the membership of specific disciplinary communities, a high degree of consensus is often ensured by selecting like-minded scholars from within well-defined disciplinary boundaries. If one surveys a few journals that regularly publish articles on discourse analysis, one is likely to find that although all of them publish articles on various aspects of discourse, they have their own set of reviewers to certify accounts of knowledge claims for inclusion in the journals. If one encounters names like Cazden, Geertz, Goffman, Gumperz, Hymes, Milroy, Saville-Troike, Scollon, Tannen and Zimmerman on the editorial committee of a journal, one could safely guess that they will be unlikely to accept articles outside a sociolinguistic orientation to discourse analysis. Articles on other aspects of discourse are more likely to be discouraged and even rejected. If on the other hand, one finds names like Ackerman, Bazerman, Berkenkotter, Comprone, Doheny-Farina, Huckin, Linda Flower, Miller or Odell, one would expect them to welcome papers with a strong rhetorical orientation. Similarly, if one finds names like Christie, Halliday, Hasan, Kress, Martin and Rothery, one will come to the inevitable conclusion that the journal will favour a more systemic orientation to discourse. Prospective authors in discourse studies choose their

189

journals carefully keeping in view their loyalty to any of these traditions. After peer review, the next important intervention comes from the editors, who enjoy all the power one can imagine to maintain the identity and integrity of the research article genre. Berkenkotter and Huckin (1995) document an in-depth and fascinating study of this kind of editorial control to maintain generic integrity. They point out that for the construction and dissemination of knowledge 'textual activity' is as important as the 'scientific activity'.

CITATIONS AND REFERENCES

The second indication of the power of genre is illustrated in the importance of citations and references in research publications. Swales (1981a) was probably the first one to study at length the description of previous research in the rhetorical activity of knowledge dissemination as distinct from knowledge creation. In order to become acceptable to the community of fellow researchers, one must relate his or her knowledge claims to the accumulated knowledge of others in the discipline, without which his or her claims in the field are unlikely to find recognition through publication. In this context it is hardly surprising that literature review occupies an important place in the researcher's repertoire of skills in most academic disciplines. Referring to the importance of citation in scientific research activity, Amsterdamska and Leydesdorff point out:

> In a scientific article 'the new encounters the old' for the first time. This encounter has a double significance since articles not only justify the new by showing that the result is warranted by experiment or observation or previous theory, but also place and integrate innovations into the context of 'old' and accepted knowledge.... References which appear in the text are the most explicit manner in which the arguments presented in the article are portrayed as linked to other texts, and thus also to a particular body of knowledge.
>
> (Amsterdamska and Leydesdorff 1989: 451)

A necessary consequence of such requirements for the acceptance of academic claims by the wider professional community is that sometimes these requirements lead to undesirable gate-keeping. Berkenkotter and Huckin (1995) in their study of such a process at an academic convention, i.e. the study of abstracts submitted for the Conference on College Composition and Communication (CCCC), discuss interesting instances of the power of generic control in well-defined contexts. On the basis of their analysis of the process of the selection of papers for the CCCC convention, they claim that:

190

1. The high-rated abstracts all addressed topics of current <u>interest</u> <u>to active, experienced members of the rhetoric and composi-</u> <u>tion community</u>; the low-rated abstracts often did not.
2. Almost all of the high-rated abstracts <u>clearly defined a problem</u>; the low-rated abstracts often did not.
3. The high-rated abstracts all <u>discussed this problem in a way</u> <u>that would be seen by experienced insiders as novel and</u> <u>therefore interesting</u>, whereas virtually none of the low-rated abstracts did.
4. The high-rated abstracts usually <u>projected more of an insider</u> <u>ethos</u> through the use of terminology, special topoi, and/or explicit or implicit references to the scholarly literature of the field than did the low-rated abstracts.

(Berkenkotter and Huckin 1995: 102, emphasis added)

They also point out that often 'the genre was shaped significantly by the interests of the program chair'. This is generally done through the theme statement issued when papers are invited for the convention. Depending upon the interests of the program chair or of the discourse community one represents, the emphasis can shift from one year to the other. Based on their study of CCCC abstracts for four years between 1988 and 1992, they find two main levels of gate-keeping:

> (a) the external reviewers and (b) the program chair. We have observed many cases where the reviewers rated an abstract Excellent and yet it was not included in the program. Presumably, the chair disagreed with the reviewers' judgements. ... In short, each convention bears the stamp of its principal gatekeeper.

They further point out that:

> In one particularly unfortunate case, a very interesting abstract was submitted to the Technical Communication area one year, where it received an Excellent rating from a reviewer and the program chair but was not included in the program (presumably because of a bad 'fit'). It was revised slightly and resubmitted the following year to the Discourse Analysis area. Again it received an Excellent rating, but again it was not included in the program. The author of this abstract probably never knew that she had written an outstanding abstract. All she would have been told was that her paper had been rejected for the program.
>
> (Berkenkotter and Huckin 1995: 115)

Another interesting case of such a gate-keeping encounter, though of a slightly different nature, between two different discourse groups was referred to by William Bright (1996). Giving his view of 30 years of American Linguistics, he referred to the following extract from a letter written by Chomsky:

> ... the level of rumour-mongering and of personal hostility ... outright falsification so scandalous that they raise serious questions about the integrity of the field ... I do not want to be associated with a journal ... which publishes flat lies ... couched in rhetoric of a sort that might be appropriate to some criminal, but that one is surprised to find in a scholarly journal.

It is not surprising that Chomsky never published in the journal, not because he was kept out, but he decided to keep himself out. Gate-keeping obviously can work both ways. Let me now turn to another professional context.

(B) Legal culture

SHARED KNOWLEDGE – PRIVILEGED ACCESS TO INFORMATION

If generic conventions, on the one hand, give suitable expression to the communicative intentions of genre writers (who are members of a particular discourse community), then on the other hand, they also match their intentions against their intended reader's expectations. This is possible only when all the participants share not only the code, but also the knowledge of the genre, which includes the knowledge about its construction, interpretation and use. A necessary implication of this shared genre knowledge is that it is not routinely available to the outsiders, which creates a kind of social distance between the legitimate members of a discourse community and those who are considered outsiders. Although this creates conditions of homogeneity between the insiders, it also increases social distance between them and the outsiders, sometimes resulting in disastrous consequences for the one who does not have access to such shared knowledge, which could be in the form of linguistic resources used to construct a generic form, or it could be in the awareness of the rules of language use, some of which are socially learnt, while others can be legally enforced, such as the ones associated with courtroom procedures. Allen and Guy (1989) report an excellent example of the lack of shared knowledge from their account of the courtroom interaction:

> An off-duty policeman in a store had shot and killed an intruder. Investigation had shown a set of burglar tools at the back of the store. The prosecutor was trying to show that there was no ground

for presuming criminal intent, and that this was cold-blooded murder. The victim's wife was testifying for the prosecution. Here she is being cross-examined by the defense.

Defense Lawyer: *Could you tell the court and the jury what your husband's occupation was?*
Wife: *He was a burglar.*

This supported the defense's contention of criminal intent, and secured acquittal for the policeman.

        (Worthington, 1984, personal communication)

If only the wife had been slightly more familiar with the conventions of the courtroom examination, the task of the defence lawyer would not have become that easy. Another example of the use of privileged access to knowledge can be illustrated by the following headline from an advertisement for 'The Schroder Singapore Trust', which reads,

The Schroder Singapore Trust Has Grown Over 60% in 3 Years

The information here can be extremely misleading, except to those who are well aware of the discursive practices of the professional community of financial managers. Anybody trying to make sense of this statement should know that this 60 per cent growth in three years couldn't be taken at its face value. Although it carries the usual statutory disclaimer in the form of a note in small print saying, 'Past performance is not necessarily a guide to future performance, the price of units may fall as well as rise and cannot be guaranteed', a lay person might still be led to think that his investment will probably get him close to 60 per cent return. The fact, on the other hand, could be that the unit value might have declined by more than 60 per cent in the last one-year or so, and may still be showing the downward trend at the time of the advertisement. There could be several other possible scenarios which will only be accessible to those with the inside knowledge of the way these genres function.

POWER AND CONTROL IN LEGISLATIVE CONTEXT

One of the most noticeable characteristics of any professional community is the availability and typical use of a range of genres, which serve the goals of the community. The recurrent use of such discoursal forms creates solidarity within its membership giving them their most powerful weapon to keep the outsiders at a safe distance. If it is true of other professions, it is all the more true of the legal profession. The main purpose of legislation is to govern the behaviour

193

of individuals and institutions in society through the use of rules and regulations. In order to keep control firmly in the hands of the legislature rather than the judiciary in a parliamentary democracy, statutory acts are written not only clearly, precisely and unambiguously but also all-inclusively. This rigour and adequate specification of scope in legislation helps the legislature to control a totally subjective and idiosyncratic interpretation of the statute book.

In this context, it is hardly surprising that most of the attempts by the powerful reformist lobbies in many western democracies to introduce plain English in legislative contexts are seen as imposition from outside and have been firmly rejected by the professional legal community. All attempts to reform legislative language, including the ones by the plain English campaign (see Thomas 1985; Eagleson 1988; Kelly 1988), have to a large extent met with very limited success, for the simple reason that they are seen as transgression of the generic integrity of the whole tradition in the legislative process. Although the plain English movement has been quite effective in influencing the redrafting of general commercial and administrative documents, including insurance policies, residential leases, tax return forms, social benefit claim forms and other papers for better accessibility and usability by a larger section of society, in the case of legislative provisions it has not had the same measure of success. The main argument for the preservation of the generic integrity of legislative discourse is that the real legislative power in all parliamentary democracies must rest with the legislatures and not with the judiciary. This is one of the most important reasons why clarity, precision, unambiguity and all-inclusiveness are so highly prized in the common law legislative discourse, which gives a relatively high degree of transparency to legislative intentions. In the last chapter we discussed many of the situational and contextual constraints operating on legislative discourses; in this section, I would like to take it further and consider at least two 'critical sites of engagement' where such constraints have serious social implications.

The emerging complexity of dynamics of power and politics in legislative expression raises a number of distinct but related issues. Firstly, to what extent can legislative genre be made accessible to all the participants, stakeholders or victims, whatever we may call them? Secondly, assuming that it raises the issue of generic integrity of legislative expression embedded in typical legal systems, then 'to what extent is this integrity important for the survival of legal culture?' Finally, to what extent is the distribution of power through legislative expression related to the notion of transparency in expressing legislative intentions in legal documents, and in what way does such

194

a transparency empower some stakeholders at the cost of others? To illustrate these three issues, I would like to look at how legal discourse, especially the way it is constructed, interpreted and used, empowers one participant at the cost of impoverishing the other.

CRITICAL SITE OF ENGAGEMENT: LEGISLATION ACROSS LEGAL SYSTEMS

It has often been claimed that legislative writing can be written in 'plain' everyday language as used by ordinary people, and the implication is that if it is done this way it will become accessible to one and all, and that the lives of millions of people will become unproblematic. However, accessibility of legal discourse is not always the function of syntactic complexity or information loading. It is often forgotten that accessibility in legislative context has three components, readability, interpretation, and application to the real facts of life, and the last two stages are less dependent on the use of linguistic resources, but more on what an interpreter brings to the text in the form not only of knowledge of the world, but also that of the socio-cultural, political and the legal context in which it is interpreted and applied. In this context, the construction of the Basic Law of Hong Kong SAR presents an interesting case, where in spite of a low incidence of 'syntactic complexity' and exceptional 'under-specification of legal scope', the discourse has been found to be 'incomprehensible' in that it has the potential for multiple inter-pretations, some of which have been found to give more power to one institution at the cost of another. Interpretation does not seem to be the function of what the writer has put together; it seems to be the function of what the interpreter brings to the discourse, including his or her attitude towards what s/he reads, which may include his or her prejudices, assumptions, political beliefs and a number of other factors.

Let me give more substance to this. As briefly mentioned in Chapter 4, the Basic Law of Hong Kong was written by the National Parliamentary Council of the People's Republic of China as a mini constitution to come into effect immediately after the transfer of sovereignty of Hong Kong to the People's Republic of China on July 1st 1997.

CRITICAL MOMENT OF APPLICATION – THE RIGHT OF ABODE IN HONG KONG

One of the most controversial cases involving the interpretation of the Basic Law has been the one that is popularly known in the HKSAR media as the 'right of abode' case. Decided on January 29th 1999, the case brought into focus the unanimous decision of the Court of Final Appeal, which interpreted Article 24 of the Basic Law to allow residence rights to all those 'persons of Chinese nationality born outside of Hong Kong of those residents' who were permanent residents in Hong Kong, irrespective of the fact whether they acquired the status before or after the birth of the child.

The Basic Law of HKSAR: Fundamental Rights and Duties of the Residents

Article 24

Residents of the Hong Kong Special Administrative Region ('Hong Kong residents') shall include permanent residents and non-permanent residents.

The permanent residents of the Hong Kong Special Administrative Region shall be:

1. Chinese citizens born in Hong Kong before or after the establishment of the Hong Kong Special Administrative Region;
2. Chinese citizens who have ordinarily resided in Hong Kong for a continuous period of not less than seven years before or after the establishment of the Hong Kong Special Administrative Region;
3. Persons of Chinese nationality born outside Hong Kong of those residents listed in categories (1) and (2);
4. ...
5. ...

The above-mentioned residents shall have the right of abode in the Hong Kong Special Administrative Region and shall be qualified to obtain, in accordance with the laws of the Region, permanent identity cards which state their right of abode.

As one can see, the Basic Law does not specify whether it was necessary for any of the parents to have this status of permanent residence at the time of the birth of the child. The Court of Final Appeal took the generous view. According to the Government of HKSAR, this landmark decision opened up the floodgates for millions of mainland people to acquire the right of abode in Hong Kong.

Considering the socio-political implications of such a decision by the highest court in the country, the government took the unprecedented step of asking the National People's Congress (NPC) to provide the reinterpretation of the relevant section of the Basic Law, which they did. According to the National People's Congress, the Court of Final Appeal went wrong in not seeking an interpretation of the Basic

Law before deciding the case. The NPC also reinterpreted the relevant section conservatively by ruling that the intent of the section in question was to allow only those people to acquire the right of abode whose parents had already acquired the status of permanent residence in Hong Kong before the birth of the child in question. The Government of Hong Kong was delighted at the reinterpretation of the relevant article of the Basic Law. However, it did raise a number of crucial issues relevant to the questions of power and control in conflicting legal and socio-political contexts, which are central to our concerns here.

One of the main issues brought into focus in this controversy was the question of who should have the final authority to interpret the Basic Law: the highest Court of Final Appeal within the common law system in force in Hong Kong, or the National People's Congress, which operates within a very different civil law system? Although the Basic Law empowers the Government of HKSAR with a very high degree of autonomy in a number of areas, including the matters of law and justice, at the same time it makes the NPC the final interpreter of the Basic Law. A serious consequence of these provisions is that since the Basic Law has been a mini-constitution written by the NPC in the tradition of the civil code used in the PRC, it only gives provisions in terms of broad principles, without any specifications in detail, which is the general practice in the common law system in use in Hong Kong. The real issue at stake thus is that a number of such unpleasant controversies and decisions could have been avoided, or at least minimized, by drafting the Basic Law in a legislative style that did not conflict with the normal expectations of the legal system within which it is likely to be interpreted and used. By incorporating, as far as foreseeable, the necessary constraints and qualifications operating on such provisions, one would have made the laws more transparent and less controversial. Obviously, there may be several other factors, in addition to syntactic complexity and density of information, that tend to make legislation inaccessible to its intended audiences with varying degrees of legal expertise and different kinds of stake in the use of legislative provisions.

Instances such as these clearly point out that, in the absence of an all-inclusive detailed specification of information, it is always possible for the legislature or the executive arms of the government to assume greater control over judicial processes. Although the conflict between the two legal systems, the civil code used in the People's Republic of China and the common law used in Hong Kong SAR, also contributed to this legal controversy, the case also reiterates that the interests of the executives in the government, the judiciary and the legislature can be

197

at cross purposes, because empowerment of one institution will invariably mean impoverishment of the other. Absolute transparency, which is almost impossible to achieve in most forms of legislative instruments, seems to be in the best interests of the legislature, but anything less than that will bring some advantage to the other, especially the judiciary. If the judiciary is absolutely independent, then it will be viewed as empowering judges at the cost of the legislature; however, if the judiciary is committed, then the real power goes to the executive, or the government. Underlying the issue of power in legislative contexts is the contestation or challenge to the generic integrity of the legislative genre. The legislative community views the language reform movement as an attempt to undermine the long and established conventions of legal writing, which have stood the test of time for centuries, and have been successful in providing power and solidarity to its members, helping the community to establish a culture of their own.

7.2   Genres in translation and document design

Genre theory, as outlined in this study, has interesting implications for all forms of recontextualization, whether it is translation (which involves two languages), simplification or easification of professional texts, or even designing of professional documents (in one or more languages). Genres are embedded in professional or social practices, and hence they tend to derive additional meanings as a result of their association with professional or disciplinary cultures. Texts rarely have such associations, and hence realize only textual meanings. In the process of recontextualization of written discourses, whether in the same language or in another language, as in translation, it is important to maintain the generic integrity of the source text in its recontextualized form, so that one can convey not only the textual meaning, but also the more conventionalized generic meaning of the source text. To illustrate the importance of maintaining the generic integrity of the source text, I would like to take an example from an investment brochure (original version of the interest section).

The Bonds bear interest from 5th January, 1994 at the rate of 5.25 per cent per annum payable in arrears on 5th of January, 1995; 5.5 per cent. per annum payable in arrears on 5th January 1996; and 5.75 per cent. payable in arrears on 5th January 1997 and each 5th of January thereafter (each such date being referred to an "Interest Payment Date"), provided that, notwithstanding the foregoing, interest on the Bonds will be payable at 5.75 per cent. per annum from, and including, the IPO Listing Date. The Bonds will cease to bear interest (i) on the Interest Payment Date last preceding the Conversion Date (as defined below) subject to conversion of the relevant Bond in accordance with the provisions of Condition 7 (c) and subject to the provisions of Condition 7 (c) or (ii) from the due date for redemption thereof unless, upon surrender in accordance with Condition 10, payment of full amount due is improperly withheld or refused or unless default is otherwise made in respect of any such payment. In such event referred to in (ii) above, such Bonds shall continue to bear interest at the rate most lately applicable (both before and after the judgement) until one of the following dates, whichever is earlier of (a) the day on which all sums due in respect of such Bonds up to that day are received by or on behalf of the relevant holder and (b) the day seven days after the Trustees or the Principal Paying Agents has notified Bondholders of receipts of all sums due in respect of all the Bonds up to that seventh day (except to the extent that there is failure in the subsequent payment to the relevant holders under these conditions). If interest is required to be calculated for a period of less than one year, it will be calculated on the basis of a 360-day year consisting of 12 months of 30 days each and, in the case of an incomplete month, the number of days elapsed.

This is an extract from a company investment brochure from Hong Kong and outlines a very detailed set of rules to calculate interest on bonds. As one can see, this is written in a typical legislative style to give a clear, precise, unambiguous and all-inclusive account of the procedures to regulate the calculation of interest on bonds and is meant to stand in a court of law. However, in doing so, it also becomes almost entirely inaccessible to ordinary or lay readers. But the main purpose of the section is to protect the interests of the company against any possible dispute or litigation. It is possible to make the document more reader-accessible without sacrificing the precision, clarity, unambiguity or the specification of scope intended by using easification devices, such as textual-mapping strategies to clarify the cognitive structure of the text. Here is another version of the same text:

5.1 The Bonds bear interest from 5th January 1994 per annum payable in arrears at the rate of

  (a) 5.25 per cent. on 5th of January, 1995;
  (b) 5.5 per cent. on 5th of January 1996;
  (c) 5.75 per cent. on 5th of January 1997 and on each 5th of January thereafter,

  (*each such date being referred to an "Interest Payment Date"*).

5.2 Notwithstanding the provisions of section 5.1 above,

  (a) *in the case of IPO listing*, interests on the Bonds will be payable at 5.75 per cent. per annum from and including the IPO Listing Date,
  (b) *in the case of conversion under the provisions of Condition 7c*, the Bonds will cease to bear interest on the Interest Payment Date last preceding the Conversion Date,

  and

  (c) *in the case of redemption*, the Bonds will cease to bear interest from the date Bonds become due for redemption.

5.3 *Where, upon surrender in accordance with Condition 10, payment of the full amount is improperly withheld, refused or otherwise defaulted*, Bonds shall continue to bear interest at the rate most lately applicable (both before and after the judgement) until one of the following dates, whichever is earlier,

Either (i) the day on which all sums due in respect of such Bonds upto that day are received by or on behalf of the relevant holder,

or (ii) the day seven days after the Trustees or the Principal Paying Agents has notified Bondholders of receipts of all sums due in respect of all the Bonds up to that seventh day (*except to the extent that there is failure in the subsequent payment to the relevant holders under these conditions*).

5.4 *If interest is required to be calculated for a period of less than one year*, it will be calculated on the basis of a 360-day year consisting of 12 months of 30 days each and, in the case of an incomplete month, the number of days elapsed.

Easification of the original interest section

Although the two texts, the original and the re-written easified one, display somewhat different use of linguistic resources for their textualization, the communicative purposes that they serve are essentially the same. Both contain the same degree of specification of scope and are equally transparent and can provide a similar degree of protection in a court of law. Both of them serve a similar communicative purpose and hence can be regarded as instances of the same genre, although the second one is in a form that is a lot more reader accessible than the first one. Let us now look at another version of the same text, which has been made rhetorically simple for easy accessibility to lay persons:

Q: Will the bonds give me interest?
A: Yes, the Bonds will give you yearly interest from 5th January 1994.

Q: When will the interest be paid?
A: It will be paid on the 5th of January each year.

Q: At what rate?
A: At the rate of 5.25% in 1995, 5.5% in 1996, and 5.75% in 1997 and after that.

Q: What will happen if the bonds are listed as IPO?
A: You will get interest at the rate of 5.75% from the date the Bonds get listed.

Q: What happens if I get the bonds converted?
A: *You* will stop getting interest on the 5th of January proceeding the date on which the bonds are converted

Q: What if I get the bonds redeemed?
A: You will stop getting interest from the date of redemption.

Q: What will happen if I surrender the bonds and still I am not paid in full?
A: In that case, you will continue to get interest at the rate which was applicable when you surrendered the bonds.

Q: How long can I continue to get my interest?
A: You will be paid till the day you are paid in full.

Simplification of interest section

Although the main substance in this simplified version is more or less the same as that in the two earlier versions, it is still very different from the other two. The differences are not simply in the textualization of the document but also more seriously in the communicative purpose it is meant to serve. For a start it undermines the value of detailed specification in legislative documentation. It is mainly meant to serve the information-giving function rather than to govern the legal relationship between the company and the clients. Besides, it is not meant to serve as a legal instrument in a court of law, and hence represents a very different kind of generic integrity than that of the earlier versions. The original and the easified versions serve a legislative function, whereas the simplified version serves a more informative function. Hence the importance of maintaining generic integrity in all forms of recontextualization, whether translation or simplification.

7.3 Genres in applied linguistics

Genre theory, as developed here, raises a number of potential issues relevant to applied linguistics, three of which I would like to take up for further discussion here. The first issue emerges from our concept of the real and the pedagogic worlds, which, to a large extent, raises the question: 'To what extent should pedagogical practices reflect or account for the realities of the world of discourse?' The second issue arises from the two distinct yet overlapping discourse perspectives we proposed in our discussion of genre practice, which makes a distinction between the social and the individual constructions of discourse, leading to a tension between the *socially constructed discourse forms* and the *private intentions* of those who have the ability and the socially assigned power to exploit such social constructions to achieve private ends. In applied linguistics, this reflects the tension between *generic integrity* and *generic creativity*, and also brings into focus the process of *generic transfer*. And, finally, there is the question of reconciliation between the real and the analytical worlds, which raises the question: 'To what extent should the *analytical procedures* account for *the full realities of the world* of discourse?' Or in other words, 'To what extent is it necessary or even desirable *to see the whole of the elephant*?' These are some of the fundamental questions in the context of applied linguistics, but have often been ignored in applied linguistics literature. Although genre theory has considerably developed in the last few years and still continues to make further progress, I still feel that at the present state of our knowledge of theory and practice, we are not in a position to see the whole of the elephant, and I am not sure if we will ever be in a position to achieve this, though we will continue to strive in that direction. Most of these issues and questions, however, are reflected in the over-arching question:

Is generic description a reflection of reality?
Or
Is it just a convenient fiction invented by the teacher?

The recent developments in genre theory discussed in earlier sections contribute significantly to our understanding of a number of areas of applied linguistics, such as language teaching and learning in general, teaching and learning of language for specific purposes, translation and interpretation in professional contexts, communication in professional organizations, document design and interpretation in professional contexts, the plain language movement, language use in advertising and marketing contexts, and several other areas relevant to language use. In this book, since our focus has been on written professional discourse, I would like to focus on only some of these areas especially relevant to the teaching and learning of LSP and communication in professional contexts; however it is possible to extend the discussion to make it relevant to other areas of application. The three broad issues identified above are associated with three main aspects of applied linguistics in general, and language teaching and learning in particular: curriculum concerns, disciplinary conflicts and analytical options. Let me discuss them one by one.

(1) Curriculum concerns

Emerging from the tension between generic integrity and generic creativity as discussed in Section 3 above, one can identify a variety of theoretical issues concerned with the development of language curriculum and teaching pedagogy, especially in the context of ESP. Let me focus on those concerned with language curriculum first.

EDUCATION V. TRAINING

Although ESP (or more generally LSP) training has a fairly long history of development, we still have few research insights indicating to what extent ESP development is a matter of education within the classroom or of job training at the workplace. There is enough evidence to show that both types of activities, formal education in the academy as part of or in addition to educational degree and in the workplace as part of job training, contribute to the development of specialist expertise in a specific professional or workplace context, but there is no conclusive evidence to suggest that one could manage with either of them on its own. We often find professionals from the workplace complaining about the inadequacy of new graduates to come to grips with the day-to-day problems of communication at work. As suggested in Chapter 5, the explanation in part lies in the fact that professional practice does not seem to play any significant role in most frameworks for the analyses of professional discourse. Lave and Wenger (1991) seem to emphasize this when they propose their theory of *legitimate peripheral participation.*

LINGUISTIC SKILLS V. COMMUNICATIVE BEHAVIOUR

Similarly, there has always been an unresolved tension between the teaching of language primarily as acquisition of linguistic skills and communicative behaviour. As discussed in Chapter 1, the history of applied discourse analysis shows a gradual development from linguistic skills to communicative competence, but a considerable degree of disappointment with communicative language teaching in recent years has raised serious doubts about any attempt to undermine the contribution of linguistic form to the acquisition of communicative behaviour. It is primarily because the language teaching profession has emphasized only one of these at various points in the history of language teaching, i.e. either linguistic competence or communicative competence. Linguistic competence is often too narrowly defined, and hence is inadequate to develop a reasonable capacity to handle specialized professional communicative tasks. Communicative competence, on the other hand, is too broadly defined, and hence is too challenging for second language learners to develop, and even if they manage to do that, it leaves them far from any capacity to handle specialized genres.

LANGUAGE V. DISCIPLINARY KNOWLEDGE

Thirdly, we still have little understanding of the relationship between language as communication and language as vehicle for the expression of disciplinary knowledge. ESP practitioners still get nervous about having to deal with disciplinary knowledge as part of linguistic training. Although there is some awareness of the need to integrate language training with the communication of disciplinary knowledge, in practice it is still considered a difficult task. In order to move in that direction, the first step will be to bring various stakeholders together, which include not only language teachers and learners, and subject teachers from the academy, but also professionals, employers and practitioners from the workplace. An additional factor that makes this task even more difficult is the awareness of disciplinary tensions across genres, which implies that learners may need multiple literacies

204

along disciplinary boundaries rather than a uniform ability to use language across the board. A multi-perspective understanding is necessary for any satisfactory and effective resolution of this concern.

CLASSROOM (ACADEMIC CONTEXT) V. REAL-WORLD (PROFESSIONAL CONTEXT)

Finally, we still need to resolve the tension between the classroom and the workplace, the academy and the profession, and language teaching and communication training. Often it has been claimed that these two aspects of language training are the two halves of the same discipline (Brumfit 1984), however in practice there is a great divide between the two positions. In fact, for the development of adequate control over professional genres and practices, which include the ability to produce and use specific professional genres, linguistic ability is only one of the factors; perhaps far more important than that is the ability to understand the conventions and the constraints, the concerns and the practices, the values and the culture of specific professional communities.

The other aspect of curriculum is the area of language pedagogy. Some of the major tensions that have been identified, established and partially resolved are as follows.

WRITING AS PRODUCT V. WRITING AS PROCESS

One of the major controversies that applied linguistic research has documented in the last two decades has been concerned with arguments in favour of writing as process, as against writing as product, until we discovered that the truth was somewhere in between, and that we needed to take into account not only the process and the product, but also the purpose as well as the participants (Bhatia 1999a). In fact, even today, as is obvious from some of the discussions about generic integrity in Chapter 5, we seem to be a long way from an adequate understanding of questions such as these: 'Why and how do specialists write their discourses the way they do?' 'Who contributes what and at what stage to the process of writing?' 'How do these specialists negotiate or evaluate the contributions from others involved in the process?' Once again, the answers may lie in multidimensional and multi-perspective analyses of professional genres.

INDIVIDUAL V. COLLABORATIVE WRITING

Language teaching, including ESP, has always treated writing as an individual activity, and it is only recently that we have discovered that

205

out in the world of work, professional writing is invariably collaborative (Gollin 1999). Whether it is in the context of a business organization, a legal firm, or a newspaper office, texts are increasingly being written on the basis of information provided by different people with different kinds of expertise, often representing different departments. So when our well-trained students go out to the professional world, they are often shocked by the degree of disparity they find in the expectations of the workplace and what they have learned in the classroom.

TEXTS V. TASKS

Furthermore, much of the work that ESP teachers do in the classroom focuses on the use of texts, though sometimes tasks also take a central role. However, these tasks, or text-task relationships (Swales 1990), also have limited relevance to the real world of professions, which is much more complex than we language teachers often imagine. In a typical legal activity of *conveyance of a property*, as reported in Candlin and Bhatia 1998, one may find a number of interdependent communicative stages, in which participants may be required to use not only several languages and modes of communication, but also a variety of legal genres, all of which contribute to the accomplishment of the professional activity. Some of these communicative stages may include receiving instructions from clients, negotiating terms of sale and purchase agreements, inventing titles and raising requisitions, drafting sale and purchase agreements, arranging mortgages, completing conveyance by undertaking and then finally replying to the clients, which may include billing the clients as well. At various stages, a number of different genres are used, written and interpreted, all of which contribute to the accomplishment of the activity. The professional expertise therefore does not depend entirely on the mastery of texts or linguistic tasks, but is the end result of a complex and interesting integration of all these aspects to make the whole activity meaningful and pragmatically successful (see Candlin and Bhatia 1998 for details).

SCAFFOLDING V. CREATIVITY IN GENRE LEARNING

Yet another interesting pedagogic debate concerns the issue of teaching genres in the classroom (Reid 1987). It started with the explicit teaching of school curriculum genres within the systemic-functional linguistic framework in Australia, where some curriculum genres are seen as 'privileged in society' and hence the belief that their 'mastery confers power' (Freedman 1994: 191). There seem to be two schools of thought:

those who believe in the explicit teaching of genres, especially the regularities of textual form and typifications, and the others who see this as too constraining and advocate free expression. The truth, however, rests somewhere in the middle. All genres, primary as well as secondary, involve conventionalized processes and outputs, which must be learnt by any one aspiring to be recognized as a member of any disciplinary community. It is only after one has developed considerable awareness of these conventions that he can exploit them innovatively. As Bakhtin (1986: 80) points out 'genres must be fully mastered to be used creatively'. The issue however is whether scaffolding can help one to master genres. This issue is also relevant for the teaching and acquisition of professional genres, where explicit genre-based language teaching and learning has often been criticized for being prescriptive and hence too constraining. In practice, however, it depends on the language teacher whether to use it for innovative exploitation of generic resources, or for a limited exposure to standardized genre contexts. Although it is essential for the learner to be familiar with specific generic conventions associated with a particular professional setting, it is neither necessary nor desirable to restrict the experience of linguistic behaviour to just the conventionalized and standardized aspects of genre construction and use.

How can one bring in creativity in genre-based language teaching and learning? Since genre analysis gives a grounded description of linguistic behaviour in professional settings, it is possible to bring in a fair amount of creativity in language teaching by adjusting communicative purposes, the nature of participation in a particular communicative setting, the social and professional relationship between the participants taking part in a particular genre-construction exercise, and above all, by bringing in variability in the use of generic strategies to achieve the same communicative purposes. However, in order to use genres creatively, the first prerequisite is to have an awareness of the conventions that are situated within specific disciplinary cultures. Bazerman attempts to resolve this tension between institutionalized expression and individual expression when he points out:

> ... the individual learns to express the self against the compulsive society. ... We are not ourselves because we set ourselves apart from each other. We become ourselves as we realize ourselves in relation to each other. The social is everything we do with each other and what we become as we do it. We individuate by identifying ourselves on a social landscape, a landscape we come to know as we interact with it. We discover and create others and ourselves by what we do with each other.
>
> (Bazerman 1993: viii)

There are at least three things that stand out clearly from the foregoing discussion: firstly, language learners need to become aware of the conversations of the disciplinary community of which they aspire to be members, which could be done through 'centripetal participation in the learning curriculum of the ambient community' (Lave and Wenger 1991: 100). Secondly, acquisition of genre knowledge, which leads to an understanding of generic integrity, is necessary but not sufficient for any subsequent exploitation or manipulation of generic conventions in real-life professional contexts. And, finally, genre knowledge should be best viewed as a resource to exploit generic conventions to respond appropriately to the requirements of professional practices rather than a blueprint for replication.

To conclude, in recent applied linguistics literature, especially in the areas of specialist language teaching and learning, we notice that hidden underneath some of these conflicts is a movement from the idealized world of the classroom towards the realities of the world of work. Often based on sound pedagogic principles, the world of the classroom is often interpreted as idealized, simplified, controlled and largely predictable. The world of professional practice, on the other hand, is largely characterized in terms of the realities of professional life, which are not only complex, but also dynamic, flexible and unpredictable, though regulated by the conventions of disciplinary cultures.

(2) Disciplinary conflicts

Within the second category of issues mentioned above are those arising from disciplinary knowledge. It is possible to identify three different, though related, types of disciplinary conflicts:

- general v. discipline-specific conflicts;
- contrasts between specific disciplines, such as between 'business' and 'law';
- theoretical v. applied disciplines.

One of the earliest concerns in language teaching, especially ESP research, was the tension between general and specific disciplinary knowledge. The very beginning of ESP is attributed to functional description of language use in terms of specialist knowledge or disciplines. Disciplinary cultures constrain discourses in different domains, and that was the main reason for the emergence of ESP as a discipline. However, in recent years the picture has become increasingly complex, with recent research leading to the establishment of generic differentiation within and across disciplines, on the one hand,

and disciplinary conflicts within genres, on the other. Similarly, interesting contrasts have been identified between theoretical and practical disciplines, such as pure and applied mathematics, economics and marketing, linguistics and applied linguistics and several others (Bhatia 1998a, 1999a, 2002). There may also be interesting differences between genres within a discipline. Textbooks, for instance, are likely to pose different challenges to the uninitiated student reader to the ones he or she is likely to face in the study of research articles, even though they may be located in the same discipline (Myers 1992, 1995).

Underlying these conflicts one may discover two types of interesting disciplinary relationships, other than those commonly observed in disciplinary cultures, as in the case of legal and business studies. As discussed in Chapter 2, these are generic differences within disciplines, on the one hand, and disciplinary conflicts within individual genres, on the other. All the three types of differences are interesting for ESP research and practice. It is interesting to note that ESP discourses across disciplines make use of their typical genres that Bazerman (1994) refers to as 'genre systems'. Typical genres used in law, for example, are cases, statutes and judgments, whereas in business, one is more likely to find letters, business reports and memos. If we go to social and public administration, the typical genres are likely to be media reports, government documents, policy statements and government treaties. Of course, there are typical academic genres common to most disciplines, such as textbooks, research articles, essays and examination questions. However most of them invariably display disciplinary differences, often leading to major tensions in the way discourses are constructed, interpreted and used in the contexts of specific disciplinary cultures. In many cases, these conflicts are so pronounced that they often lead to serious problems in the design and implementation of ESP programmes. Bhatia and Candlin (2001) report that it is often the case that in most interdisciplinary academic programmes ESP learners are required to handle not one discipline but several in the course of a single day, especially in business studies, which incorporates some aspects of law, in addition to several others. On further investigation it becomes obvious that ESP, especially in the context of interdisciplinary programmes and in workplace contexts, is not a matter of acquisition of a single literacy, or even an extension of a single literacy, but more a matter of multiple literacies embedded in different disciplinary cultures, often overlapping but generally differentiated.

(3) Analytical options

Finally we come to the third type of conflict, which I have put together under the category of linguistic analysis. The earliest tensions between analysis of language as linguistic form and function, text and discourse, register and genre, or discourse and genre are all part of the development of the discipline and have been resolved over a period of time. More recent, and perhaps more interesting from the point of view of recent developments in ESP, are conflicts between individual genres and mixed genres, embedded genres and the whole process of appropriation of genres. In the classroom context, it is pedagogically convenient to take examples of idealized individual genres, as they tend to be perfect illustrations of generic constructs. However, in the real world of discourse we often come across genres that are mixed (Bhatia 1995, 1997a), embedded (Bhatia 1995), or what Fairclough (1993, 1995) calls hybrid genres. These differences once again lead to a bigger picture focusing on the conflict between the classroom genres and the real-world genres.

The main difference in these discourse analytical frameworks is that one draws its inspiration from linguistics or text-linguistics, whereas the other relies more on socio-pragmatics. One is more concerned with linguistic (which includes functional and discoursal) form, whereas the other focuses more on the values these discourses carry in real-life contexts. One focuses essentially on surface-level patterns, whereas the other aims at a thicker and deeper understanding of the discourse in question.

Emerging from the three interrelated concerns, conflicts and options, we notice a number of overlapping tendencies that contribute to our understanding of the way ESP has developed. These tendencies contribute to our understanding of a number of different aspects of ESP theory and practice, some of which include the context in which a particular ESP effort is situated, the world that guides the effort, the nature of discourse that controls the input, the aspects of linguistic theory which inspire applications, and the desired outcome of the entire ESP effort. The conclusions and the values drawn from various conflicts can be summarized in terms of two rather different views of ESP worlds, one that is prevalent today, and the one we, as ESP practitioners, would like to move towards tomorrow. The two worlds, one representing the language description as ideal or fiction, and the other as representation of reality, can be summarized as in Diagram 7.1.

To summarize, the foregoing account, though brief in a number of ways, of some of the major conflicts and the possible negotiating prospects underpins several insightful conclusions one may draw from

210

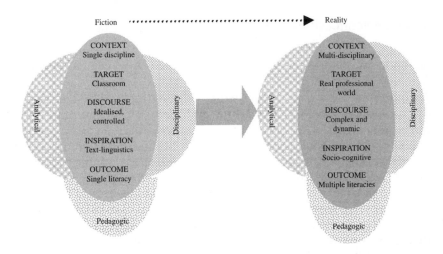

Diagram 7.1 *Registers, genres and disciplines in academic discourse*

past strengths, and may use them to further consolidate ESP, or more generally LSP, theory and practice for the next phase of its development. Some of these include the following.

MULTIDIMENSIONAL AND MULTI-PERSPECTIVE APPROACH TO DISCOURSE VARIATION IN PROFESSIONAL COMMUNITIES

Studies of discourse variation in professional communities continue to provide rationale for the design and execution of ESP programmes for a variety of narrowly focused and specifically differentiated audiences in terms of their disciplinary requirements. These include:

- use of multidisciplinary, multidimensional and multi-perspective analytical procedures to provide thicker description of language use;
- better and more insightful understanding of the realities of the world of professions through collaborative work;
- accommodation and understanding of cross-cultural and intercultural variations in disciplinary discursive practices.

These measures would necessarily facilitate a better understanding of the concerns of specific disciplinary cultures, eventually leading to a better integration of ESP practice and professional practice. In this context, genre analysis needs to be developed further to offer much thicker descriptions of language use that take into account the

211

pervasive complexities and dynamic exploitation of language use in discursive practices in specific disciplinary contexts.

ESP AS MULTIPLE LITERACIES

As indicated earlier, the ESP world is becoming increasingly multi-disciplinary, on the one hand, and multicultural, on the other. The professional world is becoming multidisciplinary because of the nature of changing job descriptions in the world of professions, where lawyers need an understanding of business practices, and management experts must have a reasonable knowledge of the intricacies of legal requirements in their typical workplace contexts. The academic community in the last few years has readily responded to such requirements by designing and offering multidisciplinary programmes, incorporating several disciplines within the same qualification.

In addition to these developments, the professional world is also becoming increasingly multicultural because of the new trends in favour of corporate mergers, often dismantling national borders to create massive multinationals. The corporate world is fast becoming much more global than it was some ten years ago. One of the strongest implications of these trends for the ESP community is to take a serious view of the diversity of cultural input to discursive practices.

In order to meet these requirements, which are distinct in terms of the disciplinary cultures they tend to serve, on the one hand, and interdisciplinary, in that most of these professional concerns are becoming increasingly interdisciplinary, on the other, ESP must develop expertise in handling not simply a single literacy but a combination of multiple literacies depending upon the typical set of competencies considered necessary for a specific professional culture.

INTEGRATION OF ESP WITH PROFESSIONAL PRACTICE: TOWARDS A SHARED VISION

Finally, the foregoing discussions of discursive practices of profes-sionals and the procedures they use in the context of authentic and critical moments of professional engagement are likely to lead ESP theory and practice towards a more realistic and shared vision of professional expertise, rather than conflicting views of who contributes what to the development of professional competence. The ESP profession can no longer position itself on the sidelines serving disciplinary requirements from the outside. The profession must participate more actively and collaboratively in the concerns of the specialist disciplines to develop a deeper and insightful understanding of some of the following questions:

- Why do these professionals use the language the way they do?
- How can we develop an understanding of what they do and how they do it?
- How can we create a common discourse that makes sense to us and at the same time to the members of the disciplinary culture we collaborate with?

Attempts to answer these interesting and challenging questions will lead to the development of a shared vision that serves both the ESP community and the disciplinary culture we tend to serve.

Questions like these may be considered from the point of view of two rather broad perspectives: a socio-critical perspective and a pedagogical perspective, so that whatever analytical procedures one may choose to employ are essentially constrained by the purpose or application of the investigation. As far as applied linguistics, especially language teaching and learning, is concerned, the main source of strength will continue to be the functional language description embedded in textual space, but moving across the tactical space, and exploring the professional space, as far as possible. If, on the other hand, the main objective is socio-critical, the investigation might begin with and concentrate on social space, but certainly move across the tactical space, but rarely cross into the textual space. The use of socio-cognitive space in the four-space model proposed in this volume is centrally relevant to all forms of genre construction, interpretation, use and exploitation in the achievement of professional objectives by members of most communities of practice, and this is the main argument for the integration of discursive and professional practices.

References

Abercrombie, D. (1967) *Elements of General Phonetics*. Edinburgh: Edinburgh University Press.

Allen, D. E. and Guy, R. F. (1989) Non-routine conversation in operational crisis, in H. Coleman (ed.), *Working with Language: A Multidisciplinary Consideration of Language Use in Work Contexts*. Berlin, New York: Mouton de Gruyter.

Amsterdamska, O. and Leydesdorff, L. (1989) Citations: indicators of significance?. *Scientometrics* 15, 449–71.

Archer, J. (1986) *A Matter of Honor*. New York: Pocket Books.

Bakhtin, M.M. (1986) *Speech Genres and Other Late Essays*. Austin: University of Texas Press.

Barber, C. L. (1962) Some measurable characteristics of scientific prose, in *Contributions to English Syntax and Phonology*. Stockholm: Almquist & Wiksell, 1–23.

Bargiela-Chiappini, F. and Nickerson, C. (eds) (1999) *Writing Business: Genres, Media and Discourse*. London: Longman.

Bazerman, C. (1988) *Shaping Written Knowledge: the Genre and Activity of the Experimental Article in Science*. Madison: The University of Wisconsin Press.

Bazerman, C. (1993) Foreword, in N. R. Blyler and C. Thralls (eds), *Professional Communication: The Social Perspective*. London: Sage Publications, vii–viii.

Bazerman, C. (1994) Systems of genres and the enhancement of social intentions, in A. Freedman and P. Medway (eds), *Genre and New Rhetoric*. London: Taylor and Francis, 79–101.

Bazerman, C. (1998) Editor's Introduction, in J. Swales, *Other Floors, Other Voices: A Textography of a Small Building*. London: Lawrence Erlbaum Associates, ix–x.

Bazerman, C. and Paradis, J. (eds) (1991) *Textual Dynamics of the Professions: Historical and Contemporary Studies of Writing in Professional Communities*. Madison, WI: University of Wisconsin Press.

Beaugrande, R. A. de and Dressler, W. U. (1981) *Introduction to Text Linguistics*. London: Longman.

Berkenkotter, C. and Huckin, T. N. (1995) *Genre Knowledge in Disciplinary Communication – Cognition/Culture/Power*. Hillsdale, NJ: Lawrence Erlbaum Associates.

Bhatia, V. K. (1982) *An Investigation into Formal and Functional Characteristics of Qualifications in Legislative Writing and its Application to English for Academic Legal Purposes.* Ph.D. thesis, University of Aston in Birmingham.

Bhatia, V. K. (1983) Simplification v. easification: the case of legal texts. *Applied Linguistics* 4/1, 42–54.

Bhatia, V. K. (1984) Syntactic discontinuity in legislative writing and its implications for academic legal purposes, in A. K. Pugh and J. M. Ulijn (eds), *Reading for Professional Purposes.* London: Heinemann Educational Books, 90–6.

Bhatia, V. K. (1992) Pragmatics of the use of nominals in academic and professional genres, in Pragmatics and Language Learning. *Monograph Series Volume 3*, eds L. F. Bouton and Y. Kachru. Urbana-Champaign, USA: University of Illinois, 217–30.

Bhatia, V. K. (1993) *Analysing Genre – Language Use in Professional Settings.* London: Longman.

Bhatia, V. K. (1994) Generic integrity in professional discourse, in B.-L. Gunarsson, P. Linell and B. Nordberg (eds), *Text and Talk in Professional Contexts.* Uppsala, Sweden: ASLA, Skriftserie nr 6, 61–76.

Bhatia, V. K. (1995) Genre-mixing in professional communication: the case of 'private intentions' v. 'socially recognised purposes', in P. Bruthiaux, T. Boswood and B. Bertha (eds), *Explorations in English for Professional Communication.* Hong Kong: City University of Hong Kong, 1–19.

Bhatia, V. K. (1996a) Methodological issues in genre analysis, in *Hermes, Journal of Linguistics* 16, 1–21.

Bhatia, V. K. (1996b) Nativization of job applications in South Asia, in R. J. Baumgardner (ed.), *South Asian English: Structure, Use and Users.* Urbana: University of Illinois Press, 158–73.

Bhatia, V. K. (1997a) Genre-mixing in academic introductions. *English for Specific Purposes* 16, 3, 181–96.

Bhatia, V. K. (1997b) Power and politics of genre, in *World Englishes* 16, 3, 359–72.

Bhatia, V. K. (1997c) Genre analysis today, in *Revue Belge de Philologie et d' Histoire* 75, 97, 629–51.

Bhatia, V. K. (1998a) Discourse of philanthropic fund-raising, in *Working Papers*, IU Center for Philanthropy, University of Indiana, Indianapolis.

Bhatia, V. K. (1998b) Generic conflicts in academic discourse, in I. Fontanet, S. Posteguillo, J. C. Palmer and J. F. Coll (eds), *Genre Studies in English for Academic Purposes.* Castell: Universitat Jaume I.

Bhatia, V. K. (1999a) Integrating products, processes, purposes and participants in professional writing, in C. N. Candlin and K. Hyland (eds), *Writing: Texts, Processes and Practices.* London: Longman, 21–39.

Bhatia, V. K. (1999b) *Analysing Genre: An Applied Linguistic Perspective.* Keynote address given at the 12th World Congress of Applied Linguistics in Tokyo (1–6 August, 1999).

Bhatia, V. K. (1999c) Disciplinary variation in business English, in M. Hewings and C. Nickerson (eds), *Business English: Research into Practice.* Harlow: Prentice Hall, 129–43.

215

Bhatia, V. K. (2000) Genres in conflict, in A. Trosborg (ed.), *Analysing Professional Genres*. Amsterdam/Philadelphia: John Benjamins Publishing Company, 147–62.

Bhatia, V. K. (2002) Generic view of academic discourse, in J. Flowerdew (ed.), *Academic Discourse*. London: Pearson Education, 21–39.

Bhatia, V. K. and Candlin, C. N. (eds) (2001) *Teaching English to Meet the Needs of Business Education in Hong Kong*. A project report to the SCOLAR Language Fund, Government of Hong Kong, published by the Centre for English Language Education and Communication Research, City University of Hong Kong.

Bhatia, V. K. and Swales, J. M. (1983) An approach to the linguistic study of legal documents. *Fachsprache* 5, 3, 98–108.

Bhatia, V. K. and Tay, M. (eds) (1987) *Teaching of English in Meeting the Needs of Business and Technology, Volumes 1 and 2*. Singapore: Department of English Language and Literature, National University of Singapore.

Boswood, T. (2000) *Strategic Writing and Organizational Identities*. Unpublished Ph.D. thesis submitted to City University of Hong Kong, Hong Kong.

Bresler, K. (1998–2000) Pursuant to partners' directive, I learned to obfuscate. *The Scribes Journal of Legal Writing*, Vol. 7, 29.

Bright, W. (1996) The view from the editor's desk: 30 years of American linguistics. Talk given at the City University of Hong Kong.

Brown, G. and Yule, G. (1983) *Discourse Analysis*. Cambridge: Cambridge University Press.

Bruffee, K. A. (1986) Social construction, language and the authority of knowledge: a bibliographical essay. *College Composition* 48, December, 730–90.

Brumfit, C. J. (1984) *Common Ground: Shared Interests in ESP and Communication Studies*, edited by R. Williams, J. Swales and J. Kirkman. Oxford: The British Council and Pergamon Press.

Burchfield, R. W., Onions, C. T. and Friedrichsen, G. W. S. (1972) *The Oxford Dictionary of English Etymology*. Oxford: Oxford University Press.

Burgess, G. (1914) *Burgess Unabridged: A New Dictionary of Words You Have Always Needed*. London: Frederick A. Stokes Company.

Caldwell, R. (1982) Specialist informant interviews, reported in Bhatia 1982.

Canale, M. and Swain, M. (1980) Theoretical basis of communicative approaches to second language teaching and testing. *Applied Linguistics* 1, 1, 1–47.

Candlin, C. N. (1995) General Editor's Preface, in N. Fairclough, *Critical Discourse Analysis: The Critical Study of Language*. London: Longman, vii–xi.

Candlin, C. N. (1999) How can discourse be a measure of expertise? Paper given at the International Association for Dialogue Analysis, University of Birmingham, UK, April 8–10 1999.

Candlin, C. N. (2000) General Editor's Preface in K. Hyland, *Disciplinary Discourses: Social Interactions in Academic Writing*. Harlow: Longman Pearson Education, xvii.

Candlin, C. N. (ed.) (2002) *Research and Practice in Professional Discourse.* Hong Kong: City University of Hong Kong Press.

Candlin, C. N. and Bhatia, V. K. (1998) The Project Report on *Strategies and Competencies in Legal Communication: A Study to Investigate the Communicative Needs of Legal Professionals.* Hong Kong: The Law Society of Hong Kong.

Candlin, C. N., Bhatia, V. K. and Jensen, C. (2002) Must the worlds collide? Professional and academic discourses in the study and practice of law, in G. Cortese and P. Riley (eds), *Domain-Specific English: Textual Practices Across Communities and Classrooms.* Bern: Verlag Peter Lang AG, 101–14.

Candlin, C. N., Bruton, C. J. and Coleman, M. (1980) *Dentist–Patient Communication*, a report to the General Dental Council. Lancaster: University of Lancaster.

Candlin, C. N. and Hyland, K. (eds) (1999) *Writing: Texts, Processes and Practices.* London: Longman.

Candlin, C. N. and Maley, Y. (1997) Intertextuality and interdiscursivity in the discourse of alternative dispute resolution, in B.-L. Gunnarsson, P. Lineel and B. Nordberg (eds), *The Construction of Professional Discourse.* London: Longman, 201–22.

Candlin, C. N. and Plum, G. A. (1999) Engaging with challenges of interdiscursivity in academic writing: researchers, students and tutors, in C. N. Candlin and K. Hyland (eds), *Writing: Texts, Processes and Practices.* London: Longman, 193–217.

Catford, J. C. (1965) *A Linguistic Theory of Translation.* Oxford: Oxford University Press.

Chomsky, N. (1965) *Aspects of the Theory of Syntax.* Cambridge, MA: MIT.

Cook, G. (1989) *Discourse.* Oxford: Oxford University Press.

Cook, G. (1992) *The Discourse of Advertising.* London: Routledge.

Corder, S. P. (1973) *Introducing Applied Linguistics.* Harmondsworth: Penguin.

Coulthard, M. (1977) *An Introduction to Discourse Analysis.* London: Longman.

Coupland, N., Sarangi, S. and Candlin, C. N. (eds) (2001) *Sociolinguistics and Social Theory.* Harlow: Pearson Education Limited.

Crystal, D. and Davy, D. (1969) *Investigating English Style.* London: Longman.

Devitt, A. (1991) Intertextuality in tax accounting, in C. Bazerman and J. Paradis (eds), *Textual Dynamics of the Professions.* Madison, WI: University of Wisconsin Press.

van Dijk, T. (1977) *Text and Context: Explorations in the Semantics and Pragmatics of Discourse.* London: Longman.

van Dijk, T. (1985) *Handbook of Discourse Analysis*, Vol. 2. London: Academic Press.

van Dijk, T. (1988) *News as Discourse.* Hillsdale, NJ: Erlbaum.

van Dijk, T. (1993) Principles of critical discourse analysis. *Discourse and Society* 4/2, 124–85.

Donald, W. J. (ed.) (1931) *Handbook of Business Administration*. York, PA: The Maple Press.

Drew, P. and Heritage, J. (1992) *Talk at Work: Interaction in Institutional Settings*. Cambridge: Cambridge University Press.

Dubois, B. L. (1982) The construction of noun phrases in biomedical journal articles, in J. Hoedt *et al.* (eds), *Pragmatics and LSP*. Copenhagen: Copenhagen School of Economics, 49–67.

Dubrow, H. (1982) *Genre*. London: Methuen and Co. Ltd.

Dudley-Evans, A. (1994) Variations in the discourse patterns favoured by different disciplines and their pedagogical applications, in J. Flowerdew (ed.), *Academic Listening: Research Perspectives*. Cambridge: Cambridge University Press, 146–58.

Eagleson, R. D. (1988) Efficiency in legal drafting, in D. Kelly, (ed.), *Essays on Legislative Drafting: In Honour of J. Q. Ewens, CMG, CBE, QC*. Adelaide: The Adelaide Law Review Association, University of Adelaide, 13–27.

Faigley, L. and Hansen, K. (1985) Learning to write in the social sciences. *College Composition and Communication* 36, 140–9.

Fairclough, N. (1985) Critical and descriptive goals in discourse analysis. *Journal of Pragmatics* 9, 739–63.

Fairclough, N. (1989) *Language and Power*. London: Longman.

Fairclough, N. (1992) *Discourse and Social Change*. Cambridge: Polity Press.

Fairclough, N. (1993) Critical discourse analysis and the marketization of public discourse: the universities. *Discourse and Society* 4, 2, 133–68.

Fairclough, N. (1995) *Critical Discourse Analysis: The Critical Study of Language*. London: Longman.

Featherstone, M. (1991) *Consumer Culture and Postmodernism*. London: Sage.

Fontanet, I., Posteguillo, S., Palmer, J. C. and Coll, J. F. (eds) (1998) *Genre Studies in English for Academic Purposes*. Castello: Universitat Jaume I.

Foucault, M. (1981) *The Archaeology of Knowledge*. New York: Pantheon Books.

Fowler, A. (1982) *Kinds of Literature*. Oxford: Oxford University Press.

Freedman, A. (1994) Anyone for tennis, in A. Freedman and P. Medway (eds), *Genre and the New Rhetoric*. London: Taylor and Francis, 43–66.

Freedman, A. and Medway, P. (eds) (1994) *Genre and the New Rhetoric*. London: Taylor and Francis.

Gee, J. (1999) *An Introduction to Discourse Analysis: Theory and Method*. London: Routledge.

Geertz, C. (1973) *The Interpretation of Culture*. New York: Basic Books.

Giddens, A. (1993) *New Rules of Sociological Method*. Cambridge: Polity Press.

Gimson, A. C. (1970) *An Introduction to Pronunciation of English*. London: Edward Arnold.

Goffman, E. (1959) *The Presentation of Self in Everyday Life*. New York: Doubleday.

Gollin, S. (1999) 'Why? I thought we'd talked about it before': Collaborative writing in a professional workplace setting, in C. N. Candlin and K. Hyland (eds), *Writing: Texts, Processes and Practices*. London: Longman.

Gold, N. (ed.) (1982) *Essays in Legal Education*. Centre for Studies in Canadian Legal Education, Toronto: Butterworths.

Goodrich, P. (1987) *Legal Discourse*. London: Macmillan.

Gordon, S. and Dawson, G. G. (1991) *Introductory Economics*, 7th Edition. Lexington, MA: D. C. Heath and Company.

Government of Hong Kong (1984) *Sino-British Joint Declaration 1984*.

Government of Hong Kong (1990) *The Basic Law of the Hong Kong Special Administrative Region of the People's Republic of China*.

Government of Hong Kong SAR (1997) *Bankruptcy Ordinance, 1997*.

Grellet, F. (1981) *Developing Reading Skills*. Cambridge: Cambridge University Press.

Grice, H. P. (1975) Logic and conversation, in P. Cole and J. Morgan (eds), *Speech Acts: Syntax and Semantics*, Vol. 3. London: Academic Press, 41–58.

Gunderson, L. (1991) *ESL Literacy Instruction – A Guidebook to Theory and Practice*. New Jersey: Prentice Hall Regents.

Gustafsson, M. (1975) *Some Syntactic Properties of English Law Language*. Turku: Department of English, University of Turku.

Halliday, M. A. K. (1994) *An Introduction to Functional Grammar*. London: Arnold.

Halliday, M. A. K., McIntosh, A. and Strevens, P. (1964) *The Linguistic Sciences and Language Teaching*. London: Longman.

Hasan, R. (1973) Code, register and social dialect, in B. Bernstein (ed.), *Class, Codes and Control: Applied Studies in the Sociology of Language*, Volume 2. London: Routledge and Kegan Paul.

Hasan, R. (1985) The structure of a text, in M. A. K. Halliday and R. Hasan, *Language, Context, and Text: Aspects of Language in a Social-Semiotic Perspective*, Victoria, Australia: Deakin University Press, 52–69.

Hatim, B. and Mason, I. (1990) *Discourse and the Translator*. London: Longman.

Hewings, M. (1999) The academy meets the real world: response to audience in academic business writing' in M. Hewings and C. Nickerson (eds), *Business English: Research into Practice*. London: Longman and The British Council.

Hewings, M. and Nickerson, C. (eds) (1999) *Business English: Research into Practice*. London: Longman and The British Council.

Hoey, M. P. (1983) *On the Surface of Discourse*. London: Allen and Unwin

Hoey, M. P. (1986) The discourse colony: a preliminary study of a neglected discourse type, in M. Coulthard (ed.), *Talking About Text: Studies Presented to David Brazil on his Retirement*. Discourse Analysis Monograph 14, Birmingham: English Language Research, University of Birmingham, 1–26.

Hudson, K. (1979) *The Jargon of the Professions*. London: The Macmillan Press Ltd.

Hyland, K. (2000) *Disciplinary Discourses: Social Interactions in Academic Writing*. Harlow: Pearson Education Ltd.

Hymes, D. (1964) Introduction: towards ethnographies of communication, in *American Anthropologist*, 66/6, part 2, 1–34.

Hymes, D. (1972) On communicative competence, in J. B. Pride and J. Holmes (eds), *Sociolinguistics: Selected Readings*. Harmondsworth: Penguin, 269–93.

Hyon, S. (1996) Genres in three traditions: implications for ESL. *TESOL Quarterly* 30/4, 693–722.

Johns, A. (2002) *Genre and Pedagogy*. London: Lawrence Erlbaum Associates.

Johnson, R. K. (ed.) (1989) *The Second Language Curriculum*. Cambridge: Cambridge University Press.

Jordan, R. R. (1990) *Academic Writing Course*. London: Collins.

Kathpalia, S. S. (1992) *A Genre Analysis of Promotional Texts*. Unpublished PhD thesis, National University of Singapore.

Kathpalia, S. S. (1997) Cross-cultural variation in professional genres: a comparative study of book blurbs, *World Englishes* 16/3, 417–26.

Kelly, D. (ed.) (1988) *Essays on Legislative Drafting: In Honour of J. Q. Ewens, CMG, CBE, QC*. Adelaide: The Adelaide Law Review Association, University of Adelaide.

Kennedy, C. and Bolitho, R. (1984) *English for Specific Purposes*. London: Macmillan.

Kress, G. (1987) Genre in a social theory of language: a reply to John Dixon, in I. Reid (ed.), *The Place of Genre in Learning: Current Debates*. Geelong, Australia: Deakin University Press.

Kress, G. R. and Van Leeuwen, T. (1996) *Reading Images: A Grammar of Visual Design*. London: Routledge.

Lave, J. and Wenger, E. (1991) *Situated Learning: Legitimate Peripheral Participation*. Cambridge: Cambridge University Press.

Layder, D. (1993) *New Strategies in Social Research: An Introduction and Guide*. London: Polity.

Livesey, F. (1982) *A Textbook of Economics*. Stockport: Polytech Publishers Ltd.

Love, A. (2002) Introductory concepts and 'cutting edge' theories: can the genre of the textbook accommodate both?, in J. Flowerdew (ed.), *Academic Discourse*. London: Pearson Education, 76–91.

Martin, J. R. (1985) Process and text: two aspects of human semiosis, in J. D. Benson and W. S. Greaves (eds), *Systemic Perspectives on Discourse*, Vol. 1. Norwood, NJ: Ablex, 248–74.

Martin, J. R. (1993) A contextual theory of language, in *The Powers of Literacy – A Genre Approach to Teaching Writing*. Pittsburgh: University of Pittsburgh Press, 116–36.

Martin, J. R., Christie, F. and Rothery, J. (1987) Social processes in education: a reply to Sawyer and Watson (and others), in I. Reid (ed.), *The Place of Genre in Learning: Current Debates*. Geelong, Australia: Deakin University Press, 46–57.

Miller, C. R. (1984) Genre as social action, in *Quarterly Journal of Speech*, 70, 157–78, also published in A. Freedman and P. Medway (eds) (1994) *Genre and the New Rhetoric*. London: Taylor and Francis, 23–42.

Miller, C. R. (1994) Rhetorical community: the cultural basis of genre, in A. Freedman, and P. Medway (eds) *Genre and the New Rhetoric*. London: Taylor and Francis, 67–78.

Munby, J. (1978) *Communicative Syllabus Design*. Cambridge: Cambridge University Press.

Myers, G. (1992) Textbooks and the sociology of scientific knowledge. *English for Specific Purposes* 11/1, 3–17.

Myers, G. (1995) Disciplines, departments and differences, in B. L. Gunnarsson and I. Backlund (eds), *Writing in Academic Contexts*. Uppsala: Uppsala University, 3–11.

Nickels, W. G. (1987) *Understanding Business*. St. Louis: Times Mirror/Mosby College Publishing.

Olsen, L. A. and Huckin, T. N. (1990) Point-driven understanding in engineering lecture comprehension. *English for Specific Purposes* 9, 33–47.

Oster, S. (1981) The use of tenses in reporting past literature, in L. Selinker, E. Tarone and V. Hanzeli (eds), *English for Academic and Technical Purposes: Studies in Honor of Louis Trimble*. Rowley, MA: Newburg House, 76–90.

Pare, A. and Smart, G. (1994) Observing genres in action: towards a research methodology, in A. Freedman and P. Medway (eds), *Genre and the New Rhetoric*. London: Taylor and Francis, 146–54.

Payton, R. L., Rosso, H. A. and Tempel, E. R. (1991) Taking fund raising seriously: an agenda, in D. Burlingame and L. Hulse (eds), *Taking Fund Raising Seriously: Advancing the Profession and Practice of Fund Raising*. San Francisco: Jossey-Bass Publishers, 3–17.

Poynton, C. (1989) *Language and Gender: Making the Difference*. Oxford: Oxford University Press.

Purves, A. (1986) Rhetorical communities, the international student and basic writing. *Journal of Basic Writing* 5, 16–24.

Ranney, A. (1990) *Governing – An Introduction to Political Science*. New Jersey: Prentice Hall.

Reid, I. (ed.) (1987) *The Place of Genre in Learning: Current Debates*. Geelong, Australia Deakin University Press.

Salager, F. (1984) Compound nominal phrases in scientific-technical literature: proportion and rationale, in A. K. Pugh and J. M. Ulijn (eds), *Reading for Professional Purposes – Studies and Practices in Native and Foreign Languages*. London: Heinemann Educational Books, 136–45.

Sarangi, S. (2000) Activity types and discourse types and interactional hybridity: the case of genetic counselling, in S. Sarangi and M. Coulthard (eds), *Discourse and Social Life*. Longman: Pearson Education.

Sarangi, S. (2002) Discourse practitioners as a community of interprofessional practice: some insights from health communication research, in C. N. Candlin (ed.), *Research and Practice in Professional Discourse*. Hong Kong: City University of Hong Kong Press.

Sarangi, S. and Candlin, C. N. (2001) 'Motivational relevancies': some methodological reflections on social theoretical and sociolinguistic practice, in N. Coupland, S. Sarangi and C. N. Candlin (eds), *Sociolinguistics and Social Theory*. Harlow: Pearson Education Limited, 350–88.

Sarangi, S. and Roberts, C. (1999) The dynamics of interactional and institutional orders in work-related settings, in S. Sarangi and C. Roberts (eds), *Talk, Work and the Institutional Order: Discourse in Medical, Mediation and Management Settings*. Berlin: Mouton de Gruyter.

Sarangi, S. and Slembrouck, S. (1994) *Language, Bureaucracy and Social Control*. London: Addison Wesley Longman Limited.

Schervish, P. G. (1997) What we know and what we need to learn about donor motivation, in D. F. Burlingame (ed.), *Critical Issues in Fund Raising*. New York: John Wiley and Sons, 110–37.

Scollon, R. (1998) *Mediated Discourse as Social Interaction – A Study of News Discourse*. London: Longman.

Scollon, R. and Scollon, S. (1995) *Intercultural Communication: A Discourse Approach*. Oxford: Basil Blackwell.

Searle, J. R. (1969) *Speech Acts*. Cambridge: Cambridge University Press.

Selinker, L., Lackstrom, J. and Trimble, L. (1973) Technical rhetorical principles and grammatical choice. *TESOL Quarterly* 7, 2 (June 1972), 127–36.

Sinclair, J. M. (1981) Planes of discourse, in S. N. A. Rizvi (ed.), *The Two-fold Voice: Essays in Honour of Ramesh Mohan*. Hyderabad: Pitamber Publishing, 70–91.

Sinclair, J. (1991) *Collins Cobuild Students Grammar*. London: HarperCollins Publishers.

Smart, G. (1998) Mapping conceptual worlds: using interpretive ethnography to explore knowledge-making in a professional community. *The Journal of Business Communication* 35/1, 111–27.

Spencer, A. (1975) *Noun-Verb Combination in Law*. Birmingham: LSU, University of Aston in Birmingham.

Srivastava, D. K. and Tennekone, A. D. (1995) *The Law of Tort in Hong Kong*. Hong Kong: Butterworths Asia.

Swales, J. M. (1974) *Notes on the Function of Attributive en-Participles in Scientific Discourse*. Papers for Special University Purposes No.1, ELSU, University of Khatoum.

Swales, J. M. (1981a) *Aspects of Article Introductions*. Aston ESP Research Report No.1, Language Studies Unit, University of Aston in Birmingham, UK.

Swales, J. M. (1981b) Definitions in science and law: a case for subject-specific ESP matters. *Fachsprache* 81/3, 106–12.

Swales, J. M. (1982) The case of cases in academic legal purposes. *IRAL* 20, 139–48.

Swales, J. M. (1990) *Genre Analysis: English in Academic and Research Settings*. Cambridge: Cambridge University Press.

Swales, J. M. (1998) *Other Floors Other Voices: A Textography of a Small University Building*. London: Lawrence Erlbaum Associates.

Swales, J. M. and Bhatia, V. K. (1982) An approach to the linguistic study of legal documents. *Fachsprache* 5, 3, 98–108.

Swift, J. (1958) *Gulliver's Travels*, ed. Richard Quintana, Modern Lib. 104 (203), quoted in R. Eagleson Plain language: changing the lawyer's image and goals, in *The Scribes Journal of Legal Writing*, Vol. 7, (1998–2000), 119– 46, and 121.

Tadros, A. (1985) *Prediction in Text*. Birmingham: The University of Birmingham, English Language Research.

Tadros, A. (1989) Predictive categories in university textbooks. *English for Specific Purposes* 8/1, 17–31.

Tauroza, S. and Allison, D. (1994) Expectation-driven understanding in information systems lecture comprehension, in J. Flowerdew (ed.), *Academic Listening: Research Perspectives*. Cambridge: Cambridge University Press, 35–54.

Tay, M. W. J. (1993) *The English Language in Singapore*. Singapore: Unipress, Centre for the Arts, National University of Singapore.

Thomas, R. (1985) Plain English and the law. *Statute Law Review* 9, 3, 144.

Trimble, L. (1985) *English for Science and Technology: A Discourse Approach*. Cambridge: Cambridge University Press.

Waller, R. (1977) Three functions of text presentation. *Notes on Transforming* 2. Milton Keynes: The Open University.

Watson, D. (1996) Individuals and institutions: the case of work and employment, in M. Wetherell (ed.), *Identities, Groups and Social Issues*. London: Sage Publications, 239–82.

Werlich, E. (1982) *A Text Grammar of English*. Heidelberg: Quelle and Meyer.

Widdowson, H. G. (1973) *An applied linguistics approach to discourse analysis*. Unpublished PhD thesis, University of Edinburgh.

Widdowson, H. G. (1978) *Teaching Language as Communication*. London: Oxford University Press.

Williams, G. (1982) *Learning the Law*. London: Stevens and Sons.

Williams, R. (1985) Teaching vocabulary recognition strategies in ESP reading. *The ESP Journal* 4, 2, 121–32.

Winter, E. O. (1977) A clause relational approach to English texts: a study of some predictive lexical items in written discourse, in *Instructional Science* 6 (Special Issue).

Wisdom, J. (1964) *Gods, Philosophy and Psycho-analysis*. Oxford: Basil Blackwell.

Wodak, R. (1994) Critical discourse analysis, in J. Blommaert (ed.), *Handbook of Pragmatics*. The Hague: Mouton.

Wodak, R. (1996) *Disorders of Discourse*. London: Longman.

Wodak, R. (2002) Multinational organizations: Europe in the search of new identities, in C. N. Candlin (ed.), *Research and Practice in Professional Discourse*. Hong Kong: City University of Hong Kong Press.

Wodak, R., de Cillia, R., Reisigl, M. and Liebhart, K. (1999) *The Discursive Construction of National Identity*. Edinburgh: Edinburgh University Press.

Yunick, S. (1997) Genres, registers and sociolinguistics, in *World Englishes* 16, 3, 321–36.

Index